WHAT IT MEANS TO
BE A BUCKEYE

WHAT IT MEANS TO BE A BUCKEYE

URBAN MEYER

AND OHIO STATE'S GREATEST PLAYERS

EDITED BY JEFF SNOOK

TRIUMPH
BOOKS

Library of Congress Cataloging-in-Publication Data

Snook, Jeff, 1960–
    What it means to be a Buckeye: Urban Meyer and Ohio State's greatest players / Jeff Snook.
        p. cm.
        ISBN 978-1-60078-647-1
    1. Ohio State University—Football—History. 2. Ohio State Buckeyes (Football team)—History. I. Title.
        GV958.O35S567 2012
        796.332'630977157—dc23

                                                                2012013867

This book is available in quantity at special discounts for your group or organization. For further information, contact:

Triumph Books LLC
814 North Franklin Street
Chicago, Illinois 60610
(312) 939-3330
Fax (312) 663-3557
www.triumphbooks.com

Printed in U.S.A.
ISBN 978-1-60078-647-1
Design by Nick Panos
Editorial production and layout by Prologue Publishing Services, LLC
All photos courtesy of Chance Brockway or Chance Brockway Jr. unless otherwise indicated

To the alumni who make The Ohio State University the premier public university in the world.

To TBDBITL, members past and present, for filling autumn Saturdays on the banks of the Olentangy with the sweet sounds of tradition.

And finally, to the 78 Buckeyes who graciously took the time to tell their stories in this book.

CONTENTS

FOREWORD

What It Means to Be a Buckeye

Fɪʀsᴛ, ʟᴇᴛ ᴍᴇ sᴛᴀᴛᴇ ᴛʜᴀᴛ ᴛʜᴇ Ohio State Buckeyes were a big part of my life and a big part of our world while I was a kid growing up in Ashtabula. In fact, that would be a great understatement.

I was about 10 years old when Archie Griffin, Pete Johnson, Cornelius Greene, and Woody Hayes' full-house backfield were in their heyday. As for my tremendous admiration for Archie, I wore that No. 45 jersey every chance I got and still have that number associated with my Yahoo account. That's how much he meant to me. I remember I was in awe when I got the chance to meet him. I was a 21-year-old graduate assistant at Ohio State, and he was just a classy guy, treating me like I was every bit the veteran coach.

It is true that I rooted for both Notre Dame and Ohio State as a kid. I am Catholic, and it was just natural to root for the Fighting Irish. But I loved the Buckeyes.

Ashtabula was a great place for me to grow up. I had a great high school football coach and a great experience in high school. And I knew someday I wanted to be a coach myself. Baseball was my best sport, but I also wanted to play college football. I may have dreamed of playing at Ohio State, but I also knew I had no chance to walk on there because I wasn't in that league. So I went to Cincinnati.

I can admit that my college football experience was real disappointing. We were awful, and I wasn't a good player, at least not the player I could have been. Our program wasn't in good shape. There wasn't a commitment to excellence there, and I am blaming nobody but myself, but it just wasn't a positive experience for me.

Urban Meyer answers questions from reporters on February 1, 2012, during his first national signing day press conference as head coach of the Buckeyes. *Photo courtesy of AP Images*

In looking back, it seems it all came together for me when I came to Ohio State in 1986 to accept a graduate assistant position with Earle Bruce. I have to thank him for that. To this day, we are very, very close.

In those two years, I saw what the pageantry of college football was supposed to be like. I saw what locker rooms were supposed to look like. I saw how a team was supposed to practice during the week and play on Saturdays. It is when I learned of the Captain's Breakfast, Senior Tackle, the singing of the fight song, and later when I became a head coach, I started some of those traditions at Bowling Green, Utah, and Florida—but I learned them and how important they were in my time at Ohio State.

It also was when I got the chance to meet Coach Hayes. I went over to the old ROTC building where he had an office and met him. Then we were at a recruiting dinner at the Scarlet and Gray golf course later, and he was sitting there in his wheelchair and wasn't doing very well at the time. There was a line of about 30 people waiting to shake his hand, and my wife, Shelley, who is from Chillicothe [Hayes' hometown], said, "Let's go meet him."

I said, "I will bring you over to his office sometime"—and I still regret that to this day, because he died the next spring.

In those two years, the 1986–1987 seasons, we would be in that old locker room at Ohio Stadium, and I would keep checking the game clock and the band always came on to the field at something like 16:36 remaining to kick-off. Coach Bruce would be doing his thing, and I would shoot down the stairs and stick my head out to watch that band come on to the field, playing the fight song as they marched down the field.

Those memories came flooding back to me when I was at Florida, as we prepared to meet Ohio State in the national championship game of the '06 season. I had piped in crowd music during our practices because we heard that Ohio State fans would have most of the tickets. It was normal for us to have the audio-video guy pipe in the other school's fight song as we practiced. So I will never forget when I told them to turn up the volume for the first time that week and I heard "Across the Field" and "Hang On Sloopy."

I thought, *Oh my God, this is hard to believe: I am preparing my team to face the Buckeyes.*

Then the pregame was surreal for me. It all hit me when I walked across the field before the game to shake Coach Tressel's hand, and I looked up and saw the Scarlet and Gray right there in front of me. It was an awesome moment for me.

People always ask me when I first started to think of the Ohio State job. I never would have taken a moment to do that as long as Coach Tressel was there. He was a great coach, and I considered him a friend. When he resigned, I was with my family at our lake house in Florida, and my phone just exploded. I had it on vibrate, and it vibrated constantly—for four hours straight.

I thought to myself, *Oh my God, I can't believe it.* I was sad for him, but I would be lying if I said I did not think about the job. I absolutely thought about it. Ohio State is my home school. Then, as the days and weeks passed, I just tried to block it out and concentrate on preparing for my ESPN responsibilities.

I called the Akron game [the 2011 season opener] for ESPN, and that was the first time I had been to Ohio Stadium since 1988. I couldn't believe it. I had no idea the stadium looked like that. The end zone had only bleachers [at the South end zone] when I was here…and now it is enclosed and beautiful, and the press box is huge. But one thing hadn't changed: when that band came out of the tunnel, I teared up some. It really hit me.

I have to say that Ohio State's facilities certainly caught up fast with the rest of the college football world from when I was here. They are A-1 quality facilities now. The stadium is beautiful. The Woody Hayes Center is state-of-the-art. The weight room is fantastic. We have everything in place that we need to be successful.

I have been extremely busy since I was hired here on November 28, 2011, but I have had time to reflect that I am in a position Woody Hayes once held. I have had a portrait of him in my home or office for a long time. When I think of his teams, I think of one word: *toughness*. When I think of him, I think of how he had a sincere interest in his players off the field. His players graduated. He was very demanding on and off the field, but he made his players better people.

Those are all things I strive for as a coach.

Since I was hired, I had the chance to walk across campus a couple of times and see Mirror Lake and the Oval. It is truly an amazing campus. It has changed a lot since I was here the first time. And so far, my time has been even better than I thought it would be. The potential is here for greatness. I just want to try my best each and every day to do a good job here. I have enjoyed reestablishing my relationship with the high school coaches in the state of Ohio. Football is really important in the state of Ohio and in Cleveland, Columbus, and Cincinnati—high school football is as good here as anywhere in America. It's certainly as well-coached as anywhere in America.

My job as head coach is to put a plan together. The plan is very simple. It's not rocket science. First, you recruit really good players. If you're lucky, you recruit great ones. Second, you hire great coaches. I love to teach. I love to coach. I love to recruit. I love to build teams, and I am not a big fan of trying to fix someone else's issues. I don't worry about anything or anyone else other than Ohio State. Ohio State is still Ohio State. We will run our spread offense, but we are going to play tough and smack people at times.

Our style at Ohio State is to have an organized and clear objective. Our objective is simple: to make the state of Ohio proud of the program and to recruit student-athletes who win on the field and in the classroom. My players will have class, on and off the field. I also want clean-looking guys, respectful of their coaches, their teammates, and their university.

Urban Meyer waves to the crowd from the basketball court at Ohio State's Schottenstein Center, after introducing his new coaching staff during halftime of the Buckeyes' 80–63 victory over the Indiana Hoosiers on January 15, 2012.
Photo courtesy of AP Images

My job is to make sure that our assistant coaches' jobs are very clear. "What are you asking that kid to do, and is he getting it done?" I want that player on the edge of his seat and scared that he's going to be called upon for the answer. Four things I talk about with my assistants as far as motivating young men are these words: *love, hate, fear,* and *survival.* And if you think about it, those are the things that motivate most people. We don't just want to present things to players—we want to teach them. We want to reach them.

I want Ohio State fans to know that there never will be willful intent to break the rules on my staff's part. If a coach on my staff does it, they will be dismissed soon after my finding out. I will never hire a guy who has a reputation for that. It's no secret that my staff and I have followed the rules in the 10 years I have been a head coach.

I want fans to know that my teams will be relentless. We will play hard at all times. I want a football team that goes for four to six seconds with relentless effort on every play. You do that and you have a chance to win every game.

I know the rivalry with the team up north means everything. That's "The Game." That's the game from my memory as a kid. Thanksgiving time. Cold weather. Ohio State versus Michigan. Woody Hayes versus Bo Schembechler. I was enamored by it all, and I can't wait to coach in that game. My teams have always taken pride in performing well in our rivalry games, and at other places we had several rivalry games. At Ohio State, it is very simple which one it is. I can say that our players will be very prepared and focused for that game, but we will try to win every game.

This is the most tradition-rich program in America. We embrace it, build upon it, and I am going to make sure our coaching staff understands everything about Buckeye Grove, about gold pants, about "The Game," about those traditions, because I've lived it.

Is this the perfect fit for me? I am hoping this is the perfect fit for me and for my family. It is our chance to come back home. I have always loved Ohio State.

What does it mean to be a Buckeye? For me, it means home. It means we have an incredible obligation to the former players and to this great institution in my home state. It's an obligation I am taking more seriously than I have ever approached anything in my life.

I hate to use the phrase "dream come true," but it really is. It is a great feeling to be back home again. It is a great feeling to be a Buckeye.

—Urban Meyer

EDITOR'S ACKNOWLEDGMENTS

FIRST OF ALL, THIS BOOK, of which you are now holding the second edition, has been a popular success, and that is attributed to Buckeye fans' enduring love of the storied history and rich tradition that makes Ohio State Buckeyes football so special.

Originally, way back in the winter of 2003, just weeks from having guided the Buckeyes to their first national championship in 34 years, Jim Tressel presented me his vision for what he thought would be a pretty good read— former players putting into words what the football program and their time at The Ohio State University had meant to them. At the time, the walls of the players' main meeting room were covered with letters from hundreds of Ohio State lettermen, addressing the current players to the responsibility and opportunity they faced.

Three months later, I finished writing and editing the first *What It Means to Be a Buckeye*, featuring 76 former players whose playing careers ranged from 1934 to 2002. Eight years later, we have included 12 additional players, most of whom were stars during the 2003–2011 period.

Time and change surely shows…Ohioans say. And there has been no bigger change in the Buckeye state than the name on the door of the head coach's office at the Woody Hayes Athletic Center. Tressel's 10 years on the job concluded with nine wins over Michigan, one national title, and victories in the Rose, Sugar, Fiesta (three times), and Alamo Bowls.

A new era has arrived: Urban Meyer is now the Buckeyes' head coach. Accordingly, there is a new name on the cover of this book. I want to thank Meyer for taking the time and effort to be a part of this second edition. Growing up a fan of Woody Hayes' teams during the Archie Griffin era, Coach Meyer believes in Ohio State tradition as much as anyone, or he wouldn't have taken the job in the first place.

I also want to thank Luke Fickell, the interim head coach in 2011, who bleeds Scarlet and Gray as much as any former player. He was raised a Buckeye, his wife and kids are Buckeyes, and no matter where he may coach someday, he makes it clear—he will always be a Buckeye.

Most of all, I want to especially thank each and every man who once wore an Ohio State uniform and took the time to participate in this project.

Through your words and memories, I hope will come a better understanding of what it means to be a Buckeye.

—Jeff Snook

INTRODUCTION

O N MAY 2, 1970, a cold but sunny day, I walked into Ohio Stadium for the first time. The Buckeyes were holding their annual spring game that day, only a year and four months removed from a national championship season. Future College Hall of Famers such as Rex Kern, Jack Tatum, and Jim Stillwagon, and other All-Americans such as Mike Sensibaugh, Jan White, and John Brockington were on the field that day.

Just 10 years old, I had my picture taken with Lou Groza, whose dream to play for Ohio State was derailed by World War II. On this day, the retired NFL star was just another fan sitting in the stands, watching the action through his binoculars and studying the roster of his favorite college team.

Following the game, my friend and I had our picture taken standing next to Stillwagon outside the Biggs Athletic Facility North, an antiquated and sprawling piece of metal northwest of campus that is now the spectacular, state-of-the-art Woody Hayes Athletic Center.

Less than six months later, Stillwagon made history by becoming the first player to win the Lombardi Award and the Outland Trophy in the same season, which ended with a shocking 27–17 loss to Stanford and Jim Plunkett in the Rose Bowl. The loss ended a three-year run with a 27–2 record, with losses at Michigan in 1969 and to Stanford—costing Ohio State its chance at three consecutive national championships.

Two years later, while seeing my first game that counted in the giant Horseshoe, an unknown freshman came off the bench to rush for a school-record 239 yards against North Carolina. He went on to make history by winning two Heisman Trophies.

More than four decades later, Archie Griffin heads the largest alumni association in the world. Stillwagon, Sensibuagh, Brockington, and Kern are successful businessmen and grandfathers, on the brink of retirement.

All of them have detailed their careers, stories, and love for Ohio State, for the football program, for the university, and especially for Woody Hayes in this book.

The Ohio State football program has been hugely successful, largely iconic, and mostly stable since the World War II era, with only five head coaches since 1951.

Of course, Hayes held the position for 28 years. His dedication to his players, on and especially off the field, where he pushed the values of education and philanthropy like his offensive linemen pushed a blocking sled, was unparalleled.

Earle Bruce loved Ohio State every day before he arrived in 1979, during his nine years as head coach, and every day since he was fired unceremoniously five days before taking the field and beating Michigan.

John Cooper arrived as an outsider and became the second "players' coach" in Buckeyes history, much like Francis Schmidt six decades earlier. He recruited well, won plenty of games, was only one game away from national titles in 1996 and '98, but ultimately was fired largely for winning only two games in 13 years against the school's archrival.

Jim Tressel came along and grew into a living Buckeyes legend in his 10 years as head coach, winning a national championship in 2002. But as happened to every Ohio State head coach since the 1930s except for Paul Brown (1942–1943)—hence, the one-time tag "the Graveyard of Coaches"—he, too, was fired/resigned under pressure, but for reasons other than his teams' performance on and off the field.

Any real Buckeye knows that the final line to "Carmen, Ohio" begins with "*Time and change will surely show…*"

The seasons pass. The years roll. Time changes everything.

I remember back in January of 1979 that some fans wondered if Ohio State football would continue without Hayes. Less than a year later, Ohio State had an 11–0 record and was playing in the Rose Bowl for a national championship. The program was as strong as ever, some said stronger because Hayes was too stubborn in certain areas not to let it progress with the times. The fans were as rabid as ever. Ohio Stadium was still filled every Saturday, even though few fans knew yet how to spell the head coach's first name correctly.

Above, on May 2, 1970, All-America nose guard Jim Stillwagon poses with two young fans, one of whom is 10-year-old Jeff Snook (far right). At right, Stillwagon, the first player to win the Outland Trophy and Lombardi Award in the same season, and Snook in 2012.

Photos courtesy of Jeff Snook

That 1979 season illustrated one thing: the Ohio State football program and all that goes with it was bigger than any one man, even Woody Hayes himself.

Thirty-two years later, that scenario would repeat itself. Although Tressel was on campus for only 10 years, slightly more than one-third of Hayes' tenure, he was so successful that many identified him as the program itself. After all, he beat Michigan nine times in 10 seasons. No coach before him— not Paul Brown or Woody himself—had done that.

But Tressel, coming off an 11–1 season in which his team won the Sugar Bowl, would be gone in the blink of Brutus' eye, and fans wondered how the program would be the same. How would the Buckeyes win Big Ten championships without Jim Tressel? How would they beat Michigan without him?

Those concerns didn't last long.

A new era has arrived.

Never has a head coach arrived on Ohio State's sprawling campus with such a sparkling résumé.

Remember, most football fans didn't know Woody Hayes from Rutherford B. Hayes when he arrived in Columbus from Miami of Ohio in 1951. When Bruce succeeded him, arriving from Iowa State in 1979, he, too, was largely anonymous even though he was an Ohio State graduate. Ditto for Cooper, a Tennessean who played at Iowa State and coached at Arizona State. Tressel was a born-and-bred Ohioan, but the skeptics doubted his success at the Division I-AA level would translate to major-college football.

This time, however, the situation is *different*.

An Ashtabula, Ohio, native and University of Cincinnati grad who coached at Bowling Green, Utah, and Florida brings a résumé highlighted by two national championships won at an SEC school. He also brings a sterling reputation as one of the nation's best recruiters.

More than that, he brings hope and confidence that Ohio State football is about to enter another golden era of unparalleled success, to be filled with 50-point explosions, even more Heisman Trophy winners, and many Big Ten and national championships.

Since he was hired November 28, 2011, as the university's 24th head coach in its 122 years of football, Urban Meyer likes to claim that he is *home* again.

He is home to muster exploding optimism to a rabid and gigantic fan base. He is home to win multiple championships. He is home to beat Michigan every year.

And he is home until he retires—for good this time.

At least those are the hopes and dreams of Buckeyes fans.

"I can't look that far ahead," Meyer has said. "I am concentrating on my job at hand right now. I don't think 10 years down the road or what my legacy will be someday. Coaches like Coach Hayes left legacies. I can't worry about that because I have made mistakes in the past. I worry about today and maybe tomorrow, making sure that his great university's fans and alumni are proud of our football teams and its players—on and off the field.

"But I do know the program's past very well—and that is what makes this job so great. Growing up, I loved Coach Hayes and what his teams accomplished. I loved what he stood for."

★   ★   ★

WOODY HAYES PAID FORWARD each and every day, especially through his charitable work and endless days and nights sitting next to hospital beds brightening the day of those less fortunate. He had a temper. He hated to lose. He lashed out. The rest of the skeptical world can remember what they choose from the man called Woody, but a Buckeye remembers the essence of the man.

When I began working on this book, way back in the winter of 2003, I didn't intend for it to be a book about Hayes—and it is not—but there will be times while reading it that you believe it is. That's because the men who played for him from 1951 through 1978 respected him, worshipped him, hated him at times, and ultimately loved him. He was the most prominent figure in most of their lives, and all these years later, they have come to understand him much, much better. What's more, they miss him and think of him almost every day.

If you don't believe he was a great man—perhaps one of the greatest figures of our time—read Rex Kern's chapter. If you don't think he had a sense of humor, read Jim Stillwagon's. If you don't think he believed in education, read Brian Baschnagel's. If you don't think he believed in love and family, read George Jacoby's.

The thing is, contrary to popular opinion, football wasn't Woody Hayes' life. It was his conduit for making everyone else's lives better. He didn't care for money, because football was his currency for making everyone else's lives richer. He didn't care for his fame, using it only to benefit the poor or needy. He brought hundreds of young men on to campus because of this game, but once he got them there, he taught them the lessons that would make most of them wildly successful later in life.

He was an educator first, a father-figure second, and coach last.

As Kern reported to me, approximately 87 percent of his players graduated. They became doctors, lawyers, ministers, and presidents of their companies. And they gave back to their communities, or as Woody would put it, they "paid forward." Whether they started every game, played sparingly, or became injured, he stood by them all the way to graduation day and beyond. And if one of them hit rough times, ended up in jail, or lost his job, Hayes was there to soften the blow and to help redirect the man's future.

In the end, I often wonder if this great university and its fans ever took that man for granted until it was too late. He did so much for so many, but was remembered by outsiders for so little.

When he gave a commencement speech at Ohio State in March of 1986, just a year before his death, he said:

> Today is the greatest day of my life. I appreciate it so much being able to come here and talk to our graduating class at The Ohio State University—the great, great university that you and I love. I am so grateful and so appreciative to be here today, I just can't tell you how much. I want to start with this concept: Paying forward—that is the thing that you folks with your great education from here can do for the rest of your lives. Take that attitude toward life, because so seldom can we pay back; those whom you owe—your parents and other people—will be gone. Emerson had something to say about that. He said you can pay back only seldom. But you can always pay forward, and you must pay line for line, deed for deed, and cent for cent.

There haven't been many football coaches who can quote Emerson, to be sure, but the opening line of his speech illustrates the essence of the man. He had coached in eight Rose Bowls and won five national championships and coached four Heisman Trophy winners and met every president from Truman to Ford, but the greatest day of his life was giving a commencement speech—because advocating education meant more to him than football. That, and the fact he was giving that speech at the university he loved as part of his own family.

As I have traveled the country and lived in Florida since graduating from Ohio State in 1982, I often have been asked by non-Ohioans: "What is a Buckeye, anyway?"

If you have to ask, you'll never understand.

You are a Buckeye if the Oval is more than a shape to you. If you realize that taking the time to watch the leaves fall there on a sunny autumn day will reward you in ways you never thought possible. It is then that you know William Oxley Thompson may have the best view on earth.

You are a Buckeye if you return to campus, no matter how many years it's been since you took that final class, and you find yourself drawn to the falling water from the fountain at Mirror Lake. It truly is a mystical place, perhaps your favorite.

You are a Buckeye if you check your watch by the giant clock tower of Independence Hall.

You are a Buckeye if that giant Horseshoe is your Saturday place of worship.

You are a Buckeye if the sounds from the TBDBITL are as sweet to you as anything the Beatles or Sinatra ever created.

And you are a Buckeye if the sweetest sounds of them all are the words and music to "Carmen Ohio."

Our alma mater brings so much emotion from the toughest men. Vaughn Broadnax named his daughter after it. Jim Marshall, who left school early to play pro football in 1958, still cries when he hears it. Cie Grant is proud to claim that he has sung it in front of thousands of fans.

In this book, you will read about the many traditions Ohio State football players have embraced and nurtured through the years.

There are many references to "gold pants," a tradition started by former coach Francis Schmidt in 1934. Someone asked Schmidt how the Buckeyes would fare against Michigan that year, and he replied, "They put their pants on one leg at a time just like everybody else." From that, each Ohio State player has been awarded a gold charm in the form of a pair of football pants for each victory over the rival Wolverines. By the way, Schmidt's Buckeyes whupped Michigan 34–0 that year.

This is why these Buckeyes' words and messages are so vital today.

From Stillwagon's disdain for individualism to Randy Gradishar's intense love for tradition to Jim Otis' boyhood dreams being realized to John Hicks' love for his teammates to Brian Baschnagel's dogged determination to succeed on the field and in the classroom to Pepper Johnson's intensity—they have each contributed to the tradition that has been built day by day, season by season, decade by decade.

With the addition of 12 players—such as A.J. Hawk, Luke Fickell, Bobby Hoying, and Craig Krenzel—to this second edition of the book, this publication now represents Buckeyes who played from the 1934 through the 2011 seasons.

Ohio State football has been and is a way of life, and without it, there would be a large void.

The men who have played it come from places all over the country—from Ashtabula to Zelina, from California to New York. They arrived as big-eyed freshmen with large fears and bigger dreams, and they departed as men possessing a concrete understanding of teamwork, commitment, perseverance, and dedication.

They arrived part of one family but left as an integral and lasting part of another. They made friendships that will last their lifetimes. They sang "Across the Field," they earned gold pants, they won Big Ten titles and national championships, and they fell in love—not only with the football program but with the greatest university in the land and its unmatched traditions and ideals. They became Buckeyes, a concept they discovered lasts for life.

Here are their stories…

—Jeff Snook

The

THIRTIES

CHARLIE REAM

END

1934–1937

As I look back almost 70 years, I am proud to say that I played football at Ohio State during a time when two of our greatest traditions were created—the "Gold Pants Club" and "Script Ohio."

I arrived in Columbus from tiny Navarre, Ohio—a little place near Massillon—and nobody knew anything about me. I had listened to Ohio State football on the radio and had heard of all the big names, and it wasn't too long after I enrolled in college and walked on to the team that I was scrimmaging against those big names.

I remember I got into the Tower Club in the stadium and lived there, paying $12 a month for room and board. I always came in late for dinner and got to know the cook pretty well, and she let me eat at about 7:00 every night after practice. The food was pretty good, because I went from 175 pounds up to 218 pretty fast.

It was a great thrill to be at Ohio State. There were something like 60 or 70 players on the freshman team, and about 50 of them were handpicked by the coaches. We would practice in that big field south of the open end of the stadium. I played tackle for my first two years and later switched to end, and of course, we had to go both ways in those days.

As a freshman, one of my jobs was to clean out the stadium after a game. I remember sweeping up after one game with a teammate, Charlie Maag, and he told me, "They promised me the stadium when I came here, but they never told me I would have to clean it!"

But we didn't have scholarships then; we had to work at different jobs to make a few dollars.

Francis Schmidt was a great offensive coach, and he would hold three-hour practices. For the first two hours and 30 minutes, we would practice offense and then save a little time for the defense. I guess he just figured defense would come naturally. He was real profane, though. He spent a lot of time screaming and cussing at the referees. But the reason he had been hired is because OSU was losing to Michigan all those years earlier. People were tired of losing to Michigan.

As the legend goes, when he was hired, he said, "Michigan puts their pants on one leg at a time same as everybody else." That is what he did say. Simon Lazarus, the president of Lazarus' store, and Herb Levy, president of the Union Company, were big, big football fans. They put their heads together and came up with the "Gold Pants Club." They created this charm made of gold that would be given to every letterman who played on a team that beat Michigan.

I am proud to say that I earned three pairs—during the first three years they were given away. Today, my wife still wears a pair on a necklace.

Not only did we never lose to Michigan, but they never scored a point on us from 1934 to '37. We beat them 34–0, 38–0, 21–0, and 21–0. In that final Michigan game, I remember tackling their punter in the end zone for two points on a cold, cold day in Ann Arbor.

It was a big thing then, but now those gold pants have become really big. I get calls every once in a while that somebody wants to buy a pair. I don't even ask how much, because why would I ever want to sell a pair of them? They mean too much to me.

The biggest game we ever played in was the 1935 Notre Dame game at Ohio Stadium. It was called "the Protestants against the Catholics," and I happened to be one of the few Catholics playing for Ohio State. I think there were 90,000 fans there that day, and we jumped to a 13–0 lead at the half. But Francis Schmidt had taken out a few key players early in the fourth quarter, and the substitution rule then meant they couldn't come back in for the remainder of the quarter. In the end, they threw a touchdown pass on the final play to beat us 18–13.

That pass was from Shakespeare to Milner, and the saying went that a Protestant boy threw a pass to a Jewish boy to lead the Irish over the Buckeyes. That was the only loss we had, and it cost us the national championship. Let me tell you that we hated like hell to lose that game.

That also was the year we played the University of Chicago and Jay Berwanger, who was just a great, great player. We beat them 20–13, but Berwanger won the first-ever Heisman Trophy that year.

The next year, 1936, was when the band developed "Script Ohio," but being in the locker room, we never got to see it. I have enjoyed it ever since, however.

This was during the Depression, and nobody had any money. A ticket to the game cost $3.50, and a program was a quarter. When I was a sophomore, we had our training table at Jim Rhodes' restaurant. Jim later became governor of Ohio, but he was a big Ohio State fan before that. Before games, we would bus out to the Columbus Country Club, have a big dinner, and stay in those dorms upstairs. We would watch some film of our opponent and then go to bed.

As a sophomore, I joined the Betas and ended up living in the fraternity house on 15th Avenue the next two years. Funny thing was that Francis Schmidt's house was close by, but he had a reputation for being such a lousy driver that nobody wanted to ride home with him. We would rather walk and get there safely.

Which reminds me, Esco Sarkkinen was in my fraternity. He was my backup when I was a senior. Later on we got to be good friends, and Esco coached all those years under Woody Hayes. He must have had 20 pairs of gold pants.

The strangest thing happened to me later when I played with the Iowa Seahawks in 1942. I was in the service, and Ohio State was on their schedule. Here I was, playing my alma mater—now that was awful strange for me. Still, it was a thrill to go back to Columbus and play them, but I remember they wouldn't let me in the Ohio State locker room. That '42 team was a great one—they lost only one game and won the national championship. Anyway, they whipped us pretty badly that day [41–12]. I remember one of our linebackers would look at me and say, "Who ran by me that time?" That Ohio State team wasn't big, but, boy, were they ever fast.

I don't know if anybody else ever played for Ohio State for a career and then played against them, too. I do know one thing: I've always been proud to say that I played football with the Ohio State Buckeyes.

During Charlie Ream's four seasons, the Buckeyes had a 25–7 record and never allowed a point to Michigan. He died in 2010.

JAMES LANGHURST
HALFBACK
1938–1940

In 1937, I QUALIFIED IN FOUR EVENTS (discus, shot put, low hurdles, and high hurdles) for Willard High School to go to the state track meet in Columbus. I won the low hurdles, and a big, burly guy came up and put his arm around me. It was Francis Schmidt. "Jim, congratulations on your win. I would like you to come to Ohio State University to play football for me, my staff, the university, and for the whole state of Ohio," he said.

That one line was a thrill that I never forgot.

We had some great times and great wins, and I remember one of the funniest things that ever happened at an Ohio State football game, a few years before I played. Stan Pincura was the Buckeyes' quarterback, and he was a great cutup, a big jokester. Back in those days, they would shoot off a gun at the end of each quarter. This one time, he was running in from the sideline, and the official shot off the gun. Stan grabbed his heart, twirled around a few times, and fell to the ground. The crowd was stunned. They thought he had been shot. Tucker Smith, the trainer, and his aides ran out onto the field. "Are you okay?" Tucker said, standing over him. "I am okay," Stan answered, "but how's the crowd taking it?"

When we played Southern California in Columbus in 1938, they beat us 14–7. The winning touchdown came when we punted, and Glen Lansdale returned the punt 70 yards up the right sideline. Ross Bartschy had got trapped inside and didn't stay to the outside as he was supposed to. The next week,

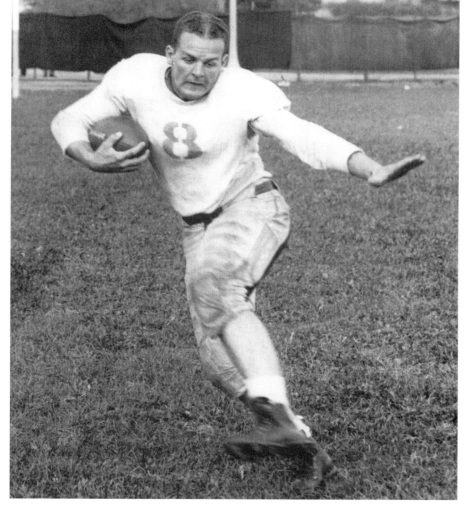

James Langhurst was sole captain of the 1940 team.

Bartschy was dropped to second team for the game at Northwestern. When the game started, the coach was sitting on the end of the bench as he always did. Bartschy saw to it that he would sit next to the coach. Throughout the game, he kept jabbing the coach in the ribs and asking him to put him in the game. He spent the whole game finding fault with his replacement. Finally, in the third quarter, the coach got up and went to the other end of the bench.

A few minutes later, he got up and walked back to Bartschy. "Bartschy," he said, "I am coach of this team. *You* go down to the other end of this bench!"

That 1938 team won only four games, but we won six the next year to win the Big Ten championship. After Michigan's Tom Harmon had won the Heisman Trophy in 1940, he told me, "Jim, I would be happy to give up the Heisman Trophy for what you got at OSU. You played on a Big Ten championship team [1939] and you were elected captain."

Nothing surpassed being named captain of that 1940 team. It's really the greatest honor a guy can have. As the years went by, I sort of became obsessed with the idea of being a captain. I figured that from 1890 through 2002, Ohio State has had 215 captains, and I am proud to say that I was one of them.

By the way, Francis Schmidt is the only Ohio State coach to shut out Michigan four years in a row: 1934 [the last time it wasn't played as the season's final game], '35, '36, and '37.

The greatest player I ever played with at Ohio State was Don Scott. He was from Canton McKinley and was our quarterback. He was about 6'4" and 220 pounds. He could pass, run, and kick…just a great athlete and a great guy. Sadly, a pilot, Don was killed in World War II.

One of the games I remember most was in 1939, when we beat Minnesota 23–20. I broke loose for an 80-yard run for a touchdown, but the official called it back for backfield in motion. He threw the flag when I was about five yards downfield. The films later showed that no one was in motion. (Ironically, in 1949, I began my officiating career at the high school level and later moved on to the college level until retiring in 1974. I have some great stories from officiating, such as the time at the Sugar Bowl when a big tackle for Notre Dame lost his false eye. We called timeout and started searching the field and finally found it. I asked him, "What would you do if something happens to your good eye." He replied, "I would become a football official!" I have to admit, that was a good one.)

Anyway, having graduated from and played at Ohio State, and having been a captain, I've always supported OSU—win or lose—and that's what a true Buckeye is all about.

James Langhurst was named MVP of the 1938 team. He died in 2008.

The FORTIES

CECIL "CY" SOUDERS
END/TACKLE
1942–1944, 1946

IN 1938 I HAD PLANNED TO GO down to LSU and play football there, until Ohio State assistant coach Ernie Godfrey came to Bucyrus and I told him what my plans were. Well, Ernie went to my high school principal and did his research and discovered that I had a steady girlfriend, Jean Hoover, who was a cheerleader.

So what did Ernie do? He visited one of Jean's classes and told her that if I went to LSU, those Southern girls wouldn't let me come back up North. "Not my guy," she told him. But then she told me, "You had better look into Ohio State." Plus, my parents were happy about that. She and Ernie won out, and I decided to head to Columbus.

I met Francis Schmidt, the head coach, and we headed to lunch driving his Caddy on the wrong side of the street, down Neil Avenue with streetcars going full blast. Ernie told him to slow down and watch where he was driving. I thought we were going to have a bad crash before I became a Buckeye. Schmidt was a rough, old cob. He was a wild man, a wild driver, and a wild talker. Every other word out of his mouth was a cuss word.

But I had made my decision. Sorry, LSU. I began my football career at Ohio State in the fall of 1939. They told me they would get me a job there, and it was sweeping the stadium. On Saturdays after games, I had to sweep up all the peanut shells, but I always found a few coins to keep me going.

My freshman year, I was on the taxi squad coached by Ernie, and our job was to go against the varsity offense. One day, I stopped about six straight plays, and Francis Schmidt stopped practice and yelled, "Who in the hell is that kid? Get him the hell out of here right now!"

Later during that fall, Jean and I decided to run off to Kentucky to get married, and we didn't return to school for three years. By that time, we had a young daughter, Sharon. I got back in 1942, and Paul Brown was the head coach. I think Paul was very similar to Jim Tressel—he was strict and a very mature man. He ran a tight ship.

That group in 1942 was a great group of boys. They were all first-class types of people, and school was the major thing for all of us. I played behind Bob Shaw that year, but I played in every game. We lost only one game, at Wisconsin, when everybody got sick. At the time, we thought we got sick from the water at the hotel, but I had read years later they discovered it was from the water on the train ride up there. They said they forgot to change the water, and it became stagnant. Well, I don't know of anybody on that team who didn't get sick that day.

That was our only loss, and as everybody knows, the '42 team became Ohio State's first national champion. Paul Brown left after the '43 season.

I played the first three games of the '44 season, and I reported to the Navy right after the Wisconsin game. It was then that I played for Paul Brown's Great Lakes team. Ironically, in the first game for Great Lakes, we went up against Wisconsin—a week after Ohio State had beaten them in Columbus. This tackle for Wisconsin asked me, "Do you have a twin brother who plays for OSU? You look just like this guy I played against last week in Columbus."

When I got out of the Navy, I was drafted by the Washington Redskins, but I wanted to come back to Ohio State to play one more season. I had a good year in 1946, and I am sure glad I did. The down part of that was that Michigan ran right over us [58–6] that year, but I ended my career with two pairs of gold pants.

I also remember playing the Chicago Bears in the All-Star Game in front of 105,000 at Soldier Field.

Being inducted into the OSU Athletic Hall of Fame was a tremendous honor for me and for my family. To me, it was already a great honor just play-ing football at Ohio State. I was from the little town of Bucyrus and didn't

12

Cecil "Cy" Souders warms up his kicking leg before a home game in 1942. *Photo courtesy of Cecil Souders* know much about college football. You just work your way along and do the best you can do.

Well, Jean and I celebrated our 63rd anniversary when Ohio State won the national championship, and the whole family was in Phoenix to see it. We'll always be Buckeyes.

Cecil "Cy" Souders, the Big Ten's Most Valuable Player in 1946, was inducted into the Ohio State Athletic Hall of Fame in 2002.

HOWARD TEIFKE
CENTER/LINEBACKER
1943, 1946–1948

T HE FIRST TIME I HEADED TO OHIO STATE, I took a bus from my hometown of Fremont. It was the fall of 1943, and I rode the bus all the way to downtown Columbus, not realizing it could have dropped me off near campus. So then I had to find my way back…. I was just a young kid lost in the big city. I was kind of homesick right from the start, and my uncle was very sick once I got there. He passed away a short time later, so I returned home. I was only 17, and I wasn't turning 18 until that October. The team was a bunch of kids that year; the season after that they won the national championship, because everybody else was in the war.

Bill Willis was playing and so was Gordon Appleby, but the rest of us were just kids. We weren't old enough to be drafted yet.

We had 33 guys on that '43 team, and I got to play a little bit, but most of the starters played both ways in those days. I remember hitting Elroy Hirsch once that season, and he bounced off of me and just kept going. I think he may have been the greatest player I ever saw.

The next year, I enlisted and headed overseas.

I remember we were somewhere in the Atlantic that November of '44 and we had the Ohio State–Michigan game on the radio. The guys loved the fact that I had been there playing a year earlier. I remember it was a close game at the half, and then we got out of range and lost the reception. It was much

14

Howard Teifke's Ohio State career was interrupted by his two years of military service during World War II. *Photo courtesy of Howard Teifke*

later when I found out that Ohio State had won 18–14, and I think Les Horvath had a big game that day.

I was in the Air Force—a gunner on a B-24—and I flew 26 missions near the end of the war. We still lost planes, but it wasn't like it was a year earlier. At that time, they had a bad ratio of being shot down, but we never were attacked by German fighter planes. I was still in Italy on V-E Day, and they sent us to California to retrain us on B-29s and we were headed for Japan. Then they came over the PA system at the base: "Fellas, the war's over. Stay on the base and everything will be free tonight." That was V-J Day. It was pretty wild, and I had wanted to go into L.A. so bad that night, but we stayed on the base.

After the war, I thought about going to North Carolina, but finally I said, "I am going back to Columbus, if Ohio State will take me." We were on the GI Bill, and you could go wherever you wanted to go. That next spring, we had 220 guys go out for spring football—a dozen centers, a dozen right guards, a dozen left guards, and so on.

Paul Bixler was the head coach by that time, and Paul just couldn't handle the talent. He wouldn't let anyone play but the starters—guys like Tony Adamle, Cy Souders, Joe Whisler, and Chuck Csuri. I was playing behind Tony Adamle, and he got his teeth kicked out in the Minnesota game. Four or five plays later, he was right back in the game. We were ahead of Illinois late in the game that year, and we threw an interception that they turned into a touchdown. The next week, we were so down that Michigan beat us 58–6. It was 55–6, and they kicked the final field goal. I remember screaming at one of those Michigan players: "What the hell is wrong with you guys?"

Wes Fesler came in to coach the '47 team, and he installed that 5–4–2 defense. They couldn't run against us, but they could pass it on us. We didn't have much of a team that year [2–6–1], but we got better by the next season. I remember we were beating Pittsburgh so badly [41–0] that some of their players told us, "You guys are the best team we've ever seen."

But we never beat Michigan in my time, and I never got a pair of gold pants. I thought we were primed to beat them in '48 in Columbus when they were ranked No. 1, and we jumped ahead 3–0, but lost 13–3. That was my last ballgame. It was a very sad day for me. Nobody likes to lose to Michigan.

All in all, it was a great adventure to go to Ohio State. I wouldn't have gotten there, or stayed there, without football. The farthest I had ever been was Cleveland, but because of Ohio State—and the war—all of that changed.

Over the years, I haven't missed too many games. The '68 team was a great team, and the '69 team was one of the best, too. I remember we were at the '69 Michigan game at Ann Arbor, and my wife said before the game, "We don't look like we want to play today." Sure enough, we lost a tough one.

I still go to most every game, because I am a Buckeye to the core. The tradition, so great for so many years, will live on.

Howard Teifke started at center and linebacker in 1948, a season in which Ohio State finished 6–3.

BOB BRUGGE

HALFBACK

1944, 1946–1947

When I arrived at Ohio State in 1944, I was just a kid—and I didn't have any confidence. I was going to go to Baldwin-Wallace because I didn't think I was good enough for Ohio State. I was just a Podunk player from Podunk Parma, Ohio. Nobody knew where Parma was, but my teammate and good friend Les Horvath was from there, too. We grew up about two streets apart from each other.

As every Buckeye knows, Les became Ohio State's first Heisman Trophy winner that season. Les was a great guy, but he really was just an average runner, an average passer. But there was nothing average about that man's smarts. He was the smartest guy playing football. He was a great tactician who could outthink the opponent.

It is no wonder he became such a great dentist. I remember Les was going to dental school at the time, and when I kept getting teeth knocked out playing football, Les would fix them for me. I would go see him, and he would fill my cavities with gold fillings. I would say, "Les, I can't afford these fillings. How can I pay you?" He said, "Don't worry, this one's on the school."

Our coach, Carroll Widdoes, was such a nice person. He was almost too nice, almost like a second father to everyone. Everybody loved him. He's the reason I went to Ohio State. But you know, he just couldn't take the pressure. It ate him up.

I was the right halfback, and behind Les that year we won 'em all. Didn't lose a game and won the Big Ten championship. I remember the Illinois game was moved to Cleveland, and we played in front of about seventy-five thousand at old Municipal Stadium. Being from Parma, that was tremendous. Plus, Les and I scored all the points that day, and we beat the Illini 26–12. It was a great day.

Big Bill Willis was a great player on our team. He was big and fast and quick as a cat. I was pretty fast back then, ran about a 10.2 hundred-yard dash. I remember in spring practice once, I ran a sweep and cut the corner and took off. The defensive back stopped, and Coach Widdoes asked him what he was doing. He simply said, "Coach, have you ever seen somebody catch Brugge from behind?"

Anyway, we went on and beat Michigan and finished the season perfect, and Coach Widdoes was named Coach of the Year. I guess now we are one of the greatest teams in Ohio State history, but we didn't even realize it back then. We were just having fun and winning football games.

After that, Les and I went to the East-West Shrine Game in San Francisco. We had such a great time. We were out there for a month practicing and having fun. We could go into restaurants with our "East All-Stars" leather jackets on and eat free. The game was played January 1, 1945. I remember that Bob Waterfield was the head coach of the West team. He was married to Jane Russell at the time, and we had this dance after the game. She danced with every player but me and the Wisconsin quarterback because we were the only players who were not 18 yet.

The next year was different. With the war going on, I was about to go into the Navy, but Paul Brown called me and said, "I got it arranged. You are going to come up to Great Lakes and play for my team." Then he called me back when it didn't work out. He said, "That SOB admiral is not an athletic man, so he won't let you play for me." Now Coach Brown never swore much, so you knew he was mad. Anyway, I didn't get to play for Paul Brown.

In 1945 I played for Camp Perry in Williamsburg, Virginia, and following the end of the war, I had three years of eligibility left and a choice to make. I had great offers from all these schools in the South that would pay me to come play for them. North Carolina offered me $10,000, a car, and, if I got married, free tuition for my wife. They said they would make the check out to my dad.

So I sent a letter to Coach Widdoes and said I was going to North Carolina. He called me back and asked, "What do you want to be when you are finished with college?" I wanted to coach. He said, "Well, who will know you down there? You need to come back to Ohio State."

So Coach Widdoes got me a job; I was the PR man for the old Deschler Wallick Hotel downtown. Then I worked at the University Theater off of Neil Avenue. But Coach Widdoes left that year to go to Ohio University as athletics director, and Paul Bixler became the coach. We didn't respect him too much. After one game at Illinois, he came into our Chicago hotel and was just sloshed. That didn't sit too well with the guys who didn't drink or smoke.

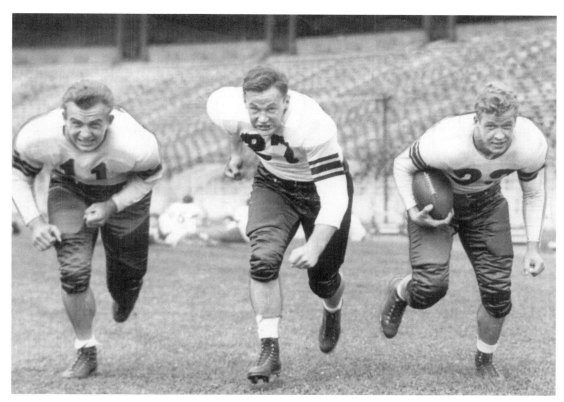

Bob Brugge (left) played for three head coaches—Carroll Widdoes, Paul Bixler, and Wes Fesler—in his three seasons.

The game I remember most in '46 was at Southern California. We had about ninety-two thousand in the stands, and I hurt my Achilles tendon. Ernie Biggs taped me up good, and I averaged about seven yards per carry. We won 21–0. Only one thing bothers me to this day. I never scored against our biggest rival. Never scored against Michigan.

One home game I remember the most was when we were playing Minnesota and we fell behind in the first quarter. I was engaged then to Lois, who became my wife for life, and she was coming to the game. In the second quarter I threw for a touchdown, ran for another, and set up a third. The crowd was going crazy. After the game, I asked Lois what she thought, and she said, "Well, I didn't get to the game until halftime, but I loved the second half."

It was the greatest thrill of my life, playing football for Ohio State. Something like that stays with you for life.

Bob Brugge was a starting back on the 1944 team, which had a 9–0 record but finished ranked No. 2 behind Army.

JOE WHISLER

HALFBACK/DEFENSIVE BACK

1946–1948

THE GREAT PAUL BROWN RECRUITED ME to Ohio State in 1943, but I never got to play for him.

I did play freshman football at Ohio State for Ernie Godfrey, but we never saw Coach Brown much. I have to tell you, that '43 freshman team was loaded with talent. The sportswriter Paul Hornung claimed that was the greatest freshman team he ever saw. We were larger and faster than the varsity squad, which had won the national championship earlier. Lou Groza was on that team, but he went into the service and never came back, and we had other great players. I think we could have beaten most varsity teams.

We played three freshman games that year and won all three of them, beating Indiana, Pittsburgh, and Michigan.

Anyway, I received my draft notice and entered the Navy the following year during World War II. My experiences in the Navy weren't too bad. I was on a landing ship tank, which transported troops to battle, and we saw a lot of storms. There were times cracks went through our ships.

After the war, I was 22. I was sadly out of shape, but I had three years of eligibility remaining. I was 5'11" and weighed about 240 pounds, because there really was nothing to do on the ship but eat. So I came back to Ohio State and worked out on the track all summer and got down to about 212 pounds.

I had a great start to the '46 season, scoring both touchdowns in the first game [a 13–13 tie with Missouri] and all three touchdowns in the next game

22

Joe Whisler finds running room during a 1948 game. *Photo courtesy of Joe Whisler* at Southern California [a 21–0 win]. That made it the first five touchdowns of the season. What I remember most was that trip to Los Angeles. We took three DC-3s to get there, and we stopped off in St. Louis. Then we went on to somewhere like Albuquerque, but before we got there, so many of the players got sick on the plane. Hal Dean had been a paratrooper during the war, and he got sick! Oh, that poor stewardess…she got sick herself just because she smelled everybody else getting sick. I felt so bad for her. We then spent a night in New Mexico and practiced there before heading on to California. Out there, we just ran right by USC.

There was one game I don't remember. At Northwestern that year, I started to make a block, and the linebacker's knee hit me in the head. It knocked me out cold. I woke up wearing street clothes, and I was sitting on the bench. Later, they put me back in, and I scored another touchdown.

We had some fun while traveling in those days. On this one trip back from Pittsburgh in '47, we had this little prop job of an airplane and we were delayed for some reason. Well, the boys went to the gift shop and bought all these windup turtles. Here they were having turtle races right out there near the runway by the airplane.

23

What still doesn't sit well was I didn't have the honor of beating Michigan. We lost to them in '46, '47, and '48. My senior year, we scored first and went ahead 3–0, but we just didn't finish the game. I thought that would be the year we would beat them. They were our rival, and I sure didn't get a pair of gold pants. That was one thing I didn't understand about Wes Fesler. In his first practice of the season, the emphasis was on beating Michigan. I thought that was really premature. I think he was 0–3–1 against them, so it didn't work much.

I guess I had a pretty good year in '48 [Whisler rushed for 579 yards on 129 carries], because they voted me MVP of the team. That was quite an honor.

Playing at Ohio State was a great, great experience. I got my bachelor's degree in education in 1949, and even though I left Ohio State, I never stopped rooting for the Buckeyes.

Joe Whisler led the team in scoring in 1946, '47, and '48 and was named MVP of the '48 team.

WILLIAM "BILLY" NEWELL

DEFENSIVE BACK

1947–1949

I LIKE TO SAY THAT MY FAMILY HELPED BUILD Ohio Stadium. My Ohio State tradition is a family tradition, starting with the construction of our now famous "Shoe." My father's OSU civil engineering classes on reinforced concrete included survey labs involving the construction of the foundation for Ohio Stadium from 1916 to 1918.

It would turn out to be a place over the next 80 years where I came to play, watch, and love the game of football. Buckeye football.

I have always been a Buckeye fan. Upon graduation from Columbiana High in 1946, there was no question where I was headed.

Football tryouts were much different then because the war had just ended, and many, many men who had previously served were there to play football. Not many of us had just come from high school. Cuts were based on wind sprints and who was the fastest. If you weren't in the top 20 of your group, you didn't make it to the next round. I wasn't very big, weighing only 165 pounds, but fortunately I was fast enough, so I made the team and became a starting defensive back my junior and senior years. In fact, I don't think we had anyone on the line who weighed more than 235 pounds. Just compare that to today's players.

FUCHS (C)—M.

WERTZ—O.

NEWELL—O.

Billy Newell gains yardage against Missouri in 1949. *Photo courtesy of William Newell*

Coach Wes Fesler had a tradition of rewarding players with silver dollars for good plays. In my case, I earned one for each interception. Problem was, they didn't pass as much as they do today, so my chances were limited. For my career, I earned 13 silver dollars, which held the OSU career record for interceptions for some time. My final interception came in the 1950 Rose Bowl, setting up a touchdown in our win [17–14 over California]. That was a great day.

Both of my brothers, John and Richard, served in World War II and then attended OSU and graduated with me in the College of Engineering.

What I am proud of is the fact that my two sons continued our Ohio State tradition. My oldest, William F. Newell Jr., worked in the athletic training program for three years, beginning during Ernie Biggs' last year. Bill Junior taped Archie Griffin's ankles during his freshman season. My second son, Marvin, worked on the equipment staff with longtime equipment manager John Bozick. Both graduated from OSU.

Through our association with Ohio State, either as a player, training staff member, or equipment staff member, we each experienced the honor and tradition of running out of that tunnel at the 'Shoe on game day. Nothing in the world compares to that feeling.

As the years have gone by, my love for my school has never diminished. I have had some heart problems, and it took three nitro tablets to get me through the 2002 national championship game. I have been, and will always be, a Buckeye. The Ohio State University is the best, and it deserves the best.

William "Billy" Newell earned three varsity letters.

The FIFTIES

GEORGE JACOBY

LINEMAN

1951–1953

I GREW UP IN TOLEDO and always wanted to go to Ohio State, but by the time I was a senior, I had considered West Point. Problem was, you couldn't go to West Point and be married, and I was very serious about my girlfriend, Nina. My childhood dream had always been to play football for the Buckeyes, and I wanted to stay close enough so my dad would be able to see the games.

Coach Wes Fesler recruited me to Ohio State, and I arrived in 1950. Wes was a fine man and a top-notch gentleman, but he made people mad at him at that point and he wasn't going to last. Why? He had lost to Michigan again [Fesler had an 0–3–1 record against Michigan]. That was the famous Snow Bowl, and it turned out to be Wes Fesler's final game.

I'll never forget our first meeting with the incoming coach. I was sitting in the front row, and Woody Hayes looked at me and asked, "Jacoby, is that you?"

"Yes, sir, it's me," I replied.

"I told you I would get you sooner or later," he said. Woody had recruited me when he was at Miami. It was the beginning of a long relationship.

When Woody was hired, everybody said, "Oh God, he'll never fill the shoes Fesler left behind. It will be a disaster." The fans were tough as hell on him those first three years, but Woody got through it. After my freshman season, he called me for a talk one day. I had been an honor student at Toledo

George Jacoby was an All–Big
Ten tackle in 1952 and 1953.

Photo courtesy of George Jacoby

29

Libby, but he said, "Jacoby, I see your grades have fallen down here; now what's going on?"

I told him I kept going home to Toledo on the weekends to see my girl-friend. "Is it serious?" he asked.

I told him it was.

"Then why the hell don't you marry her and bring her down here?" he told me.

So we got married on August 11, 1951, and Woody was largely the reason.

Once we were married, we ended up doing our laundry at his house. Anne Hayes was just a lovely lady, probably Ohio State's best recruiter. And she was a great cook, too, even though Woody always had me dieting. I played a lot that sophomore year, going both ways as everybody did. I was an offensive tackle and a nose guard. I was 5′11″ and about 225 pounds, but I could have been a lot heavier if I didn't watch what I ate.

At the time, we were recruiting Hubie Bobo, and they put him up in a hotel. Well, one of those Southern schools came up and stole him away. So they got Hubie back up for another visit. We lived in this little apartment on

High Street, and Woody called me. He said, "Jacoby, I got a favor to ask of you. You and your wife need to take Hubie Bobo back to your apartment and keep him there. Don't let him out of your sight." Nina was up all night long, checking to make sure nobody got to Hubie, but we got him signed.

The thing about that High Street apartment was there was no parking. I would park on the street and get parking tickets all the time—must have had 10 or 12 of them. I called Woody about it once, and he just said, "I'll take care of it." He did, but I had to run extra laps for it.

We had one rule that seemed excessive back then, the so-called Tuesday rule. [Assistant coach] Bill Arnsparger would knock on our door and remind us, "No sex after Tuesday." My wife and I really didn't understand that rule, and we always wondered who was telling that to all the single players, but Woody really liked Nina.

She would come to practices, and if Woody was in a good mood, he would look at her, wink, and nod toward the bench. That meant it was okay for her to go sit down. We used to go downtown to check into the hotel before games, before we would go eat dinner and see a movie as a team. One night, Woody, who never had any money on him, said, "Jacoby, let me borrow 10 bucks." I said I didn't have any money but my wife did. "Where's your wife? Get her, because I need some money to get back to campus," he said. Nina gave him the money, and Woody said, "I'll send you a check this week." Sure enough, a check came in Wednesday's mail.

The most embarrassing time of my career was when I missed the Purdue game in '52 with a freak injury. Our kicker, Thurlow "Tad" Weed, was one of my fraternity brothers. I was always kidding him that kicking was easy and that anybody could kick, so one day in the front yard of the fraternity house he told me, "Okay, Jacoby, you think it's so easy, let's go." So what did I do? I broke my toe. There was a picture in the newspaper of me at the Purdue game, sitting on the bench in a suit with my big toe all bandaged. In the stands that day, some guy a few rows behind Nina was telling the story: "I heard Jacoby got hurt by chasing his bride around the bedroom and he tripped on the vanity stool." Just then, Nina stood up and told him, "No, he didn't break it from chasing his bride around the bedroom. How do I know? I am his bride!"

Anyway, Woody was a little ticked off at me for that injury.

I can always say that I blocked for two Heisman Trophy winners, Vic Janowicz and then Hoppy. They were great players. Man, Vic could do anything—he just ran like a deer. The game I remember most was when we beat Michigan 27–7 in my junior year. It was Woody's first win over Michigan. I was playing nose guard and dropped into coverage on this one play. The quarterback looked right at me, and I was thinking, *Damn, he's going to throw it right to me.* He did, and I got a big interception. The next year, I was the team's MVP and a cocaptain with Rock Joslin. Both of those honors are very special to me to this day.

After I graduated, we continued to go back to home games. One time, Nina was pregnant with our first son, and we stopped by to see Annie after the game. We were getting ready to go home, and she said, "George, Nina can't ride all the way up to Toledo like this. You just take one of Woody's double beds in the front bedroom. Don't worry about it—Woody watches film all night, and he won't be home until about 6:00 in the morning."

Woody had this big bedroom in the front of the house with two double beds in it. Well, Nina and I were sleeping in one of them, and sure enough, at about 6:00 AM, the door opened and in came Woody. He went into the bathroom and then sat down on the edge of the bed. It was still dark. My wife woke me up. She said, "George, Woody's here. He's on the end of the bed."

I said, "Coach?"

He said, "Jacoby, what the hell are you doing in here?"

This was after I was gone, but he still recognized my voice.

When Annie would come up to Toledo, she would always tell people, "My husband got into bed with this man's pregnant wife." She always thought that was funny.

Years later, as our boys, Jeff and Douglas, started to grow up, we would take them to campus. Woody would pull them aside and tell them about how important it was to get a good education. Then we would get in the car and they would say, "Dad, Woody says we have to mind you and be good boys."

He was a great man. I see a lot of him in Coach Tressel in the way he runs a program, too. Nina and I have been loyal fans of Ohio State since I graduated, and we will be until the day we die.

George Jacoby was MVP of the 1952 team and cocaptain in '53.

ROBERT "ROCK" JOSLIN
END
1951–1953

BEING FROM MIDDLETOWN, I was deciding where to attend college. I was signed, sealed, but not yet delivered to Purdue when Wes Fesler talked to me. "You're an Ohio boy and you need to be loyal to your state school," he said.

And after thinking about it for a while, I knew I had to attend Ohio State.

That first year, Coach Fesler spent a lot of time after practice working with me to groom me to replace Vic Janowicz a few years down the road, and I have to say right here and now that I have played with many great players like Hop Cassady and others, but Vic was the best there ever was. He was just the best and was always helpful, but I never got to replace Vic because Coach Fesler left and they brought in a new coach before the 1951 season.

We had heard a lot of stories about Woody Hayes before he arrived at Ohio State, like the time he got into a fistfight during a Miami of Ohio–Cincinnati game, but we really didn't know what to think of him. As a matter of fact, most of us didn't want to play for him.

I remember one of his first temper episodes came when Bill Wilks got Woody upset during a practice. Well, Woody told him, "Take this football and stick it up your ass." Bill left the field and never came back, but he did go on to become a great basketball player.

Well, I got along with Woody pretty well because I was very self-disciplined and was tough on myself, so I didn't need anybody else to be extra tough on me. But he was a tyrant in those days. He was tough. And you know how some guys were tough but fair? Woody really was tough and unfair at times. I remember we were going up to play Michigan, and you could dress 38 players on the road back then. Well, he was planning on not dressing Bill Mott. Now Bill Mott didn't play much, but he was one of the greatest guys on the team and he was a senior. It was his final game! I told Woody, "The guy's a senior and his parents are going to be up at the game. You just can't tell him he can't dress for his final game." I told him to not dress some sophomore, and he finally agreed.

Anyway, Woody came in that first year and changed our offense from the single wing to the T formation. He converted me from halfback to end, and I think I was the only starting sophomore on that '51 team. It's a great trivia answer, but I scored the first touchdown at Ohio State under Woody Hayes. I ran this little hook pattern, and Tony Curcillo threw it low, just off the grass. I got my hands down and picked it right from the grass and rolled over for the touchdown. We beat Southern Methodist 7–0.

When Woody changed the offense, he converted Vic from a single-wing, Heisman Trophy winner to the left halfback position in the T. Now there were jokes going around that there was only one man who could stop Vic and that was Woody Hayes. That first year under Woody, we lost 7–0 at Michigan, and there were not a lot of happy people in town. I remember one game at the stadium, and I am not sure exactly when it was, but the crowd was chanting, "Good-bye, Woody! Good-bye, Woody!"

The worst blowup I saw from Woody came after we played at Pittsburgh. He came in after the game, and the locker room door was still locked. He knocked the door off the hinges to get in. He told the starting offensive guys to go sit down, and then he started in: "You look like bunch of fucking clowns out there." He really let them have it. And we had won that game [16–14].

That next season, we played without a captain after Bernie Skvarka was elected. He had a kidney removed and represented us in street clothes for the season. I was injured in the Purdue game, tearing a knee ligament. So we headed into the Michigan game, and the doctors weren't sure if I could play. Well, Dean Dugger got coldcocked right away, and they carried him off the field. I told Woody, "I need to get in this game. I can play; send me in." So he put me in there, and Michigan had this All-America safety by the name of Perry. I went down as a decoy a few times, but I thought I could get behind him. So we called the play, John Borton hit me on a pass, and I just

Robert "Rock" Joslin was an end for three years and cocaptained the 1953 team with George Jacoby. *Photo courtesy of Robert Joslin*

got my feet in before the end line. Thirty-three yards and a touchdown! I caught another touchdown later and ended up with 10 catches. We won 27–7, and it was Woody Hayes' first win over Michigan.

Woody came up to me after the game, happy as can be, and all he said was, "Joslin, you were right." He later told John Borton, "Joslin personally saved my job." I guess he was real worried about getting fired in his second season if we lost that game to Michigan.

In those days, when you went to the movies, they would show newsreels before the movies. So I had a date with this nurse, and we went to the movies. The newsreel they showed was a recap of the Ohio State–Michigan game and it was: "Joslin catches touchdown passes to lead Ohio State over Michigan." You could just say that it ended up as a great date. Now you can't get any better than that. But the best thing was pleasing my parents. My father was a great fan, and he went to all the games. I know I made him proud.

One time, my dad came up to town and took a few of us out to dinner. We ended up drinking beer and eating ribs somewhere downtown. He dropped us off, drove 90 miles back to Middletown that night, and then went to work the next day at the steel mill, telling his friends, "I was out having a beer with Vic Janowicz last night...." He was proud of me.

My senior year in 1953, George Jacoby and I were elected captains. George basically took care of the defense, and I took care of the offense. They put in a new rule that limited substitutions that year to just one player, and John Borton was the one who came out of the game. I really struggled on defense. I weighed about 190 pounds. Michigan ran the single wing, and I was not that good of a defensive player, and we lost our final game [20–0].

Woody was always good to me, though. Years later, I worked in Ashland, Kentucky, and I sat on a few boards back then, and the school football team was having a banquet. They came to me to get a guest speaker, and I called Woody. He said he had just had his gallbladder taken out. I remember waiting at the airport in Ashland, and Woody's plane rolled in. He said he had to go to the men's room, so I went with him and he opened up this briefcase. He pulled out a needle and gave himself an injection. I said, "Coach, what are you doing?"

He said, "I've been a diabetic all my adult life."

I never knew that, and I thought I was pretty close to him. I just never knew. Anyway, he gave a great talk that night about education and making the kids study and taking good courses. The parents loved him.

Another time, we had a captains' reunion in downtown Columbus, and Woody and I happened to park next to each other. As we got out of our cars, he started in on this *Hustler* publisher Larry Flynt. He got up to speak that night, and he took off on this long tirade about Larry Flynt. As we walked back to our cars later, he asked me, "Was I out of place about that Flynt stuff?"

What could I tell him? "Of course not," I said. "Coach, that was great."

After all these years, you really don't remember the surgeries, lacerations, broken bones, and all the bruises. But you don't forget that 33-yarder that helped beat Michigan. I refer to "Carmen Ohio" for the words, "While our hearts rebounding thrill…"

My heart still rebounds with thrill. It really does.

Robert "Rock" Joslin, who led the team in receiving in 1951, scored the first touchdown in Woody Hayes' Ohio State career.

HOWARD "HOPALONG" CASSADY
HALFBACK/DEFENSIVE BACK
1952–1955

Growing up in Columbus, I visited Ohio Stadium often as a kid, sneaking into the giant Horseshoe to watch the games with other kids. We would climb over the fence a few hours before the games and hide somewhere in the stadium until they opened the gates. Then we would keep moving throughout the game, just so we didn't get caught. Ohio State was a great team, the hometown team, so it was just natural to want to see them play. I liked all the big players, like Curly Morrison, Les Horvath, the Hague boys…we really didn't have heroes who were ballplayers in our day; we just loved watching games and rooting for the Buckeyes.

I never figured I would go to college, because nobody in my family ever went to college. Why would I go to college? But I played football, basketball, and baseball, and I pole-vaulted on the track team at Columbus Central, and suddenly I realized I had a chance to go someplace. I visited Notre Dame, Bear Bryant at Kentucky, Wisconsin, Indiana, and Ohio University. I knew I wanted to play baseball in college, as well as football. There were times I didn't figure I was good enough for football, because I was never that big. I weighed about 155 pounds, and everybody in college football was so much bigger than I was.

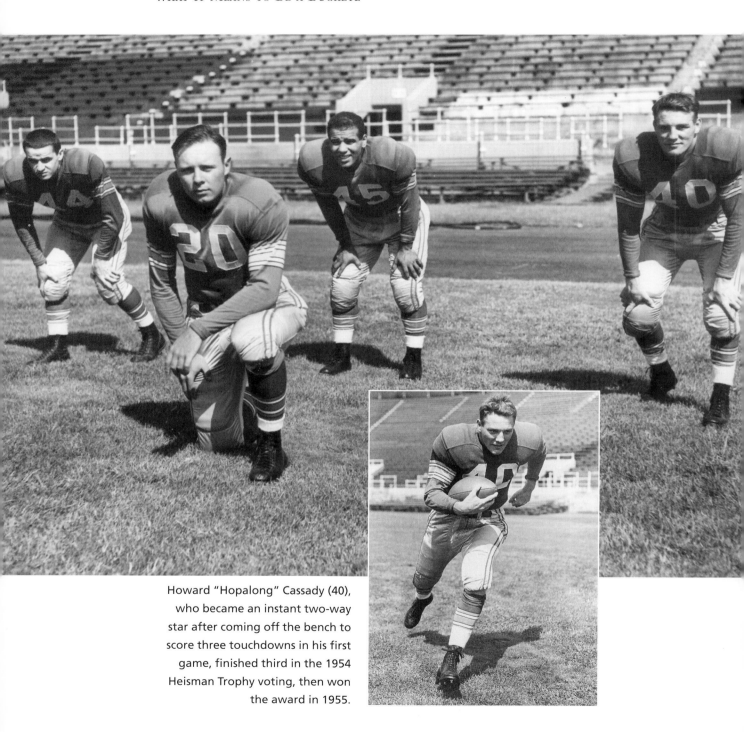

Howard "Hopalong" Cassady (40), who became an instant two-way star after coming off the bench to score three touchdowns in his first game, finished third in the 1954 Heisman Trophy voting, then won the award in 1955.

Woody Hayes invited me and my high school coaches to meet him for lunch downtown one day. It was at the corner of Broad and High Streets, right there on the northwest corner. Esco Sarkkinen was with him, and Woody just said, "I want you. You can do it." Heck, I figured if I didn't make it at Ohio State, at least I was still home. I always loved Ohio State as I grew up. Dave Parks and Frank Howell [Cassady's high school coaches] were there with me, and they handled everything for me. I guess in the end it was a group decision about what would be best for me—I was going to Ohio State to play football and baseball.

I graduated from high school in January of 1952 and enrolled at Ohio State in March, and one thing Woody didn't want me to do was sit on the bench for baseball as a freshman instead of playing spring football. You have to remember that Woody Hayes didn't have the power at that time that he did later. This was his second season, and what was their record in his first? [It was 4–3–2]. He was humble at that time, and it seemed he was fighting an uphill battle. The newspapers and fans were on him pretty good, and nobody knew if he would make it.

When I showed up for camp that summer, I was cannon fodder for the varsity. We were to open the season against Indiana, and I was running Indiana's offensive plays against the varsity. Funny thing is, we were beating them with it. I never even had a uniform until the Thursday before that Saturday opener. I remember that if you dressed for the game, your parents got tickets, and that was my goal for that first game. On Thursday, Woody told me, "Hop, go down and get a uniform; you are going to play on Saturday."

This was my choice—No. 13 or No. 40. I sure as hell didn't want No. 13, and I knew that Route 40 runs right through Columbus, so that was how I got my number.

In the Indiana game we were getting beat 13–0 at the half, and the crowd was unhappy, when I heard Woody yell something like, "Get the redhead up here!" He meant me, and I don't think the other coaches had any idea who the hell he meant. I went in for Fred Bruney, and remember we played both ways back then. As I was headed out for one of the substitutions, Fred grabbed me and said, "You're staying in here and playing the rest of the way—both ways."

I scored three touchdowns, including one on an interception, and we came back to win [33–13].

I played in 36 of the next 37 games over four years, missing that West Coast game [at California] my freshman year with a broken shoulder. They taped it down, and I played the next week against Illinois. Even though I scored a lot of touchdowns and accumulated a lot of yards, I can say that I really loved playing defense more than I loved playing offense—after getting hit, you could hit back.

In those four years, we didn't lose many games. We went from nothing to national champions.

We won 'em all in '54, but the thing I loved about it most was beating the heck out of Michigan [21–7] in Columbus. That team up north—there's nothing like whipping them.

There wasn't that much TV then, but definitely the Heisman Trophy was the top award to get if you were a college player. But the only way I knew much about the Heisman Trophy then was because I finished behind [Wisconsin's] Alan Ameche that year. It really didn't bother me at all about not winning the Heisman—I had baseball season and started right into it. I do remember I returned an interception 88 yards and we beat Wisconsin 31–14 that year, but they voted for Ameche.

In '55 we knew we couldn't go to two Rose Bowls in a row, so spoiling Michigan's season and winning as many games as we could was the big thing for us. They were supposed to beat us pretty good that year, but I don't think they crossed the 50-yard line the whole day, if not for one penalty, and we beat them 17–0. We didn't go to the Rose Bowl, but neither did Michigan.

When I went to the Downtown Athletic Club for the Heisman, [assistant coaches] Esco and Gene Fekete went with me. Woody was too busy recruiting. I can only say it was a great honor for me, and it's something you appreciate as the years go on.

Our teams were a great success story in Ohio State history, and Woody said many times later that I was a large part of his success when he first got to Ohio State, and that always made me feel honored and awfully proud. I was one of his first recruits, and he often said later that was the start of Ohio State football as we know it, and I was more than happy to be a part of it.

What can I possibly say about Woody Hayes? He kept on me from day one all the way through, but I never gave him any reason to get mad at me. I never argued with anything that man said. He handled everything for me. He was a great man—the greatest I've ever known.

He was always out to help people wherever and whenever he could. He was always visiting the hospitals, and over the years, I signed a lot of footballs for him to give away. He taught all of us well. He taught us how to be a success and how to give back to other people. After I came back when my playing days were over, Woody and I would have lunch two or three times each week. I could talk to him at any time, any day, any place. I got into a little trouble a few times, and Woody was always there for me. He was up-front, honest, and straightforward.

They just don't make 'em like him anymore, do they?

He was a Buckeye's Buckeye. A real man. A great man. He lived and died the way he was, and he never changed in between.

The day he died, March 12, 1987, I was in Fort Lauderdale with the Yankees, and my family called [my wife] Barb, and she then told me. I won't forget the sadness of it—it was one of the saddest days in my life.

I am just like the rest of his players—we loved Woody, and we loved Ohio State. Everything that happened to us at Ohio State helped make our lives easier. It worked out really well for me, and I have told every coach at Ohio State that I am always there for him if he needs me to do anything. Being a Buckeye is something that never leaves you. It is a large part of me, and it always will be.

Howard "Hopalong" Cassady, nicknamed after the famed movie cowboy Hopalong Cassidy, finished his career with 2,466 rushing yards. He was a two-time All-American and became Ohio State's third Heisman Trophy winner, winning in 1955 by what would be the most lopsided vote in the award's first 33 years. He also was named the Associated Press Athlete of the Year and won the Maxwell Award in '55. Cassady is a member of the Collegiate Football Hall of Fame and the Ohio State Athletics Hall of Fame. A first-round pick in the 1956 NFL Draft by the Detroit Lions, he played 10 seasons in the NFL—eight with Detroit, one with Cleveland, and one with Philadelphia. A shortstop at Ohio State, he was a longtime employee of the New York Yankees.

GALEN CISCO
FULLBACK/LINEBACKER
1955–1957

I WAS FORTUNATE THAT MY HIGH SCHOOL coach at Saint Mary's, Ohio, was Jack Bickel, who had been a halfback at Miami, Ohio, under Woody Hayes. He coached a lot like Woody did, so I knew what to expect if I ever went to Ohio State. Well, sure enough, Woody recruited me, and I looked at plenty of other schools, but I had no intention of going anywhere else.

When I first met Woody, what impressed me was how much he knew about me. He made it seem that he couldn't do without you. And he made it known that Ohio State would be good for you. He said, "Ohio State could do more for you after you graduate, because you are from Ohio, and you probably are going to stay in Ohio after you graduate. Why go anywhere else?"

I am glad I took his advice.

I arrived in 1954, thinking that the campus looked bigger than the whole state. It really was unbelievable that all those students could go to one school. It was just mind-boggling to me.

As freshmen, we got to go against that national championship team in practice, and we got beat up, but that helped us in the long run.

As a sophomore, I had worked my way up to second team and was doing pretty well, but during this one practice, I was lined up with the first team. We didn't have pads on, just our helmets. [Jim] Roseboro was at right half-back, Hop [Cassady] was at left half, and I was the fullback. Woody called a

Galen Cisco cocaptained the 1957 national championship team with Leo Brown.

Photo courtesy of Galen Cisco

sweep to the right side, and I thought it was a sweep to the left. Well, Cassady and I bumped heads, and Hop went down. Woody was shaking me and standing over me and screaming at me. I just kept thinking, *Get up, Hop! Get up!*

Finally, Hop got up and he was fine. He never said anything to me about it. I really thought I had screwed up big-time, but four plays later, Woody asked me, "Do you know these plays now? Well, get in there."

To start that season, we played Nebraska and beat them at home before we went to Stanford. Stanford had John Brodie at quarterback, and we held them to six points but lost 6–0. An outside linebacker, that was the first time I got to play, but from then on I played most of the games there. We lost to Duke, and those were the only losses that season, but the Big Ten had put us on probation, and we couldn't go to the Rose Bowl.

I still don't know what that was all about. From what I heard, a lot of athletes had jobs and some didn't show up for work but still got paid. But we weren't on scholarships then. [The Big Ten adopted a grant-in-aid for athletic scholarships, based on need, in 1956]. We had put together a pretty good streak in the Big Ten [17 consecutive wins] until Iowa beat us 6–0 in '56. We also lost the Big Ten title that day, and we were so flat after that, we got shut out the next week by Michigan, 19–0.

We had ended the season on a real down note, and we were picked in the middle of the pack for 1957. I had been chosen a cocaptain with Leo Brown, and it was a big honor. I don't know what I did to deserve it, but I always cherished that. We opened with TCU; they had a great back in Jim Shoffner, and he tore us up. We lost 18–14.

We went to Washington the next week, and that is when Don Sutherin, our place-kicker, turned it around when he ran about 67 yards and got us going. We won 35–7 and then got on a real roll in the Big Ten. We were real fired up for that Iowa game because of what happened the year before. I remember Richard Nixon was in the stands for the game, and Iowa was ranked fifth, and we were sixth. That game decided the Big Ten. We were trailing 13–10 when Bob White came in and just started running over people. Here was this big powerful fullback, and on that final drive, he must have carried seven or eight times for 70 yards, and Dick LeBeau carried only once on that drive. We won and then kicked Michigan 31–14 to put us in the Rose Bowl.

We had a great defense that year. We must not have allowed 100 points the whole season. [They allowed only 92.] I know one thing: we didn't give up many points in the fourth quarter that year. Woody's theory was, "Whoever wins the second half wins the game," and that applied to that team.

We had some great players then, because I think I counted once that there were 21 guys in professional football that I had played with at Ohio State. Anyway, we won a national championship in '54 when I was a freshman and in '57 when I was a senior. That was a great way to begin it, even though freshmen couldn't play, and a great way to end it.

After my eligibility was up, I had about two quarters left to graduate and I was signed to play baseball. Woody called me in and asked, "After the baseball season, what are you going to do? How about coming back and help coach freshman football and you can pick up a few classes while you're at it?"

Ernie Godfrey was the freshman head coach, and he had plenty of assistants, but that was Woody's way of making sure I graduated. After the next season, he asked, "Now what are you going to do? Come back again, because you did such a good job." I ended up coaching the freshmen from 1958 through the 1961 season. And I graduated.

Those days at OSU completely organized my future, and the whole scenario of it set me up for life. I learned that you could cope with everyday things that you run across in life. You become better prepared to deal with any setbacks. I ended up coaching in the major leagues and had a great career, and I really have Ohio State, Woody Hayes, and all of my teammates to thank.

45

Galen Cisco, captain of the 1957 national championship team, spent 30 years as a pitcher and manager/coach in professional baseball.

AUREALIUS THOMAS
LINEMAN
1955–1957

I WAS BORN IN OKLAHOMA, but I was destined to be an Ohio State Buckeye. I played football at Manual Training High in Muskogee, Oklahoma, for a coach named Walter W. Cox, who was a graduate of Oberlin College. Coach Cox first recommended that I consider moving to live with my sisters in Ohio to try to earn a football scholarship.

This was in the early '50s, and the schools were segregated in Oklahoma at that time. He knew I would have more options if I would be living in a place like Columbus. At that point, I decided to go to spend the summers with my sisters and work, and then I would return to Oklahoma. Before my junior year, I decided to stay in Columbus, and I attended Columbus West. My coach there was Mack Pemberton, and he was convinced I should attend Ohio State.

Coach Pemberton called Woody Hayes, and we scheduled an appointment. Most of Woody's linemen at that time were about 6'3" and 240 pounds, but here I was, a 6'1", 195-pound tackle. When he saw me, Woody wasn't convinced Ohio State was the place for me.

So I decided I was headed to Cincinnati. I had been selected to play in this high school All-Star Game in August of '53. While preparing for that game, [I found out that] a lot of the players there had scholarships to Ohio State. I was outperforming a lot of the fellas there, and the Ohio State coaches noticed it. Once they saw that I could get the job done, they made me an offer. My brother had played at Maryland State, which is now Maryland Eastern Shore, and he was an All-American. He taught me so much about technique as a lineman, and I made up for my lack of size with good technique and plenty of hustle.

In the fall of 1954, the week before the opening game, I was supposed to be on the second team, but Jim Reichenbach was injured and couldn't play, so I was elevated to first team. We were having a scrimmage at the stadium, and it was about 105 degrees that day. I worked about 45 minutes with the first team that day during the scrimmage, and then they called for the second team. Well, I was a second-teamer, too, so I stayed on the field and worked with them for another 45 minutes. Then, after the scrimmage, we did our running around the field. When it was all over, I went into the locker room to get an orange juice, and the next thing I know I am waking up in University Hospital. I had heat exhaustion and had lost too much water.

I was there for 28 days. It was a serious situation, and it took that long for my body chemistry to adjust. I had lost about 15 pounds. About four or five other players had heat exhaustion, too, but my case was severe. I remember waking up in the hospital, and I moved my fingertips to open my eyelids; they were open but I couldn't see. They had two tubes going into my arms to get me the necessary fluids. Woody and all the other coaches would visit me, and they made it clear that I had my scholarship whether I ever played football again or not.

Things changed that day from the standpoint of how they tried to prevent problems with the heat and how everyone looked at practicing in those conditions.

The doctors at Ohio State began researching it and doing scientific studies. They took that problem and made it a big project. They started to weigh players before and after practice. They convinced the coaches that players must have as much water as possible during practices. Before then, we couldn't have water, period. They started giving them salt. They even changed the uniforms. They used to make the jerseys that were real thick so they could be worn for five years. They recognized that once the jersey got wet with sweat, it was like having a big wet blanket over your body and your skin could not breath. So they started making the uniforms lighter.

Doctor Bob Murphy then went around to other universities and taught these new principles and told about his research. When I look back on it, I realize I am blessed because others have passed due to heat exhaustion.

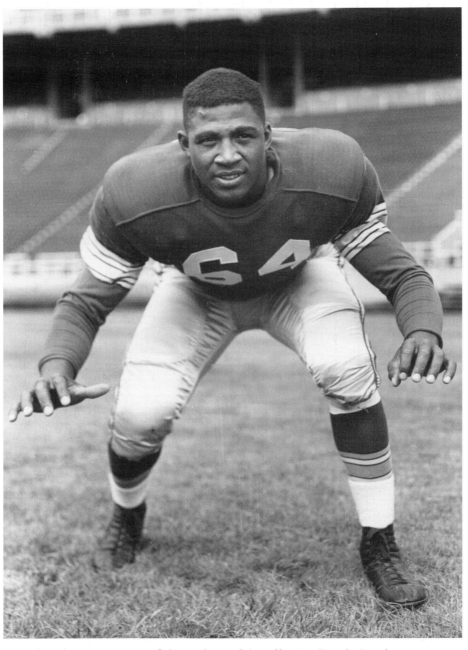

Aurealius Thomas was one of the anchors of the offensive line during the 1957 championship season. *Photo courtesy of Aurealius Thomas*

I slowly worked back the energy and stamina and began my playing days in 1955.

Woody was known for his detail and his no-nonsense planning. We made a trip to the West Coast for a game, and in the air he had us extremely busy. We didn't waste any time. We were eating, getting our ankles taped, and having various kinds of meetings with our coaches. We landed and then went directly to the locker room and practiced. When it was over, we were riding on the bus to the hotel, and I won't name the guy, but he told me he made a date with the stewardess. I said, "We were getting taped, having all those meetings with the coaches, and all that; how did you find the time?"

I averaged 52 minutes a game during my senior season, playing guard on offense and nose guard on defense. I made All-America, and we won the national championship. Because of my problem, I studied health in college and paid very close attention to my health from that day forward.

I am proud to say that I still feel very close to the university and I look upon my days at Ohio State with great fondness.

Aurealius Thomas was named an All-America guard in 1957. He was elected to the College Football Hall of Fame in 1989.

JIM MARSHALL

LINEMAN

1957–1958

DURING MY SENIOR YEAR at Columbus East, I had made high school All-America and could have played at several colleges, but I knew two places I wouldn't dare visit. Woody Hayes had talked to me often, and he said, "You visit any school you want to, but don't you dare go up there." I don't think he said the word Michigan, but I knew where he meant. He didn't want me visiting Michigan or Michigan State. I think he did say once, "We don't give a damn for the whole state of Michigan."

I had visited the Ohio State campus so much; I was impressed with the Oval, and I loved going down to Mirror Lake. The kids were sitting around it and just being mellow. I would walk over to see the buckeye trees planted for each All-American. The tradition and history of the place impressed me from the beginning. Bill Willis had gone to my high school, and I knew he was like a legend around there, and I really wanted to follow in his footsteps.

It just seemed natural for me to become a Buckeye, because I already felt like one.

That freshman year, Jim Parker taught me how to be a man. He kicked my ass every day in practice. We would scrimmage against the varsity, and Jim beat on me every day. He wanted me to answer the call. I knew if I ever could beat him, I could beat anybody. I remember many years later, he was with the Colts and I was with the Vikings, and I had sacked Johnny Unitas.

Jim Marshall was an All-America selection at tackle in 1958. *Photo courtesy of the OSU Archives*

As I rolled over and looked up, there was Jim Parker just nodding, like, "You have come of age."

The next year, when I was a sophomore, we won the national championship. I can still remember how well the Rose Bowl treated us—they gave us these cashmere blazers and a pair of binoculars.

I remember the first time I got an A in English. Woody had never shown too much emotion with me, but he looked at my grades and then looked up at me. He just gave me that look that he was proud of me. I will always remember that.

After my junior year, I left school to sign with Saskatchewan of the Canadian Football League [CFL]. I got a signing bonus of $3,000, and I bought a Pontiac Bonneville convertible. Later, I might have regretted leaving school early, but now I don't because I was one of those guys who had to go through the school of hard knocks.

It's like that song Sinatra sang: "Mistakes…I've made a few, but too few to mention."

You can imagine, Woody didn't like me leaving early, but he stayed in contact with me throughout my career. Woody Hayes would never abandon you even if he felt you made a mistake on the field or off of it. He was always on me to come back and get back in school. Just before he died, he called me and told me, "Jim, I have been asking you this, how many times; it is time for you to come home." I really didn't know what he meant, but I think he wanted to see me before he passed on. I didn't go back. I had been in an airplane crash and had so many injuries that needed to heal.

This is what I still remember when I think of my college days: the fanatical dedication of the Ohio State fans, "Carmen Ohio," the band in a quick march with a whispered version of "Fight the team across the field, show them Ohio's here…."

Whenever I hear either one of those songs, they bring tears to my eyes.

Those are feelings that will always be there for me.

Jim Marshall, after playing one season in the CFL, went on to have a brilliant NFL career, playing one season with the Cleveland Browns and 19 with the Minnesota Vikings. At the time of his retirement, he owned the NFL career records for most consecutive starts (270) and games played (280).

JIM HOUSTON
END
1957–1959

Y OU WANT HUMBLE BEGINNINGS? I started my illustrious football career at Lorin Andrews Junior High in Massillon as a seventh grader. At the time, my older brothers were playing on the high school team, and my oldest brother, Lin, was playing for the original Cleveland Browns.

I had to play football!

Guess what? I was cut from my seventh-grade team because I was too small. I didn't like to be hit, either. I remember coach Roger Price telling me that I wasn't good enough, so he cut me. I was humiliated. What would my mom, dad, brothers, and friends say?

Things changed, fortunately. After my Massillon High days, I was looking forward to college. Two of my brothers had gone to Purdue. Woody Hayes came to my house to recruit me and never said anything to me other than the normal greeting. But he convinced my mother that Columbus was much closer than Purdue. My mother simply said, "It is closer than Purdue." So I agreed with her and became a Buckeye.

I remember when they first called my name to come off the sideline at Ohio State. I almost peed my pants. As I ran out to the huddle to take my position at end, I couldn't remember any of the plays. Once the quarterback started his cadence, it suddenly came back to me. Ross Bowermaster was starting ahead of me, but he got hurt in the third game of the season. So I

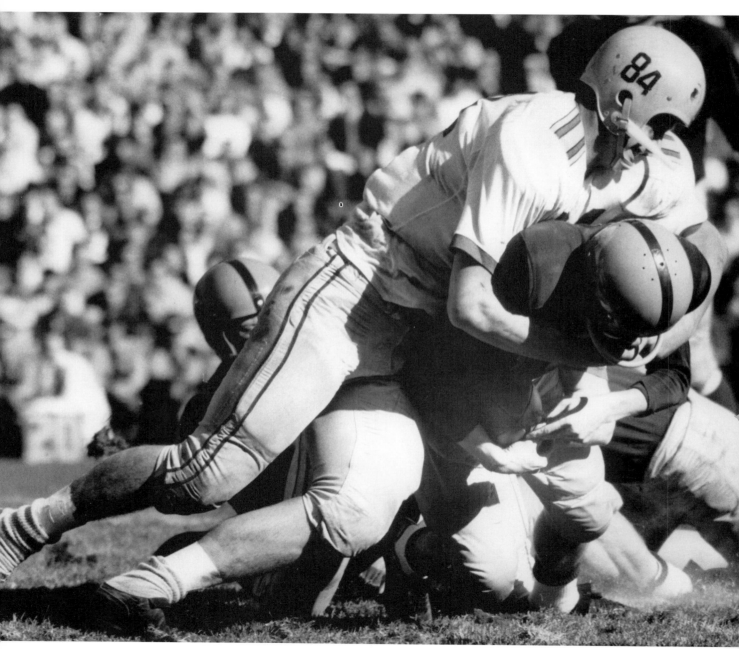

Jim Houston (84) starred at end for the Buckeyes from 1957 to 1959 and was a two-time All-American. *Photo courtesy of Jim Houston*

played the rest of the season both ways, averaging 44 minutes every game, and I played all 60 at the Rose Bowl [a 10–7 win over Oregon].

One of my teammates, Dick Schafrath, was a very good blocker. We were both about 6'3", 220-plus pounds—which was good size back then. He had calls so that we could define our blocking scheme. "Run it" was if he was facing a six-man defensive line, man-on-man blocking. "Rack it" was a double-team block by the tackle and the end. Schafrath would make the calls.

Against second-ranked Iowa my junior season, we were facing Alex Karras, an All-American at right defensive tackle, and John Klein, a 6'5", 255-pound left defensive tackle. I remember Woody calling a sweep once, and Dick saw the alignment and yelled "rack it." John's first move was up, and Schaf stuck him in the chest with his helmet, and then I blew him away. I think we gained about 18 yards on the play.

A few plays later, Woody called the same play. It was his three-yards-and-a-cloud-of-dust scenario. John Klein was over Schafrath again. Dick called "rack it," and I saw John's eyes get real big and he said, "Son of a bitch." We did it to him again for a big gain. When Dick and I got back to the huddle, we couldn't stop laughing. And that went on for several plays. We won 38–28.

During my senior year, I was a captain but we just didn't get the job done. We had a lot of injuries and had to play young players. I still made All-American, but I would have taken another Rose Bowl trip instead.

There were many ups and downs, but all in all, Ohio State was a great experience. The coaching I received from Woody Hayes and [assistant] Ernie Godfrey was responsible for my later success with the Cleveland Browns. Not bad for someone who once wasn't good enough to make his seventh-grade team.

Jim Houston played 13 seasons with the Cleveland Browns. He was inducted into the College Football Hall of Fame in 2005.

TOM MATTE
QUARTERBACK/RUNNING BACK
1958–1960

COMING OUT OF SHAW HIGH SCHOOL in East Cleveland, I had several opportunities to play college football, but Woody Hayes came to my house and sold my parents on Ohio State. He didn't worry about recruiting me—he recruited my parents. He guaranteed my mother that I would graduate from college if I came to Ohio State, and once he did that, I knew where I was headed.

Woody Hayes and I hated each other for most of my career.

I was always joking with the coaches and just having a lot of fun. I got a 1.5 GPA my first quarter in school. Woody called me in and asked, "Tom, how do you like school?"

"There is Northburg and Southburg [campus bars] and a lot to do around here," I said. "I love it."

He told me, "If you don't get a 3.0 GPA, you will lose your scholarship!"

I didn't screw around with my grades too much after that. He scared the shit out of me, and that's all it took. It was the wake-up call I needed.

On the field, he switched me from halfback to quarterback, and I had never played quarterback and didn't want to play quarterback. But he put me at second-string quarterback between my sophomore and junior years. I'll never forget what he did that spring. We had two spring games, and in the first I took the second-string offense right down the field and had a great day. I threw for five touchdowns and ran all over the place. In the second

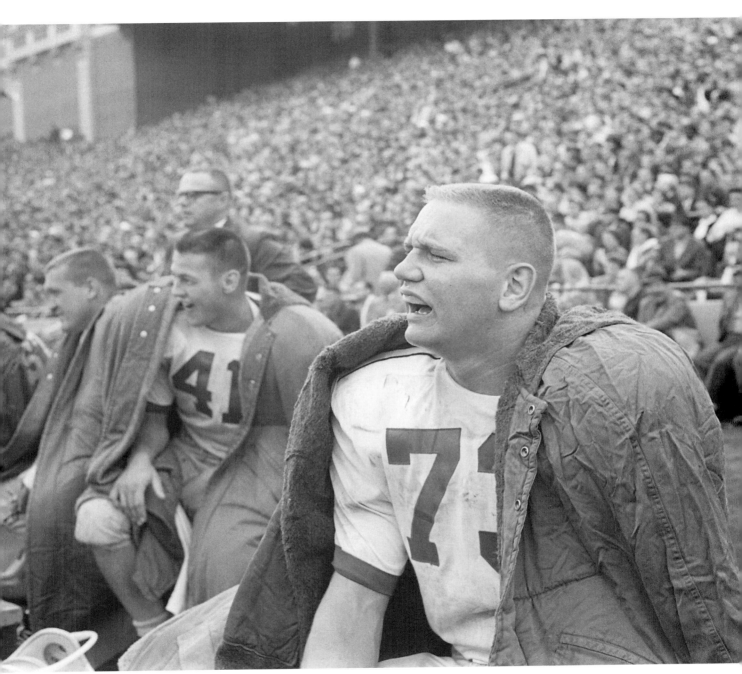

Tom Matte (41) was one of the most versatile players in Ohio State history.

spring game, Woody would call the play and then go tell the defense what the play would be. I threw five interceptions. He just made me look like a complete ass.

So we had one more practice remaining because it had been postponed due to bad weather, and I told [assistant coach] Bo Schembechler what I was going to do. Bo said, "Tom, don't do it."

"Bo, he made a complete ass out of me," I told him. So I did it—I fumbled the ball from the snap six times in a row. I would pull my hands out early on purpose and just kept fumbling.

Well, Woody got so mad. "Bo, what the fuck are we going to do? What are we going to do?" he screamed.

Then he came up and gave me a forearm shiver and hit me so hard, I could have owned the school. Now I was laughing, and he screamed again, "Bo, damn it, what are we going to do?"

Then he hit himself in the temple and went down like a sack of potatoes. Bo looked at me and said, "When he wakes up, he's going to kill you."

It turned out he had to have five stitches in his head. I went back to the dorm and went into hiding, and he came looking for me. He told me, "You will never, ever play quarterback for me." I said, "I don't want to. I want to play halfback or defensive back."

We opened up the '59 season and fell behind Duke 7–0 at halftime. It was about 98 degrees, and I was playing both ways that day. He grabbed a center and a fullback and me, and we went to our practice field right out in back of the locker room. Right out at that open end of the stadium. This is at the half! He said, "I may have to put you in at quarterback, so let's work on a few things."

We got down to two minutes to go in the game during a timeout, and he said, "Matte, go in at quarterback. Roll right, and if somebody is open, throw it. If not, run it. On the next play, roll left and do the same thing."

On one play, I went the wrong way, and it turned into a naked reverse of some sort, and I ran for about 40 yards. We won the game 14–13, and I came in on Monday and was thinking I was the cat's meow. He always had the roster posted with the depth chart, and I saw I was the third-string quarterback, but I was taken off my other positions. That season, we were 3–0–1 when I played quarterback and 0–5 when I didn't play. Now that is when we really started hating each other.

I had screwed off during my junior year. I was just always loose and having fun. I was living with a bunch of swimmers, and they were crazy guys—we got kicked out of four or five apartments. Before my senior year, Woody said, "You are worse than Vic Janowicz and Hubie Bobo combined."

Now I knew I was bad, because those were two guys who had a reputation for getting a little wild. Before my senior year, he told me, "You have a choice—you can either come live with Anne and me or you can move back into your fraternity house."

That year, I had lunch with him every day and dinner with him every night. He would tuck me in, because he gave me ulcers. We learned to get along, but he never gave me any credit. The other thing he did that really hurt me was when we voted for captains before my senior year, he told the team, "There is one guy you can't vote for, because he gets enough publicity." That still hurts.

In my senior year, I would play the game and have three hours to have dinner with my family or friends, and then I had to be back at his office to look at the film. He was like a watchdog over me, but I had a pretty good year [All-America, All–Big Ten] and it made it possible to get drafted high by the Baltimore Colts.

I had six credit hours left to graduate, and Woody called me three times during my rookie year, asking, "Are you coming back?" each time. I told him I would. As I walked off that podium with my degree that next winter, he grabbed me by the arm and took me to a telephone. He called my mom. "Mrs. Matte," he said, "your son just got his degree, and my obligation to you is fulfilled."

We ended up getting along much better after that. Later, when he came to the East Coast, he always stayed at my home. In fact, we became really good friends. He became such a special person to me. One time we talked about all we had gone through.

He told me, "You know, you were such an immature kid; you just needed guidance."

I told him, "I didn't like you at all."

"Did I get the best out of you?" he asked.

"Yes."

"Well, what do you think of yourself today?" he asked.

I told him that he helped make me who I am.

Looking back on it, I guess I just needed a kick in the ass every once in a while.

I understand him a lot better now. He was a very intelligent guy, and he made you focus. His football theories were basically military theories. He always explained himself and explained why he did certain things. He was very unselfish, and he considered us part of his family. There is no way to overestimate the effect he had on my life.

The strongest friendships I have, I made at Ohio State—my fraternity brothers, teammates, Jack Nicklaus. I am very proud of Ohio State, and I have always been proud to be a Buckeye—I can tell you that.

Tom Matte was selected in the first round of the 1961 NFL Draft by the Baltimore Colts, where he played for 12 seasons. He was named to the franchise's 50th anniversary team.

The SIXTIES

PAUL WARFIELD

HALFBACK

1961–1963

IT WAS MAY 1957 WHEN I MET a man who changed my life forever. His name was Gene Slaughter. I was in the ninth grade at Harry B. Turner Junior High in Warren, Ohio, and I thought baseball and track and field would be the only sports I would play in high school. Then my life changed in 15 minutes when Coach Slaughter talked to a group of us. He inspired me to go out for football.

After graduating from Warren Harding, I had to make a decision where to play football and where to attend college. It came down to the University of Iowa and Ohio State, and I chose Ohio State for a not-very-good reason: I wanted to stay close to my girlfriend. I guess it was a case of puppy love. To travel from Ohio to Iowa was a real journey in those days, but I-71 had been completed and I could get back and forth between Columbus and Warren.

I know this isn't original, but it was the best of times and the worst of times. I played for a very demanding head coach, and sometimes it was not a lot of fun. But you know what? Knowing what I know now, I would do the same thing all over again.

What can I say about Coach Hayes? Coach Hayes truly epitomized what a head coach should be. He worked hard. He was a perfectionist. He was a true patriot. He was a true Ohioan. He was honest. Very honest. He had so much compassion, integrity, and honesty, and those are the things that outsiders know nothing about the man. He made contributions to each and

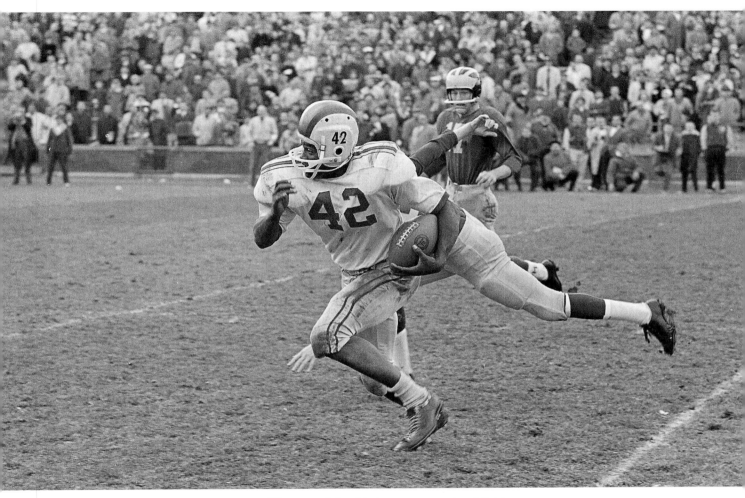

Paul Warfield shows off his graceful stride in a game against Michigan.

every athlete he brought in. The man was incredible because he touched so many lives. He made sure we were fundamentally sound on the field, and he wanted us to be an asset to the community off of it. He made sure we had the right values off the field. Education was very, very important to him. He was adamant that we get a degree from The Ohio State University through hard work in the classroom. He was a very learned man. His father was a superintendent of schools. He proved a coach could win Big Ten titles and produce national teams and yet make sure his players got the best educations. That's what makes the man stand above everyone else.

I remember one casual conversation we were having one time, and I used the word *onlyest*. He said, "What? That word doesn't exist. There is no such word." Remember, he had a master's degree in English. He knew the language.

What I learned most from him on the field was that the game of football should be played with a total team concept. I learned to do some things that do not gain much notice, such as blocking. I later became one of the best blockers in pro football because I learned how important it was at Ohio State. Remember, I blocked for such backs as Jim Brown, Leroy Kelly, and Larry Csonka. Sometimes, you just have to take an unselfish position, and that is becoming a lost concept in team sports today. For example, one thing I do not agree with in today's terms is when somebody calls a team "so and so's team. It's the quarterback's team." No, it isn't. It's everyone's team. It's their team. That's what I was taught at Ohio State, and that's how I played.

Everyone knows that Woody was famous for his practice eruptions. My first year when I was a sophomore—remember that freshmen could not play back then—on a Thursday afternoon, we were practicing for The Game. Michigan. We were practicing punt returns. Back then it was standard to employ two return men, and I was one of them. The other was Matt Snell. Now, it was one whale of a windy day. Matt went to field this punt, and it was blowing so hard, there was no way he could catch it. He dropped the punt. Woody came running down the field, and he referred to us as "jackasses." This was Michigan week, so everything had to be right. So we lined up and did it again. Matt said, "You take this one." So I dropped it, too. Woody was beside himself. This was the week before my 19th birthday, and Woody came running down the field, ripped off his hat, and started jumping up and down on it. Then he ripped it apart at the seams. I was thinking, *Wow, how could he be that angry to rip that hat apart at the seams like that?*

Now fast-forward to 20 years after that day. A friend of mine who worked for an NFL team would go to Ohio State to scout players. He always spent time with Woody. One day, they were talking for about an hour, and Woody got up and said he had to get ready for practice. He reached in his desk and there were about a dozen of those black hats with the Block "O." He grabbed one and grabbed a razor blade and started to slit the seams. He wanted it to be ready in case he needed it to prove a point. It took 20 years, but I found out how he ripped that hat apart so easily.

In that Michigan game [which OSU won 50–20 in 1961], it had been an average season for me to that point, but I had a 69-yard run, another 48-yarder, and a catch that set up a touchdown. We had so many team leaders on that team. Bob Ferguson was a great fullback. I learned discipline and sacrifice that year. I learned it was a team sport, and that team won the national championship even though we didn't get to go to the Rose Bowl for reasons I still do not fully understand. I guess the faculty council didn't think bowl games and academics mixed too well, and they didn't let us go. I remember three thousand students protesting at the student union and then marching down High Street to the capitol building.

For all four years, I was a committed dormitory resident. I lived at Park Hall, 110 West 11th Avenue, room 909. I can still remember that. It was great camaraderie. We had great debates there. I talked about everything with my teammates. I was a halfback and perhaps I didn't put the numbers on the board that I felt I should have, but it still was a wonderful experience. Woody helped make me a complete NFL player. When my playing days were over, I had a Big Ten championship ring, national championship ring, NFL championship ring from 1964 [from the Cleveland Browns], and two Super Bowl rings [from the Miami Dolphins].

I would do the same thing all over again and go to Ohio State. I came back and got my degree in education in 1966. And when I was inducted into the Pro Football Hall of Fame in 1983, I looked out in the audience when I was up on stage and you know who I saw? Woody Hayes. That really touched me. He never told me he was coming. What a great man.

And that girlfriend who made me want to attend Ohio State and stay close to home? I wasn't dating her after about one year down in Columbus. I guess everything worked out for the best.

Paul Warfield, named All–Big Ten in 1962 and '63, went on to become one of the NFL's greatest receivers, playing eight seasons with the Cleveland Browns and five with the Miami Dolphins. He is one of only eight Ohio State players or coaches inducted into the Pro Football Hall of Fame.

ARNIE CHONKO

DEFENSIVE BACK

1962–1964

Wᴇɴ I ᴡᴀs ʀᴇᴄʀᴜɪᴛᴇᴅ ᴛᴏ Oʜɪᴏ Sᴛᴀᴛᴇ, I already was a huge Buckeyes fan. My older brothers, Andy and Allan, always listened to the OSU and Notre Dame games on the radio on Saturday afternoons—either by switching channels or by using two radios. There was no TV in the early '50s. I was always thrilled to hear the exploits of Bobby Watkins, Hubert Bobo, "Hop" Cassady, and Dave Leggett, along with Jim Parker and Jim Houston, but I admit that the exploits of John Lattner and Ralph Guglielmi at Notre Dame were equally important to me.

Woody Hayes pointed out to me that Ohio State was the only place for an Ohio lad, particularly one interested in medical school. Indeed, Wayne Woodrow asked the dean of the medical school to show me around the medical school campus within a half hour of my arrival for my official recruiting visit. Dean Richard Meiling told me that I needed to maintain a 3.3 GPA to prove to the admissions committee that I was serious about medical school. I was just a quiet kid from Cleveland, and I can recall thinking that I may have bitten off more than I could chew. Of course, Woody spoke up and told Dr. Meiling that he knew that I could do that—and more—particularly with the discipline of athletics in my background.

Woody also pointed out to me that Notre Dame did not have a medical school and that he had several former players in dental school at the time. "We have the best darn medical college in the Midwest right here in good old Columbus.... So forget about even visiting that school up North!" he told me.

However, Woody was not thrilled to learn that I wanted to play baseball in the spring rather than attend spring football practices. My brothers, who had played baseball and football at Ohio University and Notre Dame, respectively, told me to insist on a written agreement from Coach Hayes prior to my signing the letter of intent. I was concerned about Woody's notorious temper, but I decided to ask for the letter. Needless to say, Woody was only mildly irked and pointed out to me that his word was his honor. I thanked him for his interest and pointed out that Coach Ara Parseghian at Northwestern and Coach Bump Elliott at Michigan had agreed to my baseball-in-the-spring request in writing. I also mentioned that both of those schools had excellent medical schools. Woody's reaction was swift and measured: he wrote a very nice letter to me, asking me to attend spring football practice during my freshman year but allowing me to pursue baseball in the spring of the last three of my undergraduate years. He also added a handwritten P.S. stating his concern that I would be making a great mistake if I attended the "school up North." What he did not know was that I hated Michigan all my life. I found it impossible to matriculate at Ann Arbor despite the greatness of the Michigan academic and athletic programs.

I was won over by the traditions of the Horseshoe—Ohio Stadium—and the sounds of that great band that I had seen on several visits to Ohio State games with my high school football team. Moreover, I sensed that Coach Parseghian would not stay at Northwestern.

Thus, a shy, pug-nosed kid from Parma followed his childhood dream and headed to Columbus to join the rigorous program of Buckeyes football...and baseball.

I worked hard in school and on the athletic fields at Ohio State. I spent 36 hours at OSU hospitals during my freshman year after suffering a concussion when tackling teammate Bo Scott in a full-scale scrimmage in the stadium on a fall Friday afternoon in 1961. When I was led into the locker room after the concussive blow, apparently Woody asked me to identify him. When I drew a blank, he shook his head and told the trainers, "Get his butt to the hospital." I awakened in the OSU neurosurgery observation ward 30 hours later in the middle of a conversation with my brother Al. The next two weeks were without serious contact for me, and it led me to wonder if I should forget football and play only baseball.

Arnie Chonko shares the Ohio State record for interceptions in a game, thanks to picking off three Indiana passes in 1964. *Photo courtesy of Arnie Chonko*

However, I can honestly say that the lure of playing on the Horseshoe grass was too great, and I pressed forward through spring practice, a subsequent separated shoulder, and Woody's wrath. He would say, "You can't make the club in the tub."

I persevered and got a break when Eddy Ulmer left school due to academic difficulties. I was inserted into the defensive backfield and won a starting job and flourished as a sophomore. I continued to work hard and improve during my junior and senior years.

Words cannot express how thrilling it was for me to play football for OSU, in the Big Ten, and in the Horseshoe along the banks of the Olentangy. I remember the courage and camaraderie of my teammates, the game-saving interceptions and tackles, and key goal-line stands that we accomplished as a team. I remember hating Woody for the grueling thrice-a-day preseason practices in the hot August and September sunshine. I still remember being "chewed out" and kicked in the ass by Woody for minor mistakes at practice and then being praised to high heaven by him a week later on his TV show! He was a volatile character, but he always meant well for his players.

And get this—he even came to several baseball games when we won the Big Ten title during my senior season in 1965, when we went on to finish second in the College World Series. Football players Bo Rein, Don Harkins, and Jim Reed also were on the team.

We all know that Woody hated to lose. Once, he almost attacked the USC Trojan mascot riding the white horse in the L.A. Coliseum when they scored a late touchdown in 1963. "I am going to knock that asshole off that goddamn horse if he comes around that fucking track again," he said. Another time, I intercepted a pass in a scrimmage at the stadium, and as I was getting tackled, I lateraled to Paul Warfield, who ran it in for a touchdown. I thought we made a wonderful play, and all of a sudden, Woody came and kicked me in the butt. "What is a smart guy like you doing making a play like that?" he said. "You could have fumbled!"

In contrast, he could be enchanting and charming while discussing Ralph Waldo Emerson's essays or the history of Western Europe following World War I and World War II.

The key to his judgment of you was giving intense effort on your part. He believed that you could "outwork the other fellow." He worked hard and expected those around him to work equally as hard. His favorite saying was "nothing good in life comes easy." His football program was an example of that philosophy. He was honest and ran a program that was academically focused and without recruiting scandals. I think the best attribute of Coach Hayes was his interest in his players' academic careers and his loyalty.

He encouraged me to aim high and pursue a career in medicine, and he was very supportive of me when I was exhausted and transiently depressed during my sophomore year in medical school. "Chonko, you damn fool, you need to learn that you cannot know everything about medicine as a young doctor—that's why they call it the practice of medicine!" he told me. "Call Dean Meiling, and he will tell you the same thing."

He bought me a new suit of clothes for graduating Phi Beta Kappa as an undergraduate and another when I graduated summa cum laude from the Ohio State College of Medicine. He even helped my wife, Barbara, find a teaching position in the Columbus area when we married after my freshman year of medical school. When you became a Buckeye, he and his wife, Anne, adopted you as family, and you were never forgotten, particularly if you were a good citizen during and after your playing days.

I have fabulous memories of my years at The Ohio State University, as an undergraduate and in medical college. All of these memories are intertwined with the figure of Wayne Woodrow Hayes.

As our alma mater states, "Time and change will surely show, how firm thy friendship O-HI-O."

It was a great honor for me to wear the scarlet and gray uniform on both the football and baseball fields. To leave the Horseshoe with the Victory Bell ringing in my ear remains an indelible memory in my life.

Dr. Arnold Chonko was Academic All–Big Ten and an All-America defensive back in 1964.

DWIGHT "IKE" KELLEY
LINEBACKER
1963–1965

I DECIDED WHERE I WANTED TO GO to college one day in Ann Arbor, Michigan. I was visiting Michigan on a recruiting trip, and it was November 25, 1961, the day that Ohio State beat them 50–20. I knew then that I wanted to play for the Buckeyes.

I came from Bremen, Ohio, a town of 1,200 people near Lancaster, and I first remember seeing Woody Hayes when he came to the Fairfield County All-County sports banquet. He was such a dynamic individual. My dad absolutely loved him, and so did my mom for that matter.

And I came to love him, too.

What can I say, Woody was Woody.

He was kind: after I came to Ohio State, my dad was watching practice in the spring on a fairly cold day. Woody noticed him and sent one of the managers in to get him a coat. I don't think people ever realized to what extent he cared.

In my four years, I remember that Woody missed practice once. On that day, he disappeared from practice, and I found out later what had happened. He had gotten word that a young student had just broken his neck playing intramural football. I guess one of the managers had gotten a message to him. Woody left practice to go to University Hospital. He took an autographed football and stayed there with that boy until his parents showed up. Woody didn't want him to be alone.

72

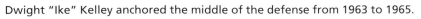

Dwight "Ike" Kelley anchored the middle of the defense from 1963 to 1965.

He was a teacher and a historian, and he always tried to make a difference.

He made sure that you knew the difference between right and wrong. Now this sounds corny, but all those lifelong lessons that he taught us, they are all true. He would say, "When you get knocked down, you only have to get up one more time." You later find out that life is like that. You get knocked down in life, you dust yourself off, and you jut that jaw out there like Woody did, and you get right back up.

And he was a competitor: in my junior year against Illinois, they had about 18 or 20 returning lettermen and were ranked pretty high [No. 2]. Dick Butkus was quoted as saying, "Ohio State's my meat, because they run straight at me and that's what I love."

Well, Woody was made aware of this. He got up in front of us and said, "Hmm, hmm, that son of a bitch won't know where we are coming from!"

He had us so sky-high for that game, we were throwing up before it. We beat them 26–0.

We had started out 6–0 that year by holding on to beat Iowa 21–19. I remember that Iowa's quarterback, Gary Snook, ran the option for a two-point conversion to tie us, and I tackled him just short of the goal line.

The next week, we got beat pretty badly by Penn State, and then we later lost to Michigan. But we beat them up there in '63 and '65, so two out of three ain't bad.

The next year, in '65, I can remember the announcement of captains like it was yesterday. Of all the great athletes we had on our team, to be elected as one of the two leaders was one of the greatest honors I had ever received. To know my teammates thought that much of me…I can't put it into words. I was just one of those crazy guys, that when I crossed that sideline, I was ready for war. Being a captain was greater than All-America status. It came from my teammates, not some sportswriter who didn't know me from Adam.

One time that season, Woody grabbed me and Greg Lashutka because we were the captains. There was some kind of demonstration on the Oval. He took us down there to speak to the group, to try to get the crowd to disperse. It's an example of how he would try to do anything he could to correct the situation any way possible. He cared about people, and he loved that university like no one else.

He was very opinionated, as everyone knows, but you never had to guess where you stood with Woody Hayes. The character and integrity of that man were above reproach. I really think that Coach Hayes had a soft spot for our class because we were so close. There were always five or six of us hanging out together—Tom Bugel, Will Sander, Greg Lashutka, Bobby Lykes, Ted Andrick, Bob Funk, Don Unverferth, Tom Barrington, and Doug Van Horn.

I also stayed very close to Woody after my playing days were done. One of the times I visited him was when they left the sponge in him after his gallbladder surgery. So I went to the hospital, and he had a nurse that looked like Sergeant Shultz outside his door. "He's not receiving visitors," she said. "Tell him it's Ike Kelley, and if he doesn't want to see me or he is tired, that's fine," I told her.

So she came back out, and I could tell that she was disappointed, because Woody wanted to see me. "Ike," he said, "do you know why I am in here? Goddamn it, you know why they left a sponge in me? Too damn many doctors. Yep, there were too many doctors. All these doctors were around there and somebody just forgot."

With me having a position at Worthington Industries in personnel, Woody would call often and ask if I knew of anything or anyplace for certain people. He would always try to help somebody get a job. One day he called me and said, "Ike, can you bail me out of jail?"

I said, "What?"

"It's one of these charity things, and I need money to be bailed out," he told me.

"What do you need, a couple of hundred?"

"No, no," Woody said. "Fifty would be great."

I remember the times he spoke at the all-sports banquets, he never charged a speaking fee. They would want to give him money, and he would donate it right back to the booster club. Woody was Woody. He was always giving back.

One time, Bruce Ruhl, Greg Lashutka, and I were involved in a children's fund-raiser and we met down at the Jai Lai. We asked Coach Hayes if we could put his name on it. Woody walked in at about 10:00 AM, and right away he said, "Well, boys, is this a good charity?"

We all said, "Absolutely."

He said, "That's good enough for me. I'll do it."

We were sitting there all prepared to give a litany of reasons to do this charity, and that's all he wanted to know. He trusted us. So then we sat there for two hours and talked about history. It got to be about noon, and suddenly he said, "Hey, you boys had better get back to work." But that's the way he was, you could sit there all day and talk to the man.

After the Gator Bowl incident [Coach Hayes' firing], he wasn't accepting calls or anything, but he had committed much earlier to speak to the chamber of commerce. Nobody was getting through to him on the phone. The president of the chamber kept calling and never got through, so he called me to see if Coach Hayes could still speak.

I went down to his house, and the shades were drawn. I knocked and I saw this little face stick out through the blinds. I heard Annie say, "Woody, it's Ike Kelley." I walked in, and a couple of other players were there. "Ike, I just kind of canceled everything," Woody told me.

I told him how they really wanted him to do this and that they would send transportation right to the house, pick him up, get him there, keep the reporters from him, then get him out the back door and right back to the house. He wouldn't have to talk to anybody else. So he called the chamber and told them that he would do it. I went that night, and I'll never forget what he said in his speech: "Expect nothing less from a man than his full potential, or that is exactly what you will get."

When Bob Funk, our place-kicker, passed away in the early '80s, I got a call out of the blue: "This is Coach Hayes; are you going down to Bob's service in Marietta? Would you mind a couple of riders?"

75

That day, Annie and Woody rode with us, and I remember we got a history lesson all the way down.

There is no way to really explain what that man meant to me, but I know I cried like a baby on the day he died.

Playing for him at Ohio State was an experience afforded to me that I never, ever thought was possible. My goal wasn't to play major college football, because I never thought I was that good. But Woody Hayes made me believe I was. It was an experience that molded my life. It gave me a direction to follow, a direction that I have used since I graduated.

As I sit here, I can't put into words what it meant for me to attend Ohio State and play football at the greatest university in the country.

Dwight "Ike" Kelley was named All-America in 1964 and '65, becoming Ohio State's first two-time All-America linebacker. He played seven seasons with the Philadelphia Eagles.

MARK STIER

LINEBACKER

1966–1968

ICAME FROM A LITTLE TOWN called Louisville up in northeast Ohio, a place where few kids ever come from and go to a major college to play football. I was ready to go to the Air Force Academy, West Point, or maybe even Kent State, and then Woody Hayes came to our high school banquet that year to speak. We had another player whom everybody was recruiting, and I think Woody wanted him, but he decided to go to Notre Dame.

It was a Cinderella thing for me. I questioned whether I was good enough to play at Ohio State, but Coach Hayes told me that night that he had seen enough of the tapes and he told me that I was good enough. He said, "Don't doubt yourself and come on."

That night changed my life.

I loved it from my freshman days all the way through. Tiger Ellison coached the freshmen, and we had a great time. I remember Woody preaching to us from the time we set foot on campus: "You can be a superstar at Ohio State, but if you don't get your degree, you are kidding yourself!"

During my sophomore and junior years, it was very tough in terms of wins and losses. We were 4–5 and then 6–3, but that sophomore class in '68 gave us a lot of expectations. We had noticed how good they were as freshmen, but we didn't know how they would perform once the real games started.

Our defensive coordinator was Lou McCullough, and Crazy Lou would work us, work us, and work us. Lou wanted his defense lean and mean. He

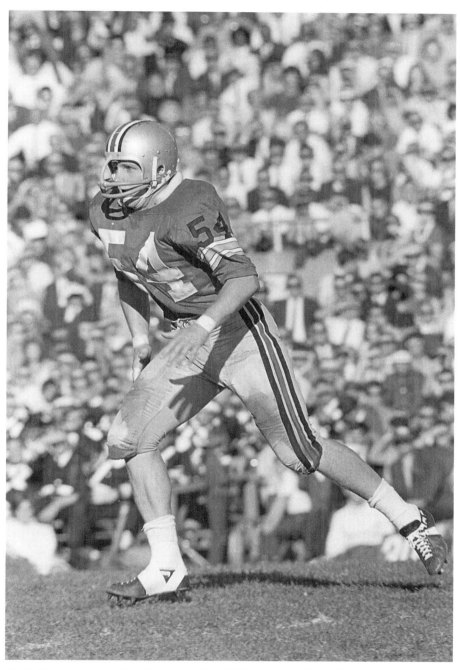

Mark Stier was one of the leaders of the 1968 national championship team.

was great in terms of our conditioning. We would run and run before practice, and we never started practice until somebody would throw up. So we had a designated thrower-upper. Somebody had to do it, because that was the signal to stop conditioning and start practicing.

I remember that after the Iowa game [a 33–27 win], the coaches weren't happy, and we had to run sprints—after the game! They wanted to make sure we were in shape, and you think we would have been by then. Our chemistry on that team was outstanding. We didn't have any racial problems. All the guys got along real well. It was a very, very close-knit team.

We always took a couple of buses wherever we went, from practice or to the airport, or wherever. The first-teamers would be in the first bus, along with Woody in the front seat. We had an assistant athletics director, and his famous line was, "All you others in the second bus." If you didn't start, you were an AYO—all you others. We had a lot of fun with that. The first bus was always pretty sedate because Woody was on it. In that second bus, we had a lot of fun.

We began 1968 and said, "Let's take them one at a time and see what happens."

We beat SMU 35–14 in that first game, and they set NCAA passing records that day [76 attempts] that lasted a long time. I had a couple of interceptions that day. I think that Purdue game, the third game of the season, was when we all realized we might have a pretty good team. They had beaten us the year before, and they came in ranked No. 1. They had Mike Phipps at quarterback, Leroy Keyes, and the whole crew. We shut them out 13–0.

Before the Michigan game, Coach McCullough would put pictures of Michigan players above all the urinals and in the lockers, and we had a special rug we ran over before the Michigan game.

We blew out Michigan 50–14 to go to the Rose Bowl. USC came in as a great team, but we played O.J. [Simpson] man-to-man in that second half and just shut them down. It was a great game, one I will always remember. That was the only time I ever remember another player coming into our locker room after the game. O.J. came in and gave a little speech about how we won the game fair and square, and he told us we were the best team. I never saw that before or since. But he went down like everybody else—he wasn't exactly hard to tackle.

I often wondered what would have happened if we had lost one game in '68, if anyone would have remembered us or if we just would have been another team forgotten over time.

I am so glad to finally say that we are not the last Ohio State team to win a national championship. Through those 34 years, we had a lot of great teams that didn't get it done. Little did I realize how meaningful that '68 team would be over time.

Coach Hayes…what a guy. I never, ever to this day have seen a guy who could swear so fluently, sentence after sentence. You know, he didn't swear much off the field, though. Off the field, he was as nice a guy as you would ever want to see. But on the field…all the shenanigans you have heard about…they are all true.

What's a Buckeye? A man of discipline, a man of character, a man who plays his hardest and has some fun along the way. He wins with compassion and loses with grace.

Ohio State has always been near and dear to my heart. That phrase, "How firm thy friendship—O–HI–O," is pretty amazing.

And it's true.

Mark Stier, twice named Academic All–Big Ten, was MVP of the 1968 national championship team.

DIRK WORDEN
LINEBACKER
1966–1968

Hardly a day passes when I don't reflect back to those experiences and memories of Ohio State. I had the honor of being named the team MVP of the 1967 season and then being named cocaptain of the national championship team in '68 [with David Foley]. To this day, I am truly proud of those honors and at the same time very humble to think that my teammates thought enough of me to bestow those titles upon me.

Ohio State football is a true lifelong fraternity, and I am proud to be part of it.

Here are some of my memories:

We struggled early in the 1967 season, starting 2–3 with losses to Arizona, Purdue, and Illinois. And the year before that we were 4–5, and everybody knows that at Ohio State, that's not good enough.

Still, it seems hard to believe now that rumors were flying throughout Columbus that a coaching change was being considered, but Coach Hayes had the class to not put any more pressure on the players and coaches. He didn't want any of that "win for me" motivation. Writers and broadcasters were really on Woody then, and we had heard he had received an ultimatum to win that game or else.

About 10 minutes before the Michigan State game at East Lansing, we had all gathered in the back of the locker room after our pregame warm-up. Coach Hayes had a great memory, and he hadn't forgotten what had happened in 1965, the last time OSU had visited Spartan Stadium. Michigan State had whipped the Buckeyes 32–7. During that game, their fans constantly bombarded the field with streamers of unfolding rolls of toilet paper every time Michigan State did something good.

In his pregame speech, Woody all of a sudden jutted out his jaw and shouted, "Do you know what today is? It's Operation Constipation! They're not going to be throwing that damn toilet paper at us this time! We are going to show them where to shove it!"

We won 21–7, and it was the beginning of our own roll. We won the next three games to finish the season, and it was the start of what later became a school-record, 22-game winning streak that spanned three seasons.

It also may well have saved Coach Hayes' job, but it was certain that it set the stage for great things to come for Ohio State football. I hate to think what would have happened if we had lost that game at Michigan State. Who knows? That may have changed the course of Ohio State football history.

Against Purdue in 1968, it was in the second quarter and we were in man coverage. I was covering a back out of the backfield, and he caught this pass in front of me. He stopped to cut, and I planted my foot and completely blew out the knee. My leg was never the same.

81

I wasn't able to contribute much, other than encouragement, for the remainder of the season, which was the remainder of my career. After the 50–14 victory over Michigan, Coach Hayes and my teammates awarded me a game ball, and I can't tell you how much that touched me. I still have it prominently displayed to this day. Then I played a little in the Rose Bowl victory over USC, a game that clinched the national championship for us, before having surgery when we returned to Columbus.

In January I had accompanied Coach Hayes to New York to the Downtown Athletic Club to receive the McArthur Bowl–emblematic of the national champions. On the airplane ride, Coach Hayes talked nonstop, and when he finally stopped, I had planned to thank him for all he had done for me and for all of my teammates. When he paused, I looked over, and there he was, sound asleep. I never saw him sleeping before, and it just never dawned on me that this man slept like everybody else.

I thought, *Damn, he is human!*

After we had beaten USC to win the national championship, Coach Hayes had called a team meeting. He simply told us, "Remember your teammates. This is the last time we will be meeting. Remember what it took to achieve

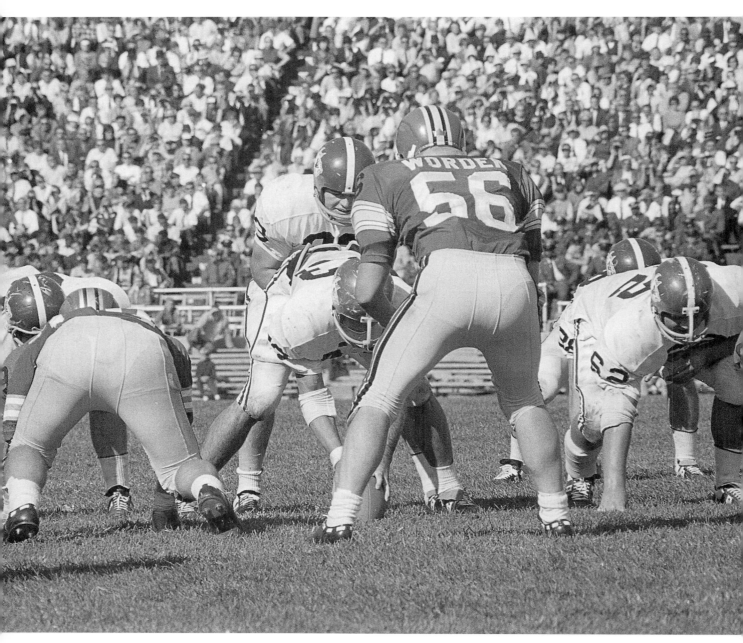

Dirk Worden (56) surveys the line of scrimmage in the 1966 season opener against Texas Christian.

the ultimate—teamwork, preparation, hard work, dedication, and perseverance. Keep these lessons, and they will help you in whatever you do in life."

I will always remember his words. He was right.

What can I say about Ohio State's fans? The Buckeye Nation is truly remarkable, the fans are everywhere, and it makes me proud to think that I once was part of something very special in so many people's lives.

For that great Fiesta Bowl, I was sitting there listening to all the Ohio State fans around me talking about the '68 team and the Rose Bowl and the last time we won a national championship, and I finally had to show them my ring. Next thing you know, there was a crowd around me to look at it. Then after the game, we went to this saloon near the stadium, and all these guys, a little older than I, were talking about that '68 team.

"Do you remember that '68 team?" one of them asked me.

Once they saw my ring, I had 10 beers sitting in front of me.

That's just the way Ohio State is—there is so much pride from the fans on to the players.

The 1968 team had carried the torch for so long as OSU's last national champions, so it was with great pride that we could pass that title on to the 2002 national champs.

Dirk Worden was named MVP of the 1967 team. He was also a tri-captain of the 1968 national championship team.

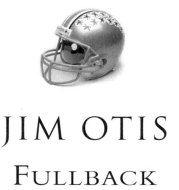

JIM OTIS
FULLBACK
1967–1969

I CAN HONESTLY SAY THAT THIS is no exaggeration, but from the time I learned to walk, I was a fan of the Ohio State Buckeyes and I knew that I would someday play football for them. And Woody Hayes was like part of my family from my earliest memories.

My dad and Woody were roommates at Denison, and he remained close to our family as I grew up. He would come up to Celina, Ohio, and we would go boating. I started attending OSU games at the age of five, and if you named the number, I could tell you the name of the player who wore it.

Ohio State football…I lived it, slept it, dreamed it. When I was 11 or 12, I would tell all my friends that I would someday play fullback at Ohio State. When we were playing in the yard, they would act like they were Jim Brown or some other great NFL player, and I always acted like an Ohio State player. Now that's tough, acting like a college player and trying to beat an NFL player!

When I got to be a high school senior, my coach told everybody I was going to Ohio State. I guess that limited the number of schools recruiting me, not that they had a chance anyway, but it limited some of the fun I could have had from those visits. Anyway, Woody came to speak at my high school banquet, and he came out to the house afterward. He pulled me aside, and he said, "I want to talk to you. I want you to know that we are recruiting other fullbacks, bigger, better fullbacks."

Jim Otis bulls his way through a hole during the 13–0 win over No. 1 Purdue in 1968.

I said, "Coach, are you offering me a scholarship?"

He said he was, and I just told him, "Well, we'll have to find out just how good those other fullbacks are."

After that freshman season, we began to find out. After that spring season in '67, I was still third-string. Woody called me in and said, "You know, you were in there on seven of the eight drives [that the first-string defense] was scored on. Now it's okay for me to be dumb, but I don't want my assistants to be that dumb."

That day, I moved up the depth chart. I got to play a lot my sophomore year, but we were having a tough year. We had lost to Arizona and Purdue, and then I fumbled in the first half against Illinois, and Woody became pretty mad at me. I didn't play in that second half, we ended up losing, and he benched me for the next two games.

We went to Michigan with a 5–3 record, and I'll never forget that first Michigan game. Woody was so intense in that locker room. He just shouted, "If there is going to be a fight today, let's do it right here in this tunnel!"

We won 24–14.

Next season was the dream season for us. That '68 team put it all together and blended perfectly, and I want to tell the real story of what happened on the famous two-point conversion play against Michigan. We were beating them 44–14 late in the game, and Ray Gillian broke a long run to get it down to the 5. We ran it three times and got nothing. We were facing a fourth-and-goal at the 5, and I just happened to be walking by Woody on the sideline. I tapped him on the shoulder and I asked, "Coach, do you want that touchdown?"

He just said, "Go in and get it! And you call the play!"

So I went in and looked around, and the best lineman in the huddle was Dave Cheney at left tackle. I looked at Dave and said, "Now Woody wants this touchdown, and he wants it over you!"

I got the touchdown over Dave, and the old stadium was rocking like it never rocked before. Kevin Rusnak was at quarterback. We probably should have called timeout right there to get organized, but we didn't. We were trained not to waste timeouts. It really was very innocent, but we lined up to run a play just to get it run before we got a delay of game. But we didn't score [the two-point conversion]. Woody had nothing to do with it, and I take the blame for it, but Woody always shouldered the blame for one of his players. As everybody knows, after the game when he was asked why he went for two points with a 50–14 lead, Woody replied, "Because they wouldn't let me go for three."

Preparing for that Rose Bowl, I just remember Woody turning up those heaters in the French Field House. It was so hot in there that we could hardly breathe, and it was snowing outside. Ask anybody on that team, and they will remember that heat. Woody turned out to be right on that one—it was 90 degrees on game day, and we ran USC off the field in the second half. Their tongues were wagging.

There is no doubt in my mind that the '69 team was the best team at Ohio State, but that Michigan game is right out of the twilight zone. Ron Maciejowski and I roomed together the night before, and we missed the bus to the stadium. It was a panicky-type of thing, with a lot of traffic ahead of us. We got the hotel guy to take us in one of those courtesy vans, and we had the guy driving on the opposite side of the highway and everything. Finally, the police nabbed us, and we explained who we were. The policeman told us, "Okay, we'll take you the rest of the way, but if you guys are lying to us, you're going to jail." We got there and snuck in the locker room, and I don't think Woody ever found out.

The game was a disaster, too. We had six interceptions in that game, and there were times that we never even threw the ball six times in a game.

For my career, I was a guy who took time off the clock, got the first down, and kept the yard markers moving. That was the important thing to me. Sometimes, great plays are three or four yards long. They didn't expect me to break a long run—they wanted me to get first downs and eat the clock. Well, in that game, we had a fourth-and-2 late in the first half, and I didn't pick up the first down. That play still haunts me to this day. If I had picked up the first down, we could have scored before the half, and that game might have been different.

It was the toughest loss of my career. Michigan wasn't even close to us in terms of talent, but it taught us a lesson. We were walking off the field, and Woody looked at me and said, "I am sorry. If you had carried 15 more times, we would have won this game." Then he walked away.

I played in the NFL, and I can honestly say there was never anything greater than playing at Ohio State. People at Ohio State sincerely care about you. The whole stadium is behind you. Everyone in that state is behind you. It's all first class.

87

Woody Hayes was the greatest man. He cared endlessly about his players. I remember one time he went around giving out neckties for Christmas. I was in the room with Teddy Provost, Alan Jack, and Chuck Hutchison. Woody opened the box, and it was full of these skinny black ties. All of a sudden, somebody started laughing. Then we all started laughing. "Well," Woody asked us, "what's so funny?"

"Coach," I said, "nobody wears those skinny ties anymore. They're out of style." He picked them up and later came back with these wider ties that were more fashionable. You can bet that somebody got chewed out on that one. He might not have been up on the current fashions, but that is how much he cared about us.

When he had his first heart attack during my NFL career, I went to Riverside Hospital to see him. The doctor told me, "Jim, just stay 45 seconds and don't let him talk."

I walked in there; the room was real cold, and he was on all those monitors. "Coach, I don't want you to say anything. I am here to tell you how much I love you," I told him. "I want you to know how much those kids need you to be ready for them, so you do what the doctors tell you to do."

As I walked out, he snapped, "Jim, when's training camp?" I told him it started in two weeks. "Damn it," he said, "are you in shape?"

We've all heard crap over the years for that Gator Bowl thing. I just tell them, "You don't know the Woody I know. Hey, Woody was a southpaw and he hit that kid right-handed." The real story is that he didn't take care of his diabetes, and the fact is that he had nodded off in the locker room before that game. His blood sugar was all screwed up, but he never told anybody that. He didn't want to make excuses.

One of the best days of my life was October 18, 1981, when my son Jimmy was born. I held him first and Woody held him second, even before his mother. Woody was in St. Louis to give a speech, and I had picked him up at the airport. Well, he had the courtesy to let me hold my son first. That great man always was and always will be a part of our family.

Jim Otis led Ohio State in rushing in 1967, '68, and '69, finishing his career with 2,542 yards and 35 touchdowns. He played with the Kansas City Chiefs, the St. Louis Cardinals, and the New Orleans Saints.

TED PROVOST
DEFENSIVE BACK
1967–1969

I WAS BETTER KNOWN FOR BASKETBALL than I was for football, coming out of tiny Fairless High, which was just south of Massillon, Ohio. I think somebody in Massillon notified Earle Bruce, who was an assistant at that time. He got the ball rolling, and then Lou McCollough, the defensive coordinator and the recruiter for our area, started recruiting me. I never met with Woody Hayes until I came to Columbus for my visit. One time, Lou was sitting at our kitchen table, and my mom called him "Hank." Michigan State was recruiting me, too, and Hank Bullough was their defensive coordinator. She just got them confused, and I said, "Mom!" It was kind of funny. Ohio University had offered me a scholarship to play both sports, but I was always leaning toward Ohio State. When Woody took me over to the Jai Lai during recruiting, we talked about math and engineering because that's what I was interested in. He kept saying how good Ohio State's engineering school was. I wondered if I was good enough to play for Ohio State.

"You come from a small school," he told me. "We are recruiting you because we know you are a good athlete. We wouldn't do it if we didn't know you could play here."

In the end, it was a pretty easy decision for me.

I had heard all the stories of how tough and mean Woody was before I got there. I had heard how hard they hit and how tough practice was. We had a

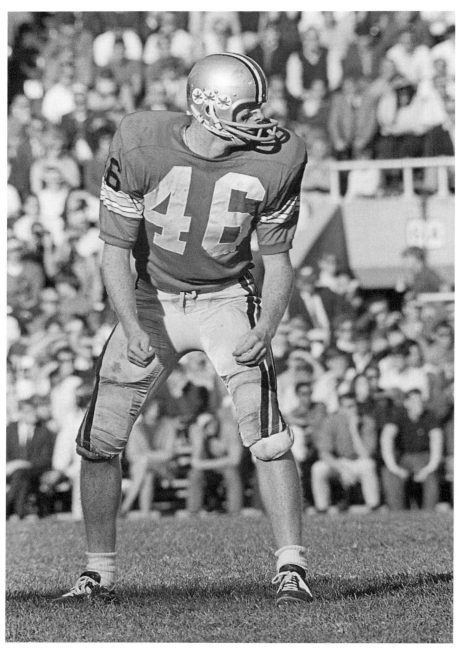

90

Ted Provost started at cornerback for three seasons.

couple of days of practice before the varsity came in. Once they got there, the hitting was probably what they said it was like.

In my freshman year, it was only Woody's second losing season [the first was 1959]. There were people trying to run him out at that point, and those airplanes were flying overhead with banners that read: "Good-bye, Woody."

He told us he was trying to put together three top-notch [recruiting] classes to get it turned around. The class before us had Dave Foley and Rufus Mayes. Ours had Alan Jack, Chuck Hutchison, David Whitfield, Jim Otis, Tom Backhus, and a few other great players. And then that sophomore class that everybody knows about put us over the top.

When things weren't going well, we saw all the bad signs of Woody. My sophomore year we had started 2–3, and Jim Otis had fumbled twice before the half. We were meeting at halftime, and Woody jumped right over two rows of people to take a swing at Otis. We lost that game 17–13. Paul Huff started that next game at fullback and got Midwestern Back of the Week.

I remember that game well because Dick Himes was an offensive tackle and he was really quiet. He never said a word. Before that game at Michigan State, he got up and told us how bad he wanted to beat them. They were favored to beat us badly that day, but we played one of our best games [21–7 win]. We won the next three games and beat Michigan to finish 6–3.

In that '68 season, the game I remember most is the Purdue game. They came in to Ohio Stadium the year before with [quarterback Mike] Phipps, and it was a real embarrassment [41–6 loss]. They could have beaten us 60–0 that day, and it made Woody point to that game for a whole year. They came in the next season ranked No. 1, and we shut them out 13–0.

The thing I remember about the Rose Bowl is that it was all business. There was no partying. We were supposed to do a press thing there when we got off the airplane, but that didn't happen. We began practicing right away, and it all paid off for us.

We were so well prepared for the game because we knew what they did with O. J. [Simpson]. We knew if we could take him away, we would win the game. I actually got my foot hurt in practice and played only for the first quarter and a half. Mark Stier covered O.J. all over the field, and I had to back him up in the secondary if he got by him. One time, I remember they threw a swing pass to him and Mark missed him, and I made an open-field tackle. O.J. got up and said, "Great hit."

I get asked the question a lot, but I do think the '69 team was better. We didn't have Mayes or Foley, but Woody opened up the offense a little bit, and it was easy for us. I think it was too easy. We beat everybody pretty badly—the closest games we had were 27 points [Washington and Minnesota].

We just had a letdown against Michigan, and I don't know why. That junior class got to come back and beat them the next year, but that was my final game. I never had a chance to come back and redeem myself. I know if we had won that game, we would have been voted one of the top teams in the century. We still have reunions for the '68 team, but not for the '69 team.

All in all, it was a great four years at Ohio State. I can say that I am a Buckeye for life.

Ted Provost was an All–Big Ten defensive back in 1968 and '69 and an All-American in '69. He is one of eight Ohio State players to record three interceptions in one game (against Northwestern in 1967).

REX KERN

QUARTERBACK
1968–1970

WHEN I WAS A BOY, my heroes had names like Havlicek, Lucas, and Roberts, and as long as I can remember, I wanted to go to Ohio State to play basketball for the great Fred Taylor. Fred was bigger than life to me. As I developed as a basketball player, he started recruiting me out of Lancaster High School, and my dreams were coming true. But I was pretty good at football and baseball, too, and I had several colleges to choose from. I could have gone to UCLA to play for John Wooden or North Carolina to play for Dean Smith. Ohio University had a great baseball program, and I considered going there, because they would let me play all three sports, and I also was drafted by the old Kansas City Athletics during my senior season.

Then Wayne Woodrow Hayes walked into my life.

It seems that everybody around me met him before I did. He came to one of my basketball games in Columbus, and I was thrilled to death, but it was a game in which I had the opportunity to tie it at the end, and I missed a free throw. "I would like to talk to Rex," he told my parents, "but if he is anything like me, he won't feel like talking after getting beat."

So he left.

One day I was walking down the hallway at Lancaster High, coming out of the locker room, and there he was, walking toward me. He just said hello and kept on walking. He was headed to the principal's office to find out what kind of person I was. He had already talked to my football coach.

Then Dad, who was a barber, got home and told me, "You'll never guess who was in the chair today."

"I have no clue," I told him.

"Coach Hayes came down and got his hair cut today," he said. "He talked about getting an education at Ohio State. He talked about paying back and paying forward, but he didn't talk much about football."

I knew where I wanted to go to college, and when I finally decided it was Ohio State, Woody and Fred agreed that I could play both football and basketball. The real thing that sold me on Ohio State: Coach Hayes and Coach Taylor both convinced me I would get a good education and the academic support would be there if I needed it. I started thinking that I would be the first in my family to get a college degree, so I told them both I would become a Buckeye.

"Okay, Rex, I need you to call these kids," Woody told me, giving me a list of recruits. "There's this kid out of Cleveland we need to get. His name is Larry Zelina. If we get him, it will complete one of the best classes Ohio State has ever had."

One of my first days on campus, I was in the physical education building and I met Rufus Mayes. I saw "Rufe" take off his shirt, and I never thought his shoulders would stop. I never saw anybody that big.

Well, we got Larry Zelina, and the amount of talent on that freshman class was phenomenal. We knew it immediately after that first day of freshman practice. We must have had 10 or 11 high school All-Americans, and I firmly believe our class was the beginning of another era of Ohio State football. These guys were so athletic that they could play any sport. Take Jack Tatum. "Tate" would have been one of the all-time best running backs if he had stayed on offense. He was that good.

As freshmen, they called us the "Baby Bucks." We would practice against the varsity defense in 1967, and one day illustrates what kind of talent we had. We were in goal-line offense, and the defensive coordinator, Lou McCullough, and our freshman coach, Tiger Ellison, were going back and forth.

"Okay, this is what Purdue is going to be running on the goal line," Lou told Tiger. "Let's see if you can score on us."

We gave it to John Brockington, and he would score without anybody touching him. "Okay, let's see what the Baby Bucks can do from the 3-yard line," Lou shouted. So they moved it back to the 3-yard line, we gave it to Larry Zelina, and he scored. They moved it to the 6, and we scored again.

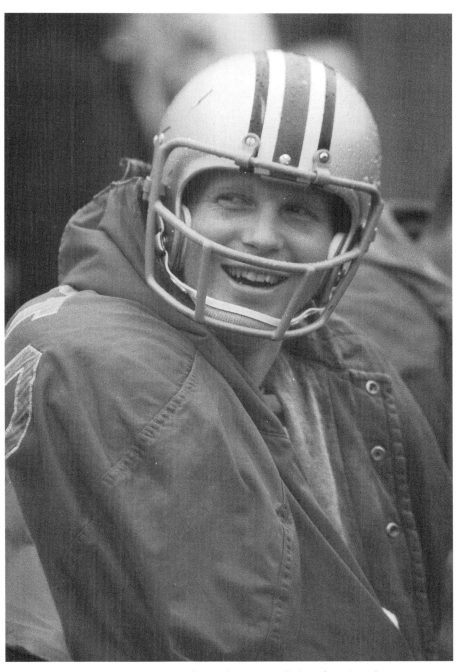

A born leader, Rex Kern was one of Woody Hayes' all-time favorite players.

Tate would score. Then Leo Hayden. They couldn't stop us. Now Lou was starting to get upset. "Dang it, Tiger, you're not running the play right; you are not blocking this the way you are supposed to," he yelled.

Tiger would just say, "You can't stop our Baby Bucks!"

Earle Bruce was coaching the defensive backs that season, and he had this tackling drill for them where they had a five-yard square. They would line up, three defensive backs in this square, give the ball to the freshmen, and then would have to tackle [the freshmen]. First Zelina, and he would get by all three. Brock would run right over them. [Ron] Maciejowski would get through. Tate would make it easy. I would make it. Earle would get so upset with those defensive backs, but they couldn't tackle us. Some of them couldn't touch us.

That next spring, toward the end of spring practice, I had what I thought was a nagging hamstring pull. It had bothered me toward the end of freshman basketball, and one day I couldn't get out of bed or even tie my shoes. So the doctor diagnosed it as a ruptured disk in my lower back. I had back surgery at the end of June, and back surgery was a big deal in those days—not many guys came back from it.

When I came out of surgery, Coach Hayes was in the room. He took my parents out in the hall and told them, "Listen, if Rex never plays a down for us, he'll get his degree from Ohio State. I'll see to that!" My dad told me that conversation later.

Heading into that fall of '68, I didn't think I would be ready, and I wasn't sure how my back would hold up. But I improved and got ready to play, and I was No. 1 on the depth chart.

Woody was such an organized disciplinarian, and we had our routine the day before the game. He even taught us how to pack our bags and what to put in them for our overnight stay. We would go to the golf course, eat filet mignon and those cinnamon rolls that everybody loved, go see a movie, and go back to the hotel. We would have a brief meeting, watch a little film, drink some hot chocolate, and eat our cookies and an apple.

Before that first game, we were opening against Southern Methodist, and my roommate was Jim Otis. Woody would come by and figuratively tuck us in. Well, let's just say that my intestines were working too frequently that night. Woody came in and said, "Jim, how are you feeling?"

"I am ready to play, but if Rex goes to the bathroom one more time, you're gonna have to sleep with him tonight," he told Woody.

"Oh, no, oh, no," Woody replied. "I got to have my fullback rested and ready to go."

Now I was thinking that Otis would be sleeping in Woody's room and Woody would be sleeping next to me. He summoned Dr. Murphy to the room, and Dr. Bob told him, "Rex will be fine. He's just a little nervous."

I remember the exciting part about that next morning: it was the motorcycle escort to the stadium. Coach Hayes was sitting in the front, and I was across the aisle from him. My eyes were as big as saucers, as these motorcycle cops led us down through campus to the stadium. Kids were clapping and rooting for us and cheering at the bus. We got off, and there was a crowd waiting to greet Woody. It seemed that Ohio State football was larger than life.

So the game started, and SMU was passing it all over the field. They set an NCAA record at that time for 76 passes in one game. Woody had told me before the season, "Rex, there will be times out there that you will notice things that me and my coaches won't notice. It will be a gut reaction, and you will have to make a decision out there to do what is best for the team."

We were facing a fourth-and-10 right before the half at about midfield, and this was one of those times. I was huddling the guys as quick as I could, but Woody was sending Mike Sensibaugh in to punt. I waved Mike and the punt team off the field and called, "Robust, fullback delay." It was a short pass for Jim Otis, who would fake block and slip over the middle. That had to be the worst call at the worst time. SMU came on a fire game from the right corner, and Otis got held up by the defensive end. I dropped back, and both linebackers were all over Otis by this time, and the corner hit me and knocked me up into the air. I did a 360 pirouette and landed on my feet. Somehow, I took off and picked up 16 yards and a first down. The crowd went wild. Then I hit Dave Brungard over the middle for a touchdown right before halftime. We won 35–14 that day, and I think it was a new era for Ohio State football. That first game had not been a sellout, and I think we started a chain of sellouts ever since.

Well, we rolled through that season, beating No. 1 Purdue 13–0 in a great defensive game. Teddy Provost made a huge interception and ran into the end zone. We knew the Big Ten championship would go through that last game against Michigan. That fall, I was going to class from 8:00 AM until practice started, and I always had to take a sack lunch with me to eat on the run. One day of that Michigan week, I didn't have time to eat. We came into the meetings, and George Chaump, the quarterbacks coach, said, "Rex, you don't look well. Are you okay?" I told him I missed lunch. So we went out to practice, and I saw this manager carrying a McDonald's bag across the field. He walked up to George and gave it to him. George walked up to Woody, and they talked before Woody called me over. He ordered, "Rex, take this bag and go over there behind those tarps and eat this and then get back in there." So I went over and ate my hamburger, ran back in, and after practice, Rufus told me, "Woody would let you eat McDonald's, but if it were anybody else, especially a lineman, he would have us eating grass if we were hungry."

Early in that Michigan game, Tate fired in on a blitz and just decleated Denny Brown—one of those crushing tackles—and I have no idea how Denny got up. But right then and there, there was no doubt in my mind we were going to beat Michigan. At halftime, we made an adjustment and went to an unbalanced line, and Michigan had never seen it. We just did what we wanted to that day [in a 50–14 win].

Woody always said, "If you are going to fight in the North Atlantic, then train in the North Atlantic." So as we prepared for the Rose Bowl to play USC, he had the heat in the French Field House turned up to 98 degrees every day. The quarterbacks were never involved in tackling drills, but one day in there, Woody said, "George, bring those quarterbacks over here and let them hit the tackling dummy." I was the first guy up and hit the tackling dummy and fell down in pain. I had dislocated my shoulder. Woody came running up and he was screaming, "Oh, shit! Oh, shit!" Our trainer, Ernie Biggs, ran over and popped it back into place, but I couldn't practice and didn't know if I would play in the Rose Bowl. But they rigged up a shoulder harness, and when we went to California, I worked my way back into shape.

I remember during practice out there, Woody had one of his megaton blowups. Paul Huff was a fullback who was injured with a bad back and watching practice from the sideline when Woody got mad about something on the field. All of a sudden, he screamed, "That's it! Everybody's running! Everybody start running!" He looked at Huffer and said, "You too! Run till I tell you to stop."

Later, I was coming out of the shower and almost completely dressed when the equipment manager came in. "Coach Hayes, would you like me to tell Paul Huff he can stop running now?" he asked.

"Yep," Woody said, "tell him to stop."

Poor Huffer had nothing to do with what went wrong on the field, and he was running all that time.

It was very hot on game day, January 1, 1969, and during pregame warm-ups, Otis said, "I am sweating so bad; these jerseys are too hot." We had always practiced in those fishnet jerseys, and we happened to have them in the locker room. Many players that day wore those fishnets in the Rose Bowl, and that was the first time Ohio State had ever used them.

When we met USC at Disneyland, I remember thinking they were the San Diego Chargers. I mean, they were huge! We were undersized on the line of scrimmage, and I was wondering what would happen during the game, but our offensive line controlled USC from the beginning. We got down 10–0 after O. J. [Simpson] busted an 80-yard run, and I got in the huddle and said, "Okay, we've been screwing around long enough. Let's go!" We got back to tie it 10–10 at the half, and then our defense turned it up a notch in the second half. We could always count on our defense.

I think at that time, that game had the largest viewing audience in college football history. We were No. 1 in one poll and they were No. 2, and vice versa. The Rose Bowl was the biggest game in the universe at that time, but I think the euphoria and excitement of beating the team up North was greater. There was nothing like beating Michigan that year. Still, I'll never forget the Rose Bowl. We won the national championship, and I met my wife, Nancy, who was one of the princesses on the Rose Bowl court. [Kern was named the game's MVP, completing 9 of 15 passes for 101 yards and two touchdowns.]

The '69 team had one of those years where we just crushed people. We were winning by three and four touchdowns, and the starters didn't play many second halves. I think *Sports Illustrated* wrote, "Kern might win the Heisman Trophy, but not play enough to earn a letter."

In that first game against TCU, on the first play, we threw a pass to Bruce Jankowski for 69 yards. It was called back for holding. So I noticed they were in man coverage, and I called an automatic: "Gold 98." Woody named it, because he always said, "This play is as good as gold." It was for Bruce to line up on the right side and run a post pattern. Bruce had tremendous speed. We hit it for a touchdown, and that was the first play of the '69 season. We won 62–0 that day.

We threw enough to keep defenses off balance, and we threw a lot on first and second down in '68 and '69.

We were 8–0, ranked No. 1, and had a 22-game winning streak heading to Michigan, as everyone knows. I have never really talked much about what happened that day, and I know people have always wondered, but here it is. The day before the game, it was chilly and moist and a cold front was coming in. Michigan had the artificial turf, and we were out there practicing and stretching on it, and I was lying on my back. My back had gotten wet from this turf, and I started to have a flare-up of back spasms. ABC wanted to do an interview that day, something with a Heisman Trophy angle. They had said that [Purdue's] Mike Phipps and I were splitting the Midwest vote and this game could change that. ABC was late getting there, and the longer I stood waiting on them, the colder it got.

The next day, I couldn't get out of bed. My back was killing me, but gradually it got better, and I was able to move around. On that first series, I had dropped back and then shot up the middle for 50 yards, but something changed after that. [Coach] Bo Schembechler had those guys so well prepared. I always heard later that we had taken Michigan lightly. That is bullshit— Michigan played the greatest game in their school's history. I swear it was like Bo was in our huddle. They knew exactly what we were going to do. It was just an ugly day and, without question, the worst loss I ever experienced. When did I get over it?

I haven't.

That '68 team was voted team of the decade by the *Sporting News* and one of the 10 greatest football teams of all time. I am here to tell you that the '69 team was much better. Woody always said it was the best team ever at Ohio State, but we didn't beat Michigan.

In the locker room after the game, Woody stood on a bench and told us, "All good things must come to an end. This is one of those. We will start preparing for those guys on the way back home." And we did. That will always be branded in my mind and ingrained in my heart.

He had given me a lot of freedom those first two years, but after that Michigan game, it changed. We didn't pass much at all in 1970, and I didn't know why until years later when I read it in Woody's book. He thought I was injured for most of my senior year, but I wasn't. It seemed he just didn't have the confidence to put it up, as we had the first two years. But we had so many great running backs…who would ever argue? We were winning, and that was all that mattered.

That year, on Thursday before the Michigan game, Woody had one of his megatons again. We were running the offense, marching down the field, and two of our guys were standing on the sideline. Now as we went down the field, they were supposed to be paying attention and moving with us, but we got down to the 45, and all of a sudden Woody noticed them over there shooting the breeze, not paying attention. Well, the old man came unglued. His play cards went up in the air, he started ripping his shirt, screaming, the watch went, he was on the ground, and then he started crying. He started crying and said to Earle Bruce, "Earle, they won't play for me! They won't play for me! My God, it's Michigan week and they won't play for me!"

Now I think that was the only time I heard him say the "M" word. He always used some other term for them, but he said it that time. John Hicks was our right tackle and he had never seen Woody like this, and John was real emotional. So was Tommy DeLeone, our center. Now both of them are about to cry. "Come on, Rex, get us ready!" Tommy screamed. "We'll play for him! We'll play for him!"

It was effective.

101

The campus started going nuts that week. On Tuesday night, there were about five thousand students trying to find where players lived...holding their own pep rally. Then there was another one on Wednesday night. Woody got word of this and decided it was time to get us off campus a night early, so we spent Thursday night at the Fawcett Center. I remember that night because at about 10:00 PM, a lot of us were hungry. The trainers told Woody that, and all of a sudden, they had to put in an order at that McDonald's down the street. Can you imagine what happened there when that order for 100 Big Macs and 100 fries came in?

We beat them 20–9 in our last game in our stadium—we never lost a game at Ohio Stadium in those three years. And it did take away a little of the hurt from the year before.

Before that Rose Bowl against Stanford, I think he made a tactical error. Woody brought the captains in to schedule the practices, and [Jim] Stillwagon said, "Coach, instead of going out 14 days ahead of the game and practicing on the first day, why don't we go out 15 days ahead and just do all the media stuff, get our pictures taken, and have a relaxing day. Then the next morning, we'll go two-a-days as long as you want to."

"By God," Woody said, "you seniors are getting smarter. I love that idea."

Well, no sooner had that airplane banked out of Columbus than the trainer came on the speaker and told us who would be getting taped first in the back of the plane. That meant we would be having practice as soon as we landed. Then during the interviews that day, Woody threw the media out, and we had a marathon practice. That set the tone for the Rose Bowl. It put us out of sync, broke our momentum, and really broke our trust.

Stanford was so well prepared. Stillwagon tells the story that [Stanford coach] John Ralston told him he had read Woody's book *Hotline to Victory* three times before the game. He prepared for us out of that book, and [Jim] Plunkett had one of his incredible days. We just weren't in the right mind-set for that game.

I look at my Ohio State days and put it into three categories. One, I got a great education. Two, I made lifelong friends from my teammates and classmates. Three, I got the opportunity to play the best football in the country. Our names became household names with OSU alumni, thousands of fans, and friends all over the world. It's just hard to put into words what Ohio State means to me. I am a product of Ohio State, and I am proud to say that three times I walked across that stage to get degrees [bachelor's, master's, and a doctorate in education]. I hope I became a good representative of our university.

Woody Hayes was such an incredible man to me. There is not enough space for me to say what he meant to me. He brought out the best in everybody.

All the stories don't do him justice.

One time he was in the shopping center in Upper Arlington, and this man came up to him and told him how much he and his wife loved the Buckeyes and how he just wanted to shake his hand. "Well, where is your wife?" Woody asked him. The man told him she was dying of cancer at Riverside Hospital. That evening, that man went to see his wife, and Woody was already sitting by her bedside. There are hundreds of stories like that. Woody used to just walk the halls at all of the hospitals and drop in to cheer people up—people he didn't know.

He would call me over after training table sometimes and say, "Rex, you got any tests you are studying for?" If I said no, he would say, "Let's go." You knew where you were going—you were going to the hospital with him.

We once had a teammate who had lost his best friend in Vietnam. This teammate went home one weekend, and there were some war protesters there, and he got into a fight with them. Well, one of them hit him over the head with a bottle, and he never played a down at Ohio State. The injury had affected his central nervous system. Years later, Woody asked me if I remembered that teammate. I did, and he said, "Well, I got him graduated today!"

That's how much an education meant to the man, whether you played football or not. During my rookie year with the Colts, I surveyed our 17 rookies. One guy from Dartmouth had graduated, and me, and that was it. I know for the first 25 years that Woody was at Ohio State, 87 percent of his players graduated. Of that, another 36 percent went to graduate school. That tells you something about what he thought of an education.

We had one linebacker who was one of the most unlikely guys to go on to law school, but he decided kind of late that's what he wanted to do. Woody went to the dean of the OSU law school. "Sorry, Coach, no way," the guy told him. Woody then called the dean of Capital's law school. The guy looked at his records and said, "You know, son, have you ever thought about another profession?" But Woody helped get him in, and he graduated in the top three of his class. He later went to Oxford, and now he is a judge in Columbus. His name is Bill Pollitt.

I looked this up once recently, and there were 11 scholarships in either Annie Hayes' or Woody's names. Eleven!

Jack Nicklaus wrote me a letter once. It read: "To me, Woody was one of the greatest people in sports history. He always told me, 'I am going to get one of your kids to come to Ohio State.' He got down to my fourth one, Gary. They had made a luncheon date in Columbus on a Friday. Woody passed away the day before. Of course, Gary went to Ohio State. I will never forget Christmas Day 1969, when my dad was dying of cancer. As we finished dinner, there was a knock on our door, and it was Woody Hayes. In his hand was his book, and he had written, 'To the best father-son team I have ever known.' That was pretty special to me. It still is."

I had a very special relationship with Woody Hayes. We both respected each other immediately. When I got my Ph.D., he had a little party for me over at the Jai Lai. That time, he told me how proud he was of me. When they left that sponge in him during his gallbladder surgery, he had to go back into the hospital. I called up and got the receptionist at the hospital. She said, "I am sure Woody would want to talk to you." He got on the phone, and he sounded very weak. "Rex, what are you calling me for?" he asked. All of a sudden he remembered my back problems. "Rex, by God, I hear you got back problems again. You know what we need to do? We need to get you back here to University Hospital and take care of that back."

Now I was thinking, *They left a sponge in you, and you want me to come back there?* But the point is, he never thought of himself. He was worried about my back.

The last time I was in Columbus prior to his death, we went to the Faculty Club for lunch. He was on his cane then, and we went to his favorite table. All of those professors would come into the club and stop by his table. That man had amazing knowledge. He could talk about sociology, business, politics, war, history, anything. We always fought over who would pay—he would never let me pay.

As we left, he said, "Rex, you haven't driven down Woody Hayes Drive yet, have you? By God, we've got to go down there!" We did, and he loved it. I took him home, and I had made up my mind I was going to tell him what he meant to me. We went to the side door, and I opened it for him. Before he walked in, I just said, "Coach, I want you to know that I love you," and I kissed him on the cheek. I think it shocked the old man. That was the last time I saw him alive.

God, I miss that man. The day he died was the saddest day of my life. Even now, it brings great sorrow to me.

After he died, I was in charge of raising money for an endowment chair in military history in his name, and it was something that Annie wanted so badly. We were $10,000 or $20,000 short, and I went to see Dick Brubaker, who was the captain of the 1954 team. Dick said, "I will take care of it." I went back to see Annie, and she was in the hospital when I told her. Tears ran down her cheek.

What a wonderful lady Anne Hayes was. She was just as good a person as he was—maybe even better, because she had to put up with him. We all did, but he made us better people for it.

Rex Kern, who led Ohio State to a 27–2 record in his three-year career, was an All-American in 1969 and team captain in '70. He played three seasons with the Baltimore Colts and one with the Buffalo Bills. He was inducted into the College Football Hall of Fame in 2007. He earned three degrees—bachelor's, master's, and doctorate—from Ohio State.

MIKE SENSIBAUGH

DEFENSIVE BACK

1968–1970

I GREW UP IN CINCINNATI as a preacher's kid, and when it came time to choose a college, I really didn't want to go to Ohio State. I just didn't want to stay close to home, so I visited Georgia Tech, Maryland, and Florida. But this man at my high school told me that you needed somebody to stand behind you in case you get hurt or they make a mistake with you. He said you have to make sure they won't run you off the football team or take your scholarship if you don't pan out. "Besides, 100 miles is far enough from home," he told me. He was talking about a first-class program like Ohio State.

I was planning on majoring in math, and when Woody recruited me, he told me, "Now math is a good subject. Either you have the right answer or the wrong answer."

He convinced me that Ohio State was the right school for me.

I remember getting some of the best advice of my life during my freshman orientation. [Assistant coach] Tiger Ellison was a super guy, and he told us, "As a freshman, you're a number. But go to class! No matter what the situation is, go to class. Don't sit in the back of the class. Sit right up front. Take notes on what is important. When that professor looks at you, you be looking back at him. That professor, or teacher's assistant, has gone through graduate school, and that subject is the most important thing in the world to him. So you have to make like it is, too."

That really stuck with me, and I shared this with my kids when they went to college.

The thing that I can remember from my first game, the season opener against SMU in 1968 at Ohio Stadium, was the roar of the crowd for the first time. It was something I will never forget. I got my first career interception and then got clobbered by Jack Tatum as he tried to peel off a tackler. The guy had me by the leg, and Jack hit me so hard I fumbled. But I recovered it, so I didn't make a complete fool of myself.

SMU must have attempted about 80 passes that day [actually 76, which remains an OSU opponent's record], and our secondary coach was Lou Holtz. After the game, Coach Holtz told me, "I couldn't grade you, son, because I couldn't even find you on the film." I guess I was lining up pretty deep at free safety.

That was the year we became humans again. As freshmen, you couldn't play back then. We just played two freshmen games and practiced all the time. So our class was really ready during spring ball. We were getting into the mix and we would be able to play—Rex Kern, Timmy Anderson, Jim Stillwagon, John Brockington, Jack Tatum…what a great class.

I remember that August when we were taking our team photo. Woody looked at me in my jersey and said, "Mike, that's not your high school number. Don't you want your high school number? What was it anyway?" I just said "10" and he said, "Oh," and walked away. Rex had that number. An interesting story: Tom Bartley was the only one not in the team photo. He had a class that day and he was a senior. He probably didn't care much at the time, but then we won the national championship, and that was the official team photo of Ohio State's last national champions.

That was a fantastic run that season. We were the last undefeated team at Ohio State until 2002. Let's face it, from 1968 until 2002 is way too long. We should have had a few in between.

I was punting some, and in the second game against Oregon I squibbed one off the side of my foot. I came off to the sideline, and Woody started beating me on my shoulder pads, screaming, "Don't you ever do that again!" The other coaches came over to me and said, "If you ever do that again, don't run off the field toward Woody!" I said, "He's going to find me sooner or later, so I might as well get it over with."

At Illinois that season we jumped ahead 24–0 at halftime. Then in the second half, Rex got hurt. Illinois scored three touchdowns and went for

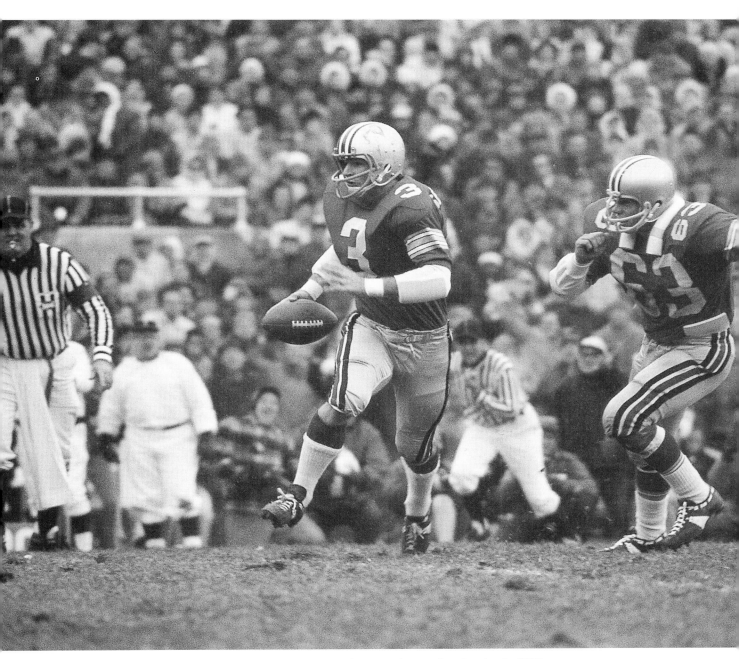

Mike Sensibaugh (3), here returning an interception against Purdue in 1969,
believed if he could get a hand on the football, he could intercept it.

two-point conversions on each and got them all to tie it. We scored again to make it 31–24 late in the game. Woody always yelled in practice, "If you miss a ball or a pass, don't beat on the ground and act like that is the first ball you ever missed. Don't do it for the fans. Just get up and make the next play."

So I had an opportunity for this interception, and I took a dive at it. It would have basically ended the game. I just missed it, and I wanted to pound my hands on the ground, but I remembered what Woody had always said in practice. So I got up, and on the next play, I intercepted a pass to end the game.

I just felt that if I should get my hands on the ball, I should catch it, and I felt that way from my first game [Sensibaugh holds the OSU record with 22 interceptions].

It takes a lot to go through a championship season. But we beat Michigan and headed to the Rose Bowl to play O.J. Simpson and USC. I didn't start the game, but Ted Provost got hurt early, and I came in and played most of the game. I remember the first time they got down there, they had a first-and-goal and they ran O.J. on two weak-side runs to my side. I scraped off and tackled him two times in a row. He had no place to go. We held them to a field goal, and it was 3–0. Now we had watched film of O.J. and knew what he could do, but seeing it was believing it. The next time, he made this lateral move, and I went for the kill. I just got a hand on him and he went 80 yards to make it 10–0.

108

We came back to win [27–16] and won the national championship. It was a great day. The great thing about that team was that there were a lot of seniors who were unselfish. Take a class guy like Bill Long. He was a two-year starter at quarterback before Rex came along. But several seniors gave up positions.

That '69 season was the most fun because we just blew everybody away…until the Michigan game. I still don't know what happened. I think Rex got hurt in warm-ups, and he still won't divulge what happened. We don't even like to talk about it after all these years. It was the toughest defeat ever.

We never even watched film of that loss. I remember after I got into pro ball with the Cardinals and one of my teammates was Dan Dierdorf. He said, "We beat your ass." I said it was only 24–12. "No," he said, "we really beat your ass physically." I guess they did. It was one of Woody's greatest teams, but that was the end of the [22-game] winning streak.

In 1978 we were playing at Canton, Ohio, in the preseason, and Jim Otis was a teammate. Woody came into the locker room to see us. Dan turned and introduced himself to Woody. Woody said, "Yep, yep, yep…we made a mistake [not recruiting] you." Then he just turned around and walked away. Woody disliked anything to do with Michigan. In fact, I never heard him say the word Michigan. He always said "those sons of bitches up North" or something like that.

We used to have to wear our names taped to our helmets during practice, and that's how I got my nickname, "Baugh." The tape with the front part of my name had peeled off, so Doug Adams and Stillwagon started calling me that. Doug Adams was the thickest-chested guy. He had upper-body strength to no end. We didn't have weights in the dorm, so he would say, "Baugh, come sit on my back," and he would do push-ups as I sat on his back. What a true friend. One of the saddest days in my life years later was the day when I heard he was killed while riding his bike.

Rex, too, was such a phenomenal person. In the locker room, they had us numerically, so with me being 3, I was next to him. During our senior year, he gave me a Bible and wrote in it: "Thanks for letting me locker next to you for the past three seasons." I still have it. What a neat man.

Another awesome player was Tatum. I really think Tatum would have been one of the best running backs Ohio State ever had. You just could not catch that man when he had the ball.

You know how I hated dropping interceptions. Well, I had pretty sticky fingers off the field, too. Our practice balls had "Ohio State University" ingrained in them, and I decided that they made great gifts for family members and friends. I lived right behind the football facility at Buckeye Village. So if I ever got a real good ball when I was punting in practice, I would shank one purposely over the fence and then come back and get it later. I sort of became known for that. I would stick them in bushes where we entered and exited during practices. You know those orange cones that block off parking lots? I would stuff a football right up there and come get it later.

One time, the equipment guys put me in the dirty-towel bin, covered me up with towels and jerseys, and then closed the locker room after practice. I slipped out of there later in the evening, but I had plenty of presents. It was like having a free shopping spree.

Good thing Woody never caught me. Can you imagine Woody today? I don't think Woody would have existed with the press today. You know how those coaches have to talk to the announcers coming off the field at halftime? Gosh, Woody would have taken one of those microphones and jammed it somewhere.

Well, I earned my degree in math and graduated in four years, and I will always be a Buckeye. I was so proud of the [2002] team. It was just time for another national championship. It brought nothing but pride. It is true that Buckeyes bleed scarlet and gray. Ohio State was the right school for me.

Mike Sensibaugh, who was All–Big Ten in 1969 and '70, holds the Ohio State career interception record with 22. He played eight seasons in the NFL.

JIM STILLWAGON
MIDDLE GUARD
1968–1970

IT SOUNDS FUNNY TO SAY NOW, but when I was a young kid from Mount Vernon, Ohio, I didn't like Ohio State. My dad went to Notre Dame.

I had gone to military school in Virginia because I didn't get along with the nuns too well at my school. But I came home one time so I could see my parents and visited Ohio State. I got recruited by Michigan State, West Virginia, and all those schools in the South.

I met Woody Hayes and went into his office. They didn't have any scholarships for me, but on that day, some other high school player had told them that he wasn't coming. So they had a scholarship for me at the last moment. I remember Woody asking me what was the last novel I had read. I don't think I had read any novels, but I said *Moby Dick*. So we spent about 45 minutes talking about *Moby Dick*. Then he said, "If you are good enough, you'll make it here. And if you're not, you won't."

So I became a Buckeye.

I remember the program was in the dark ages with weight lifting at that time. I had to bring my own weights. We had a special bond on that freshman team. We scrimmaged against the varsity, and there was a lot of pride among the freshmen. From that nucleus, we had a common goal. We were all different one way or another, but we had one thing in common: to win.

As sophomores, we all took starting positions and just had a great year. We wouldn't be denied. We just overwhelmed people. We were a horse-and-

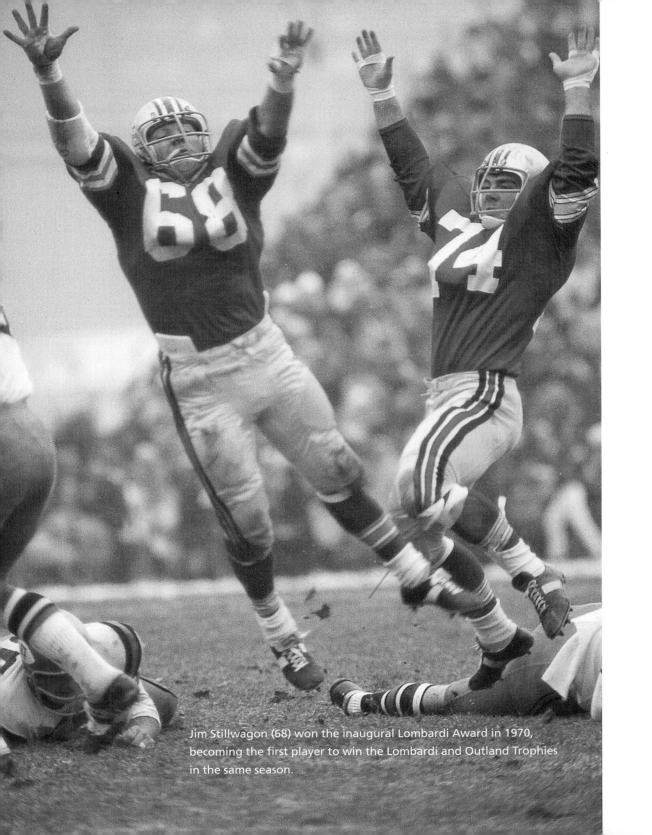

Jim Stillwagon (68) won the inaugural Lombardi Award in 1970, becoming the first player to win the Lombardi and Outland Trophies in the same season.

plow team, and Woody was a great horse-and-plow coach. We won every game. It's hard to believe that was the last national championship team from Ohio State until 2002.

But we were so worn out after the Rose Bowl [a 27–16 win over USC] that we didn't really appreciate what had happened. Woody always believed that if too much good was written or said about you, it would make you soft. That eventually wore on us.

Our junior year, we had a great season until the Michigan game. We were No. 1 in the country for every week from camp all the way through. Rex Kern was hurt in that Michigan game, and Woody was superstitious. We had attacked people all season until that game. One of his downfalls was he would outthink himself, and I think he did it in that game [a 24–12 loss]. Woody was predictable when it was close. Bo knew Woody's mind-set, too. He knew we would run right and run left. He stacked those tackles in there on the line of scrimmage. That game set us back. It set Woody back.

As seniors, however, that game motivated us. It set us up for a revenge game against Michigan, and it was one of the greatest games I played. We beat them [20–9]. We went out to the Rose Bowl to play Stanford and went through two-a-days [practices] and scrimmaged in a gymnasium with tennis shoes on. Woody loved to hit and hit all the time. It wore on us. We scrimmaged a lot and really had a minor uprising—a big team meeting—and it was never right after that. I think he lost sight of the big picture. Then in the game we sat back and didn't attack them. Stanford beat us [27–17]. I am not taking anything away from Stanford, but they played an eight-cylinder team playing on four cylinders.

113

Don't get me wrong. Woody Hayes was a great man. But was Woody Hayes a great Xs-and-Os coach? No. Was he a great leader? Yes. He could make an average player good. He could make a good player great. And he could make a great player a superstar.

I have a lot of great Woody stories, but one of my favorites is this: he always wore short sleeves no matter how cold it was. I would see him after practice in that shower for about 10 minutes, and his arms were purple like plums. Well one time he was not wearing a short-sleeve shirt, but he had on one of those mock turtlenecks. We started to call him "Woodstock" once we saw that turtleneck, and, you know, he sort of liked it.

My senior year was when there was the energy crisis, and Woody wouldn't drive because of the gas crunch. So I had this old Barracuda I was driving, and after practice one day Woody asked for a ride over to training table. He liked riding with me, so during my whole senior year he rode with me after practice. It was neat just listening to him. He would talk about all the younger players like Randy Gradishar who were going to be great.

Our talks were always interesting because Woody was always interesting. He used to talk about big battles in history and the wars. One time he was telling me about this famous guy from Ohio State who invented "WEFT," which was a way to identify enemy aircraft. It stood for "Wings, Engine, Fuselage, and Tail." Woody called it, "Wrong Every Fucking Time." He said, "By the time you figured it out with that system, the son of a bitch had dropped a bomb on you." I thought that was real funny.

So one day after practice I was in the shower and was telling the guys about Woodstock's theory on WEFT, and I noticed that he was in a bathroom stall listening. I could hear him chuckling about it. I could hear his cleats clattering on the floor because he was laughing so hard.

Anyway, after the Stanford game, Woody called me down to the office and started to thank me for all I had done, and he said, "Son, if you would have played middle linebacker instead of middle guard, you would be drafted higher. I want you to know you made a big sacrifice for the team and I appreciate it. You are going down to the Lombardi Award thing in Houston, but don't get too excited. They won't give it to no Yankee bastard." I went down there, and there were Spiro Agnew and Howard Cosell. I sat next to Red Adair, listening to him talk about eating a cold turkey sandwich off the coast of some country while bullets were whizzing over his head. It was a great experience, but I was not expecting to win this thing, and then they called my name. I was surprised.

Later, they called me up and told me I also won the Outland Trophy. It wasn't a big award back then, but now it's a part of Americana. You know, I really never liked individual awards. I am against retiring numbers. I think it is the wrong thing to do. College football is about the team. It is about playing together. At Ohio State, we had a team that won. Not just one player. That was what was always great about Ohio State. We won as a team. We lost as a team. Everybody got treated the same. Everybody respected everybody. I respected and admired the walk-ons the most. We were already on scholarship, but they would come out and get their butts killed, and they were paying their way.

Individualism really is a disease. The Ohio State program is back to being a team. It's a special place and provides a special experience. It's really too bad that everybody can't come out of that tunnel and run onto that field just one time. You come off the ground emotionally. In this whole world and atmosphere at that particular time, you are on one of the grandest stages and part of one of the biggest shows on earth. It's very special.

Looking back, I am very thankful they had one last scholarship for me.

Jim Stillwagon, a two-time All-American and MVP of the 1970 team, became the 15th Ohio State player elected to the College Football Hall of Fame.

JOHN BROCKINGTON
RUNNING BACK
1968–1970

I FIRST LIVED IN A BOARDING HOUSE in Manhattan before we moved to Brooklyn when I was seven years old. We took the BMT train to the last stop on the No. 42 bus, and that landed us at 1590 East 102nd Street—the Bayview Projects. And that is where I grew up.

There were three of us kids—my brother Freeman, my sister Linda, and me—and we grew up in the heart of this four-block area of projects. It was a Jewish neighborhood and not a rough neighborhood by any means. We could hang out all night, and nothing bad was going on. Actually, it was a great place to grow up for me because it seemed that everybody got along well.

There was a little park that took up about a third of one block, connected to a school, and that is where I learned to play every sport there was. I learned to catch a football there because we always played two-handed touch. It was concrete, so we couldn't tackle. We also played stickball with a certain set of ground rules for doubles, triples, and home runs, and as we got bigger, we expanded the ground rules. We also played handball. We played pitch and catch, and I know this is when I developed my eye-hand coordination. There is a book titled *Talent Is Overrated*, which states that practice is what makes you great at anything. And that is what we did. We played and practiced day after day after day.

When I started playing football at Thomas Jefferson High, my first position was wingback, and the coaches later moved me to fullback, and I also

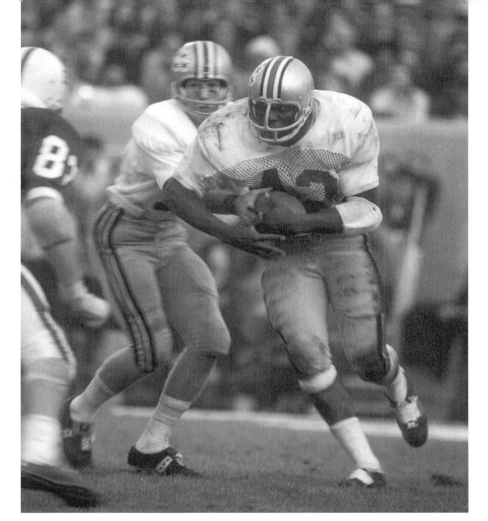

John Brockington (42) takes a handoff from Rex Kern in the 1971 Rose Bowl versus Stanford, a 27–17 loss in Pasadena, California—one of only two defeats during Brockington's three-year Ohio State football career. *Photo courtesy of Getty Images*

played linebacker. The field we practiced on was nothing but dirt, and we constantly had to water it down because it was so dusty. It was a very modest facility, to say the least, but we had some good football teams.

I remember at one point during my junior year, I was missing too many practices—I was young and immature—and my coach [Moe Finkelstein] grabbed me and said, "Son, you are always missing practice. Why is that? You have 30 seconds to decide if you want to be on this football team."

He jerked me straight with that talk. You always have a few of those moments that change your life, and this was one of them. From then on, I became a pretty good football player, and I never missed practice again.

We didn't have a lot of kids from my school going to college, but I noticed colleges being interested in me, schools such as UConn and Syracuse. Then Larry Catuzzi, an Ohio State assistant coach, came to see me. I remember we sent film of me to Nebraska, but they told me I would be a third-team running back if I went there. I didn't know about Woody Hayes, but my high school coach knew all about him. He came out and talked to my mom about my getting an education at Ohio State. He didn't talk about football, and he didn't recruit me. Woody recruited her, and he recruited her on education.

When I first went to Ohio to visit the campus, I was terrified. I had never been on an airplane before, and when that landing gear went up, I thought the thing would crash. I remember going to a basketball game at St. John Arena and seeing how beautiful everything was on campus. The grass was so green. There were beautiful trees, and the stadium was huge. I thought, *Oh my gosh, I would get to play on this beautiful green grass field, in front of all these people?*

I remember asking Coach Catuzzi, "What are the school colors—red and gray?"

He said, "No, son, scarlet and gray."

I remember seeing an Ohio State sweatshirt with those colors, and I asked the coach, "Can I take that home with me?"

He said, "Can't do it. If I give that to you, I am committing an NCAA violation."

I also visited Syracuse and met Larry Csonka, but they didn't accept me right away, and Ohio State did. There was a war going on, and I wasn't going to wait. Plus, I loved my visit to Columbus, so I was about to become a Buckeye.

One of the first nights in my dormitory, I remember heading down to the snack bar, and the first person I saw was Doug Adams. He was wearing a pair of blue cutoff shorts, flip-flops, and a tank top. He had this big barrel chest and looked like a Greek god. I thought to myself, *I am really going to have to work my butt off to play at this school. These guys know what they are doing. They are big and they are good.*

The thing is, Ohio State didn't really have a weight program at that point, but certain guys lifted on their own, and you could tell that Doug was one of those guys.

Once practices started, it was evident that we had a pretty good freshman class with guys like Rex Kern, Bruce Jankowski, Jim Stillwagon, Leo Hayden, Jack Tatum, and Tim Anderson. The varsity had all they could handle to control us [in scrimmages]. The coaches were thinking about making me a linebacker at first, but I always knew I could block and play running back, and I wanted to stay on offense.

I also didn't make mental mistakes such as jumping offside. I worked hard, hustled all the time, and did what the coaches asked me to do. I knew with coaches like Lombardi and Woody Hayes, you would stay on their good side if you did those things.

Freshmen were ineligible then [until 1972], of course, but after that first year, there was a question whether I should be at fullback or halfback. I wanted to be at fullback, but I knew Woody loved Jim Otis and had a relationship with his father that went way back. I had a great spring but came back in the fall as the No. 2 guy and thought I should have been starting.

The only time Woody ever got mad at me was one time during a drill, we were running "30 Dive," and I carried it for seven yards and then again for five yards, but my shoe came off. I went to the sideline to tie my shoe, and I could see these legs straddling me. I looked up, and it was Woody. "If you ever run the football like that again, you will never play a down at Ohio State!" he snapped. He wanted me to stop messing around and run it straight upfield.

This story shows another side to Woody Hayes. I was married to my high school sweetheart in 1967, and we had a baby girl named Kelly. On our first Thanksgiving, we were living in a small one-bedroom apartment at the old Buckeye Village, and there was a knock at the door. There was Woody, standing there with a basket full of fruit and nuts and a turkey for us. He knew we didn't have much, and he wanted to make sure we had food for Thanksgiving. That's the type of man he was.

To start my sophomore season [1968], I remember catching a 44-yard pass from Rex to set up the season's first touchdown [in a 35–14 win over Southern Methodist]. In the third game, we were playing No. 1 Purdue, and they had crushed us the year before [41–6]. Leroy Keyes had just killed us running the football. I remember the coaches preaching, "Now Leroy Keyes is a cutback runner. Don't over-pursue him. Stay in your lanes and tackle him when he cuts back."

Woody told us, "They have these big defensive tackles who are the key to their defense. We are going to run those big, fat defensive tackles to death, and then they will be too tired to make tackles." Sure enough, the coaches knew what they were talking about. Keyes didn't gain but about 24 yards that day, the defense beat [Purdue quarterback] Mike Phipps up pretty good, those defensive tackles got tired, and we won 13–0. That's when we knew we had something.

We were undefeated and practicing for Michigan when Ron Maciejowski and somebody else were fooling around in practice behind Woody's back, and he turned and saw them. He threw his cards up into the air, took his glasses off, and crushed them in his hands and started screaming, "Don't you know we are playing Michigan this week!"

We just destroyed Michigan that week, and by the end of the game it was 50–14.

We were No. 1, and that set up the Rose Bowl matchup with No. 2 USC for the national championship. I didn't play much because I had a horrible Michigan game, but I was just happy to be there. I knew we had a good thing going, and I didn't want to cause trouble and split the team up over my lack of playing time. Being young, you don't always make the best decisions, but I think I handled not playing pretty well as a sophomore and a junior, and I think Woody always appreciated the way I handled it.

I remember our defensive guys running and pursuing O.J. Simpson all over the field. One time, Tim Anderson just nailed him in the chest. Our guys could run on defense. After the game [Ohio State won 27–16 to win the national title], O.J. came into our locker room, and this is exactly what he said: "I just want to tell you guys that you are the best fucking football team I have ever seen. Congratulations!"

By the time I was a senior, Jim Otis was gone. They moved me to fullback, and I became the featured back. It was a fun season for me, getting all those carries and helping us to another undefeated season.

One game, against Northwestern at home, we got the ball on our 5-yard line, and Woody was mad at the way we were playing, so he ran me every play until we got to the 50. It must have been about 10 straight carries. We had a fourth-and-1, and he ran me again. I picked it up and came to the sideline, and he said, "I did that because of you! I did that because of you!"

I had 42 carries that day (for 161 yards) and my shins were sore after that game. Woody never forgot anything. He knew I was a good soldier the two years before and took not playing well when I could have made an issue of it. That was his way of repaying me.

It's funny because later on when I was with the Packers, my locker was next to Ray Nitschke's. He once told me, "You should go kiss Woody's ass."

I asked, "What?"

He said, "I am serious. You should kiss his ass. If he had started you for three years, you would be burned out and have nothing left by now, but you are fresh and have a lot of carries left in you."

Anyway, by the time we got to Michigan week, we were 8–0 and Woody had us each write on a piece of paper what we planned to do against Michigan. I don't know what I wrote, but Woody read it and started screaming, "Now, John Brockington, are you going to do it? Are *you* going to do it?"

Another thing that struck me during that game was when Stillwagon limped off the field. Assistant coach Bill Mallory looked at him and said, "It's Michigan! You can't get hurt today!" Jim just looked at him, turned around, and limped back to the huddle. And we won 20–9.

We had a seniors' meeting before the Rose Bowl against Stanford when Woody asked us, "Now we can fly out there on the 17th [of December] and relax and get acclimated and not practice until the 18th, or we fly out the 18th and practice that day. What do you want to do?"

121

Naturally, we chose the 17th, thinking we could go to a movie and relax a little bit before beginning practice the next day. The flight was about an hour out of Los Angeles when somebody announced, "Okay, red team, start getting taped for practice." We had a lot of ticked-off football players on that trip. We then held a meeting of the seniors, and one of the captains went to Woody and said, "You lied to us."

Woody just went off and screamed, "This is my football team! I'll do it the way I want!" You just didn't defy Woody Hayes.

We went into the game knowing that the No. 1 team [Texas] got beat and the national championship was ours if we won. We were ahead 17–13 after three quarters, but that fourth-down play at their 19-yard line changed the game. Rex audibled "Railroad," changing a "27" running play to the left to a "26" to the right, but the line didn't catch the audible. There was nothing there, and I got stopped for no gain. Then Jim Plunkett got hot and drove them down the field to take the lead right after that.

That loss [27–17] and the Michigan loss of 1969 were the only two losses of our careers. We finished with a 27–2 record and could have won three straight national championships if we had won those two games. Can you imagine, winning three straight national titles? Nobody has done that.

Woody once told us during a team meeting, "Look around this room. These people will be your best friends for the rest of your life."

You know, he was right. When I got sick [Brockington received a kidney transplant in 2001], the first people who wanted to help me were several of my old teammates, most of all Ron Maciejowski. Then another guy by the name of Jim Coburn was the first to offer his kidney. Those facts remind me that, once we all got to know each other, race didn't matter to any of us. We were all one family when we played at Ohio State, and that was the first time some white guys on the team were exposed to black players.

I don't remember the final time I ever talked to Woody, but I remember the day he died [March 12, 1987], and it was a very, very sad day for me. He was like a dad to me at times—like a dad to all of us. He taught us about life. I know he was proud of me when I became NFL Rookie of the Year with the Packers, although he never told me that, because once I saw a picture of me in my Packers uniform behind his desk. He wasn't into patting you on the back, but he felt it.

I have to say, Ohio State means everything to me. I love Ohio State. I love the football program and I love the school. I can never replace the overall experience of those four years. I had great teammates who became great friends. I was a part of something, a part of a great institution. I am so thankful for that experience. Ohio State is my school. I love the Packers today, but I *bleed* scarlet and gray for the Buckeyes.

John Brockington rushed for 1,142 yards and 17 touchdowns in 1970 and was named a first-team All-American. He finished his career with 24 touchdowns and a 4.4-yards-per-carry average. He was a first-round pick of the Green Bay Packers and was named NFL Rookie of the Year in 1971. He was named to the Pro Bowl three times and finished his NFL career with 5,185 rushing yards and 30 touchdowns. He retired from football in 1977. His foundation, johnbrockington foundation.org, provides help and hope to those affected by kidney disease.

DICK WAKEFIELD
END
1969–1971

I WAS BORN IN ROYAL OAK, MICHIGAN, and grew up in Avon Lake, Ohio, loving the Buckeyes. Not that he needed to, but Woody Hayes visited me twice to recruit me, and each time he came to one of my high school basketball games. In that first game, we got beat by Bay Village 102–47, and Woody came into the locker room after the game. He said, "I'll come back the next time you play them." The day we were to play Bay Village again, it was snowing, and I got a telegram that day: "The weather's too bad. Good luck against Bay Village!" It was signed "Woody Hayes." I was disappointed I wouldn't see him that night, but right before the game, he walked in with Rex Kern. We lost that game, too, but it was much closer—77–70. During the game, he sat next to my dad and grandmother, and he buttered her up all night. She thought he was the king of the world. My dad loved him, too. He sold the parents, but he was an honest man. I remember him telling them both: "I guarantee he will get a good education."

There was no doubt where I would spend the next four years.

Once I got to Ohio State, I was awestruck. I was from a little hick town of 6,000 people, and I remember seeing those 11-story dorms and all those big buildings, and I thought, *What am I going to do now?* That's where the camaraderie of Ohio State football came in. Most of the players bonded together, and you quickly found out that there were many more guys with the same feelings that you had. Right away, Woody laid down the law. His

Dick Wakefield was an end from 1969 to 1971. *Photo courtesy of Dick Wakefield*

124

famous line was: "You don't have to like me, just respect me." I can honestly say nobody was respected more than Coach Hayes. He also said something like, "If you show me a good guy that the players love all the time, I will show you a loser."

There's one thing that man never was—a loser. The thing that upset Woody the most was mental mistakes. He hated offside and holding, and when you did those things, he would jump all over you. I remember in one practice, John Brockington kept missing the hole. He was running with his head down and kept missing it. Finally, Woody started chasing him, screaming, "I am going to get you!" Can you picture this older man, running down the field, shaking his fist and chasing John, who probably ran a 9.7 100-yard dash?

One time we were having a bad practice, fumbling and jumping offside and not hitting the holes, and he stopped practice and told us, "I know what the problem is—you're not getting enough blood into your heads. Everybody, stand on your head!" So here we were, as a team, doing handstands. We were stopping traffic on Olentangy River Road. People were stopping their cars to watch this. And God forbid if you laughed. If you did it, you did it quietly. One time, Woody knocked the wind out of me. He hit me in the chest, and I went down. I didn't drop many passes after that. If he was alive and doing that today, everybody would be suing him.

Despite all that, he was a very caring man. One thing Woody had us do— when we flew to road games he would have us take out those life insurance policies for $10 each and make our parents the beneficiaries. I think the university paid that $10 for us. And then we always picked up a postcard and would write a note home to our parents. He wanted us to do that to stay in touch with the people we loved.

The guy was ahead of his time in a lot of ways, too. You know how the NFL has that instant-replay rule where teams are charged a timeout to review a play? Woody had that idea for college football when I played. He knew better than anyone that officials blew calls.

Which brings me to the 1971 game at Michigan. We were 6–3, having a down year because of injuries. We had 12 starters out for that game, and we were heavy underdogs. The night before the game, Tommy Marendt, a starting defensive end, came down with appendicitis, and now he couldn't play. We were just riddled with injuries, but we had them down 7–3 before they got a late touchdown to take the lead. We passed a lot that season, because we didn't have the talent or depth to line up and smash people. The tackle next to me, Merv Teague, who was a hell of a player, weighed about 220. I was a 200-pound tight end/wingback. Donny Lamka was our quarterback, and he reminded me of Bobby Douglass. He would run right over you if he had to, and he was a great field general, a natural leader.

We got to late in the game, we crossed the 50, and we had a certain play set up. We knew that if we were in a two-or-more back set, they would bring their so-called Wolfman closer to the line of scrimmage. On this play, I was at tight end on the right side, but the formation was to the left. I knew Michigan was thinking, *Why is Wakefield on the other side?* The play called for

Jimmy Lee Harris to run a go pattern on the left side, and we would run play-action, and I would come down underneath, running from the right side to the left side. Thom Darden, their free safety, read it and came up on me. It was a perfect pass, and as I was about to catch it, Darden came up over my shoulder and went over the top of me. He intercepted it right in front of Michigan's bench, but there is no doubt he interfered with me. The line judge was right there looking at it. I got up, and immediately I looked around for the flags. I saw a few and thought, *Great, now we got a first down.* Then somebody told me, "No, it's not interference—it's on your coach."

Woody just went ballistic. He grabbed those yard markers and busted them over his knee. He proceeded to get flagged two more times. I called that official everything that he was, but he never flagged me, because he knew he missed the call. I was a senior, and it was my last game, and I hated to lose to them. That play would have been a huge, huge gain—maybe even a touchdown. We busted our butts the whole game, and then we had that happen at the end.

It was not the way I wanted to end my career, but I have always been a Buckeyes fan and always will be. As I sit here at my desk, I am looking at a Woody bobblehead. You have to wonder what he would have thought about those things. After your playing days are done, you go through a secondary rush with each Ohio State game you watch. After we won the national title in the Fiesta Bowl, I was so wired that I couldn't go to bed until 5:00 in the morning. And I am here to say there are no better fans than Ohio State fans.

I live in Michigan now, and I am misplaced up here because I am a Buckeye through and through.

126

Dick Wakefield led Ohio State in receiving in 1971 with 31 receptions for 432 yards. His 11 receptions against Colorado are tied for seventh best on the school's single-game list.

STAN WHITE

LINEBACKER

1969–1971

WHAT DID I GET OUT OF PLAYING football at Ohio State? I met my wife, played on a national championship team, got an accounting degree [and later a law degree while playing pro football], and became a young man from the boy who first stepped on campus in 1968.

Most important, I played for Woody Hayes, who molded countless boys into men. We all received demands by Coach Hayes to get an education. Woody emphasized this: "The next play could be your last, but your education would never be taken away."

Those days, the athletes lived on South Campus. I lived in Stradley Hall all four years. I remember the camaraderie among all the athletes. We played basketball constantly on the 11th Avenue courts. I remember having relay sprint races down and back on the sidewalk from Stradley to Bradford Commons. Ed Smith, Jim Cleamons, Jack Tatum, and Ray Gillian were just a few who would take off their shoes at night and run…just for the fun of it.

And we had a lot of fun.

Naturally, most of my memories revolve around football. And, of course, the memories are always strongest from the Michigan games. The four during my stay were all memorable. Since freshmen weren't eligible, I watched from the stands as my varsity teammates closed out the unlikely unbeaten regular season in 1968 by beating Michigan 50–14.

The next day, Tony Mason, a Michigan assistant, called Woody "a big fat pig." Later, their whole staff was fired. The Wolverines hired Bo Schembechler, and we all remember that first Bo-Woody matchup in 1969.

After all these years, it still hurts. It hurts while I am writing this. It will always hurt. It will be in my gut for the rest of my life.

The 1970 Michigan game will also be in me the rest of my life, but this one I will carry in my heart. It was two unbeaten teams meeting in the biggest rivalry in sports. And we won 20–9. I intercepted a pass late in the game and returned it to the 9-yard line. A couple of plays later, Rex pitched to Leo Hayden on an option for a touchdown to cap off the game.

But what I remember most is the crowd. I played for 21 years, including 13 in pro football, and you know what? On that interception, it was the only time I ever heard the crowd during the game. As I jumped to catch the ball, I was struck by the booming explosion of the crowd. That moment is seared in my memory, and it is as real today as it was all those years ago.

The greatest player I played with was undoubtedly Jack Tatum. He was scary in person and downright feared on the field. He was the only player I ever saw who never had to break down when making a tackle. He could run full speed, adjust at full speed, and always delivered a lethal blow right between the numbers. He was as fast as he needed to be. In that 1968 Michigan game, there was one play I can still see. Jack blitzed on the outside from his monster position as Michigan All-American Ron Johnson found a big hole up the middle and was off to the goal line. Jack suddenly went into a baseball slide, got up, took off through the same hole, and ran down Johnson in what looked like a man chasing down a little boy. He saved a touchdown. What a player.

But my favorite player was Rex Kern. He was a brilliant ball handler, a great athlete, and the consummate winner. He later became my roommate during my rookie year with the Baltimore Colts. He introduced me to his strength, Jesus Christ. It changed my life and the purpose of my life forever.

In 1971 we had lost all of those "Super Sophomores" like Rex, Tatum, Brockington, Sensibaugh, and Stillwagon, and we had 11 knee surgeries as a team. Michigan was undefeated, we were 6–3, and the game was in Ann Arbor. But it was Ohio State–Michigan. And with three minutes left, we were still leading 7–3 on my high school teammate's [Tom Campana's] punt return for a touchdown. Michigan finally scored in the last two minutes to take the lead, and our final desperation drive ended when Thom Darden

Stan White led the 1970
team in tackles with 106.

knocked down Dick Wakefield and intercepted that last pass. Woody went berserk. He ran on the field. Jerry Markbreit, who later became a well-known NFL official whom I got to know well, called two or three 15-yard penalties on him. Some guys thought about restraining Woody, but most of us wanted him to go on. At least it delayed the end of our OSU lives.

When it did end, I cried. It's the only time I can remember doing that. My final game ended with Woody tearing up the sideline markers. Well, at least it was memorable.

I sent my son, Stan Jr., to Ohio State to play football. But I also sent him to grow as a man in body, mind, and spirit. I always wanted Stan Jr. to be a Buckeye, but it was beyond doubt when Coach Tressel took over.

People may also think it was coincidental that the 1968 national championship came in my freshman year. The next one, 34 years later, came in my son's freshman year.

I don't.

Stan White, named All–Big Ten in 1971, played 13 seasons in the NFL, starting every game over the final 12 seasons.

TOM DeLEONE
OFFENSIVE LINEMAN
1969–1971

INEVER THOUGHT I WOULD EVER BE good enough to play football in college, let alone make a living at it. Heck, I went out for my eighth-grade team and quit right away because it was a lot harder than I thought it would be. I remember I had a paper route, and my friends sort of ignored me because I didn't play football. Then in ninth grade, we had a 90-man travel squad and I wasn't one of them, but I grew between my ninth and 10th grades, and midway through my sophomore year at Roosevelt High in Kent, Ohio, the senior center got kicked off the team. I became the starter at center and played that position for the next 21 years.

My high school teammates were Stan White and Tom Campana, and everybody was recruiting them. When their films got sent around the country, some coaches started to ask, "Who's that center?"

My father had died when I was 12, and my mom worked at Kent State as a receptionist. Mom and I just figured that I would go to Kent State and keep living at home. But then I got my first scholarship offer—it was from the University of Pittsburgh. Mom sat there crying in our little apartment…I can still see her. Early on, I wasn't being recruited by Ohio State, but Woody Hayes came to our little apartment later and sat down at the kitchen table with Mom and me. He talked about history for three hours. As he got up, he said, "Mrs. DeLeone, I can promise you two things—if your son comes to Ohio State, he will graduate and he will be the starting center by his sophomore year."

Tom DeLeone (52) blocks against Minnesota in 1970 as Rex Kern takes the snap.

I don't know what he saw in me for him to say that, but I sure didn't think that way.

When I got to Ohio State in 1968, I remember the day my mom and brother dropped me off at Park Hall. I went to the cafeteria and thought, *Look at all these students....* I couldn't believe how many people were in there, but I was looking at just the football team. That was my first big shock. Right there, I wanted to go home and pump gas, but Jim Jones wouldn't let me. Jim was the study hall coach back then and later became the athletics director, but he saved me from leaving Ohio State. "Tom, if you leave," he asked me, "what are you going to do when you get back there?"

I really didn't have an answer for him.

My first practice was a real nightmare—I had to go against Jim Stillwagon. I was a freshman and he was a sophomore, and I never thought I would make it to the second day. That '68 team went to the Rose Bowl and won the national championship, but the freshmen got to go home before Christmas.

Woody was right—by the fifth game of my sophomore season, I started at center. I don't know whom we were playing, but I was sitting in front of Woody during the pregame meeting in the locker room and was hyperventilating. He looked at me and said, "You know, you wouldn't be starting if I didn't think you could do the job." That's all I needed to hear—I was fine after that.

133

That '69 team rolled through the season until the terrible loss at Michigan. I know it was the worst game I had ever played, before or since. I went against Henry Hill, Michigan's nose guard. He was a year ahead of me, and he was very, very good. Here's what I did for the next year: I cut out Henry Hill's picture and pasted it on my dorm room mirror at eye level. Every time I combed my hair or looked in that mirror, I saw Henry Hill for a year. I studied his film intently, and the next year [a 20–9 OSU win], I got a piece of him back. Let me put it this way: Henry Hill left the game in the third quarter.

That week before the game was classic Woody. We were in the offensive huddle in Thursday's practice. He fell to his hands and knees in the middle of the huddle and started crawling around. Both of his hands were touching our feet, and he would go from one player to another. "I want to feel your feet to see if you're ready," he said. He went all the way around the circle doing this to everybody. He came to me, felt my feet, and pronounced, "You're ready to play."

I don't know how he knew it, but I guess I was. Henry Hill would agree with him.

You know, I think it was the same week, but after practice, two girls came over, and we were studying in the dorm. They brought a few beers over with them, so I was sitting there drinking this beer with them in my room when I heard somebody shout, "Woody's on the floor!"

Now Woody would come down to South Campus quite a bit, and he would always bring a pizza with him. It was almost like his disguise. Everybody would always love to see Woody down there, and they would come out to greet him. So I heard this commotion and I stuck those beers under the bed and threw a blanket down there to make sure he couldn't see them. Sure enough, he opened my door and he had a big box of pizza. He just said, "Ladies, we have a big game this week and you should probably leave now."

In my life, I never saw two girls move faster than that. He didn't offer me any pizza, either. He just turned the lights out and said something like, "Get to bed." Then he closed the door. It was about 8:30! But I went to bed. That was Woody—he wanted to see how you were living. Thank God somebody yelled that he was coming, or I would have been caught with that beer.

134

I have to say that I fell in love with everything about Ohio State—the traditions, running out of that tunnel…what an awesome feeling. It is what is right about athletics. Somebody once asked me if I had any second thoughts about going to Ohio State. I said, "Are you kidding me? None." It was the greatest decision I ever made. I will always be a Buckeye.

Tom DeLeone, twice named All–Big Ten, played two seasons with the Cincinnati Bengals and 11 with the Cleveland Browns.

The SEVENTIES

JOHN HICKS
OFFENSIVE LINEMAN
1970, 1972–1973

NINETEEN SEVENTY-FOUR was my rookie year with the New York Giants, and we were playing the Kansas City Chiefs. After the game, a tackle for the Chiefs, Jim Tyrer, who had been in the league for years, came running over and hugged me. "You played a great game," he said.

That year, Doug Van Horn was one of our captains, and I took his place as the starting right guard. He wasn't mad. Generally, veterans don't have a lot to do with rookies, but Doug made it a point to look after me and help me through my rookie season. He took me under his wing, and we became lifelong friends.

You know what Jim and Doug had in common? They, like me, were Buckeyes.

If you walk into the Woody Hayes Athletic Center today, you realize the depth of Ohio State's tradition. There have been 29 College Hall of Famers, more than 130 All-Americans, and several Heisman Trophy winners. There are too many great players to mention, but when I meet any one of them, it is like meeting one of your teammates. It's hard to explain, but that's the way it feels.

I won't forget my official recruiting trip to Ohio State. It was the Michigan game in 1968, and the Buckeyes won 50–14 and won the national championship that year. Seeing the band, the crowd, and the team in those scarlet and gray uniforms running onto the field…it was the greatest experience of my life.

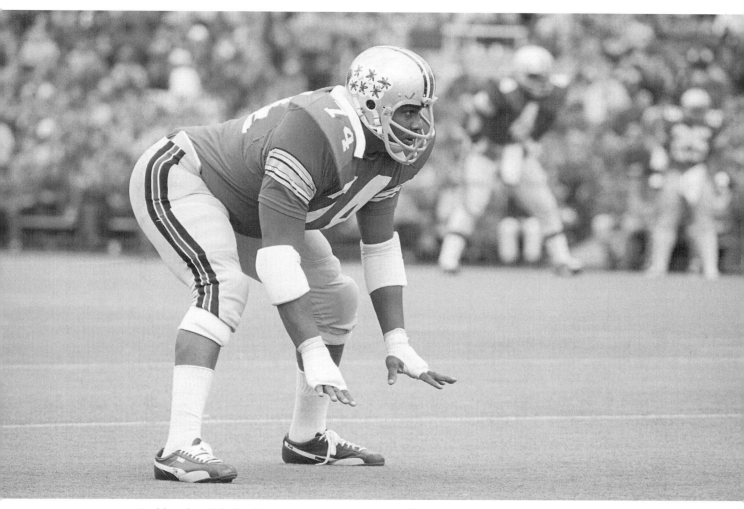

Tackle John Hicks had the size, strength, and mobility to become a two-time All-American.

Coach Hayes later met me and asked, "How would you like to be a Buck-eye?" I thought I was living a dream.

From that day I first accepted the offer, my life changed. I was a Buckeye, sure, but I really didn't know what that meant at that time.

When you play for Ohio State, you know you are special. I realized that as time went on. I remember after our freshman orientation when Coach

Hayes met with us, he seemed to be like a stately grandfather and not the crazy general that everyone made him out to be.

The team was the defending national champions, and I was scared when I walked into the Biggs Facility that first day. I started out as the third-team tackle and the third-team guard, and the freshman coaches really went after us that first day. After the first workout, I remember sitting at my locker next to Merv Teague. I turned and said, "I can't leave because I don't want to go back to the steel mill where I worked during the summer." Merv was from Youngstown and also had worked at the steel mill, and we bonded from that day forward. That was the last workout I had at Ohio State where I was third-team.

We played two freshman games that year. Remember, freshmen weren't eligible to play varsity back then. In our first game at Indiana, we were so excited we couldn't wait. The field was a mess that day, but what an experience. We beat Indiana 19–7 and were feeling pretty good about ourselves. When we came home, nobody would speak to us. Coach Hayes said we were the worst freshman team he had ever had. [Defensive coordinator] Lou McCullough had threatened to take our scholarships from us. And the varsity? Those guys just ignored us.

The varsity was beating people by 30 points or more, and they finally told us that our win was not good enough to be a Buckeye. We got the message.

We worked harder after that first game, and we had another game against Ohio University coming up. Coach Hayes and Coach Bill Hess at Ohio U. had been friends. Coach Hess used to coach at Ohio State with Coach Hayes, and he always had wanted Coach Hayes to schedule a game at Ohio State, but Coach Hayes refused because of the risk of losing to a state school. So Coach Hayes agreed that if Ohio University's freshmen played well against Ohio State, then he would reconsider scheduling a varsity game.

The week before the Ohio U. game was like Michigan week. Our freshman coach, John Mummey, had the varsity players come in and talk to us. Jack Tatum came in. Now Jack didn't say much to anybody, so we thought, *Wow, this must be a big game.* We played the game on a Friday before a home game, and Coach Hayes came out to give us our pregame speech, and the varsity showed up to watch the game. We won 56–7.

About halfway through the game, I saw Coach Hayes walking back to his office, and I later found out he had placed a call to his friend to tell him that we were beating his team so badly, not to ever call him about scheduling a game again.

At the start of my sophomore year, I had earned the starting right tackle position. I thought I was going to be nervous about my first start, in our first game against Texas A&M at Ohio Stadium. But as the week progressed, I felt like a veteran. Coach Hayes asked me how I felt, and I said I was ready to play. We beat Texas A&M 56–13. We kept winning every week. Finally, Michigan week was here. The town exploded. Michigan was undefeated. We were undefeated. Playing for the title. We had the revenge factor, and the Rose Bowl was the prize. Everyone was so uptight, but I felt relaxed. We won 20–9, and Coach Hayes later told me that I had played a great game. That was the first time I had played on a championship team.

The next season was a nightmare. I got hurt in summer practice and had to have a knee operation, which knocked me out for the season. We went 6–4. I went crazy that year. I was hurt, and we were losing. The next year, 1972, was the first year that the freshmen could play varsity, and we had some pretty good freshmen like Archie Griffin, Corny Greene, Brian Baschnagel, and Tim Fox.

In our second game, we were playing a pretty good North Carolina team that had gone undefeated the year before. We were losing, and the North Carolina players were saying we couldn't block too well. They were feeling they were going to beat us. A new chapter in Ohio State history was written that day. Archie Griffin ran for a stadium and Ohio State record of 239 yards, and we came back to win big. About halfway through the third quarter, I told the North Carolina players that they couldn't tackle too well. We finished that year by beating Michigan but losing to USC 42–17 in the Rose Bowl.

I would have been drafted by the pros, but I felt I wanted to play one more year and settle the Southern California score. So I decided to accept a red-shirt season and play in 1973. We were loaded, and we knew we were a great team. It was one of the greatest teams I had ever played on. We steamrolled our way through the season. Michigan was undefeated, too. We tied 10–10, and it was one of the toughest games I had ever played in. I figured our season was over. Well, as everyone knows, the Big Ten picked us to represent the conference in the Rose Bowl. The Big Ten had a four-game losing streak in the Rose Bowl, and they wanted a win. We had promised Coach Hayes that when we got back to the Rose Bowl, we would win the game for him.

We did, 42–21, beating Southern California, and Coach Hayes told us it was one of his greatest wins ever.

I finished my playing career 28–3–1, with three Big Ten championships and one Rose Bowl win, and I was the first player in the history of the Big Ten to have played in three Rose Bowls.

There are other things I remember most about playing at Ohio State:

After each game, Coach Hayes would meet and speak to our families. Anne Hayes would go to the French Field House before the games and speak to them. She knew everything about every family—whether a family member had died or if there was a graduation or a birth.

It was a family.

In the locker room, Coach Hayes always told us that the finest people we would ever meet would be in this room. You know what? He was right. Those teammates I had on those teams are the greatest people I have ever met. We were not a team just on the football field. We became a team for life.

Although we don't always see each other a lot anymore as we grow older, you know that we are there for each other and will always love each other. We were and still are all Buckeyes.

John Hicks won the Outland Trophy and the Lombardi Award, finished second in the Heisman Trophy balloting to Penn State's John Cappelletti in 1973, and became the 18th Buckeye inducted into the College Football Hall of Fame. He played four seasons with the New York Giants.

RANDY GRADISHAR
LINEBACKER
1971–1973

I REMEMBER MEETING WOODY HAYES like it was yesterday. I was working in my father's grocery store one afternoon in Champion, Ohio, when my high school principal called me. He said, "Randy, you need to come back to school now because Woody Hayes is here in my office and he would like to see you." Woody Hayes? To see me? I thought my buddies were playing a prank on me.

Here I was…I had never considered going to college until my senior year at Champion High School. I didn't have any clue, really, as to what my future might hold. I didn't start playing football until the ninth grade, and I wasn't highly recruited. I thought I might be better at basketball. But here was Woody Hayes, wanting to talk to me.

I went back to school, and there he was in the principal's office, waiting on me. We talked about family, education, careers, and, finally, football. Then Woody said, "Let's go see your father at the grocery store."

So we drove back to my father's store, and my dad was behind the meat counter, slicing meat. Woody joined him, and they stood there for 45 minutes behind the meat slicer, talking about World War II. My dad had been in the Army and had fought in the South Pacific on the infamous Luzon Island in the Philippines. Well, you know, Woody was a historian and a war buff and knew everything about World War II. They hit it off right away. You could say the recruitment of Randy Gradishar was under way.

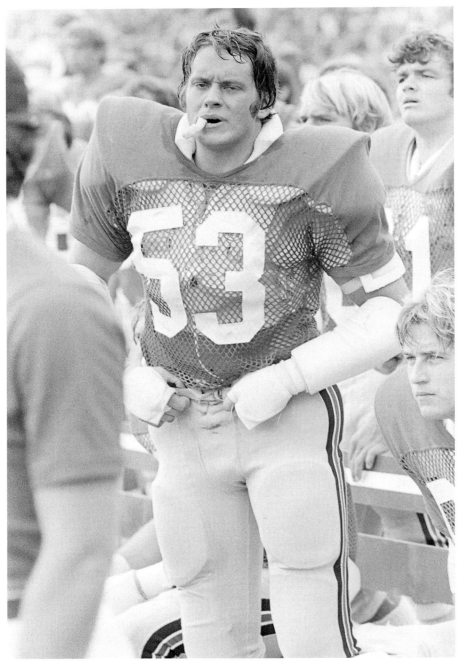

Randy Gradishar became one of Ohio State's most decorated defensive players.

Being recruited by Woody Hayes was overwhelming to me. Remember, I grew up in a quiet little community, and when we went to Browns and Indians games, I thought that was such a big deal. Being in a big city like Cleveland and eating in a restaurant was thrilling to me. So when Woody took me to the old Jai Lai restaurant, I was very impressed.

I could tell right away that Woody Hayes was a man of integrity.

What Woody stood for, believing in God and yourself, I also believed. He was always focused on education. He said, "Son, you are here for one reason, and that's to get an education. It will always benefit you." One of my goals was to graduate in four years. I remember Woody saying, "I'll give you an opportunity to play and that's all." He never promised starting positions. He made it clear that there was a price to pay and that price was hard work through discipline and that was the theme. My dad had taught me a good work ethic. Heck, I had worked in his grocery store since I was 11.

The other thing I learned about him right away was that he was very observant. One time, he said, "Son, you have some big feet there." I wore a size 14½ shoe, and I said, "Yeah, I have a good foundation with these feet." He noticed everything about you. He didn't miss a thing.

Naturally, I chose Ohio State, committing in February 1970. It was a natural fit. Once there, I really felt like I matured.

143

My military draft number was 186, and I was drafted during that summer. I moved into the dorm in August, and I enrolled in ROTC at Ohio State for the first two years. I remember all those student protests about Vietnam.

In addition to all of those changes in my life, I had to face the challenge of my own adequacy in football. While checking into my dorm as a freshman, I saw all these all-staters and All-Americans. I was all-nothing. I thought, *What in the world am I doing here?* Rex Kern and Jack Tatum were seniors and part of a national championship team, and here I was a freshman going up against them in practice. I questioned myself. One time in practice, we called a blitz, and I broke free and was just about to tackle Rex Kern when all of a sudden John Brockington came out of nowhere and hit me so hard…I thought he broke my sternum. But I healed, and I figured out I could play with these guys. It was somewhat of a turning point for me.

Woody always pushed us to be better. He really had a student mind-set, and I did, too. I wanted to get better. I wanted to learn. Woody knew how to motivate you. He encouraged you. "Goddamn it, you can do it," he would say. "You can do it!" After a while, you believed you could.

The entire playing experience at Ohio State is entrenched in my memory, but the Michigan games really stand out. In 1971, my sophomore year, we were playing in Ann Arbor, and that's when Thom Darden interfered with Dick Wakefield and the officials didn't make the call. Woody went crazy! The next year, we made a great goal-line stand that enabled us to beat Michigan and go to the Rose Bowl as Big Ten champions.

How did Woody feel about Michigan? Let me illustrate with one story. One time we were at the Quarterback Club and the team was being introduced, and a freshman had on a blue tie. Woody took one look at that blue tie, and he walked over and whipped it off that freshman. The audience went wild. We learned quickly that tradition dictated we wear ties of scarlet and gray, but we didn't know much about fashion. At the Rose Bowl one year, we went to Disneyland in those plaid coats we had to wear.

Anywhere we went, even in plaid coats, I really felt it was an honor just to represent Ohio State. I finally realized I was a part of it. I remember that John Hicks and I were chosen to be on the *Playboy* All-America team, and the honor meant a visit to the Playboy Mansion, but that magazine was not on Woody's reading list. He didn't believe it would be the right kind of exposure and it wouldn't do Ohio State, John, or me any good, so he wouldn't let us go. With no pictures of us, *Playboy* cut and pasted our heads onto pictures for that article.

In addition to graduating in four years, one of my other goals was to be on the weekly Woody Hayes TV show. We didn't do a whole lot of media interviews back then, and it was controlled, so we were real stilted on that show. But I got on it. And I graduated with a B.S. in education—in four years. I met my goals.

The last time I saw Coach Hayes was in 1983. When I realized business would take me back to Columbus, I called Coach Hayes and invited him and Anne to dinner at the Jai Lai. She did not join us, but it was typical of Woody—we didn't talk much about football or sports. He just wanted to get caught up on my life and career. Such a great man! I'll tell you one thing: he was committed to this university and to the people of Ohio. He was a real patriot who believed in the United States. He always said there was a difference between right and wrong. That man had a lot of wisdom, but what people don't understand is that he had a great sense of humility. He never thought it was all about him. Woody was like a second father to me and to most of his players.

Woody is part of the history, part of the great tradition at Ohio State. I really believe that with the long-standing tradition at Ohio State, that history will always be a part of us and we a part of it. When you go to Ohio State, you are a part of a rich history. The Ohio State University will provide the leadership and vision and will challenge you. It's about all the people, administrators, coaches, alumni, and players who care about you. It's not all about winning. It's about the values you stand for.

Living in Colorado, I find that wherever I go, whenever I mention that I am a Buckeye, eyes light up and the Ohio State tradition comes alive. It's the people and their passion for Ohio State that makes it such a great place. I am a Buckeye forever.

Randy Gradishar, a two-time All-America linebacker, became the 17th Ohio State player to be inducted into the College Football Hall of Fame. He also is a member of the CoSIDA Academic Hall of Fame and was an Academic All-American in 1973. He played 10 seasons with the Denver Broncos.

VIC KOEGEL

DEFENSIVE LINEMAN

1971–1973

WHEN I THINK OF WOODY HAYES and how he became so successful, I think it started with his recruiting. He was a tireless worker, and he didn't ever want to be outrecruited or outworked by anybody. My road to Ohio State is a perfect illustration. When I was a senior at Cincinnati Moeller, I had narrowed my choices to Ohio State and Notre Dame. Woody came down to recruit me and made three visits to my house. He went out to dinner with my parents, and I remember him ordering that bananas dish for dessert—the one with the fire flaming from the bananas. It was the first time I ever saw that. I had never been out to dinner at a restaurant like this, either. But Woody was the kind of guy who wanted to get to know your family first.

So I went on my trip to Notre Dame, and I had not yet met with Ara Parseghian. I arrived on a Friday, and the first I saw him was on Sunday. I went into his office, and as I sat there, he never looked up. He was reading this big pile of paper—my press clippings. He didn't say anything for about three minutes. Then he asked me, "Are you coming to Notre Dame?"

I told him, "I don't know right now. I want to take another look at Ohio State."

He said, "Well, let me know when you are ready to sign with Notre Dame."

And that was it. I thought, *You have to be kidding me.* I spent no more than 10 minutes in that office, and that was what he said to me. I made the decision

Vic Koegel (62) chases the quarterback during the 60–0 win over Northwestern in 1973.

to go to Ohio State pretty quickly. Woody Hayes had visited my family three times, and Parseghian never did.

Years later when I was with the Bengals, one of my teammates was Doug Adams, who was three years older than me. We were talking about Woody and recruiting, and I asked him if he had ever considered Notre Dame. "That damn Parseghian," he said. "He met with me for only 10 minutes."

That's what made Woody Hayes even greater in our eyes.

I remember when I went to campus for the first time as an incoming freshman. Ohio State had signed Randy Keith, too, and my parents took me and Randy up there from Cincinnati. We got out of the car in front of the dorm, and Woody came up to us, and there were several seniors there, too. Somebody said, "There's Rex over there." My mom turned around and said, "I don't see any dog over there." We had to explain to her: "Mom, that's Rex Kern—the great quarterback."

The big thing on your first night at Ohio State was that Woody would come around and we would go over our vocabulary book. He had sent it to us in the summer, and we were supposed to go through it and know all these words. He would walk in our rooms and ask, "Now, do you all have your books?" Then he would quiz us on the meaning of certain words. It was Woody's Word Power class.

My first impression of Woody on the field was him going berserk…just beating people up. I played for Coach [Gerry] Faust at Moeller, and he would scream at you, but he wouldn't punch you. You hear the stories about Woody before you get there, but until you see it person, it is unbelievable.

In that first year, you would fear him, in the second year, you would accept him, and in the third, you would laugh at him—but maybe not out loud in front of him.

In one game at Minnesota, during my sophomore year, we were behind at halftime. Woody gave his speech in the locker room and ended with him saying: "Let's go out there and win this game!" He started to go out, but the door was locked. So Woody broke this glass box with a fire axe in it. He got that axe and started beating this door down with it before they stopped him. We came back to win 14–12.

That was the last game we won that year. We ended by losing three in a row—to Michigan State, Northwestern, and then the Michigan game when he tore up the sideline markers.

Woody would always do something crazy on that Thursday before the Michigan game, something to get you psyched up.

Before that Michigan game, the *Lantern* had written some article with the prediction that Michigan would beat us 60–0. On the back of the bus that day, I remember Kenny Luttner was reading this article. Well, Woody went berserk, and he started ripping the newspaper out of Kenny's hands. He was screaming, "They're traitors! They're traitors!" Then before the game, his pregame speech was about Benedict Arnold.

That year was a bad year for us [6–4] because we had so many injuries. It was the first year of the AstroTurf at Ohio Stadium, and we had so many serious knee injuries. Your foot would get caught when you would cut, or you would get hit while your foot was planted. After that, they watered it down so it wasn't so sticky. But it got me in the '72 opener against Iowa. It was a bad injury, but I played through the first six games before my knee popped out for good and I had to have surgery.

The second game, against North Carolina, was the game Archie broke out [239 yards], but what is forgotten is that my roommate, Elmer Lippert, ran for more than 100 yards that day.

I ended up starting for all of my three seasons, except for those final five games in my junior year because of my knee injury. That is the one thing about Woody—when he gave you a shot, you had better be ready. If you made mistakes, you might never get in again. But he always gave everyone at least one chance. I got my first chance as a sophomore when Randy Gradishar injured his thumb.

The highlight had to be the Rose Bowl win over USC at the end of my senior season. They had beaten us 42–17 the year before, and we wanted to redeem ourselves. It was tied 21–21, and the defense wasn't playing well at all. I remember Woody went berserk on the sideline and punched Arnie Jones, and Arnie punched him back. But [defensive coordinator] George Hill had a good game plan. He would drop our ends—Van DeCree and Jim Cope—into coverage, and it confused Pat Haden. Haden would drop back and see four linebackers there. We shut them down after that and beat them 42–21.

After the game, I told Woody, "Thanks for a great four years." He said it was the best win he had ever had. That team was good enough to win the national title, but we had that 10–10 tie at Michigan.

I really believe that when they won the Fiesta Bowl, and the 2002 national title, it was a victory for anybody who ever wore the scarlet and gray. We all took it personally—all the great players who have come through Ohio State. Just take a look at Woody's teams after 1968—almost any one of them could have won the national championship but didn't. So it was long overdue that we got one in 2002.

It was a proud moment for that team, but it was a proud moment for any of us who ever played football at Ohio State.

Vic Koegel, who as a sophomore led the 1971 team in tackles with 126, was an All–Big Ten linebacker in '73.

BRUCE ELIA

FULLBACK/LINEBACKER

1972–1974

I WAS A SMALL-TOWN JERSEY KID who was used to hanging out with his friends on the street corner until 1:00 in the morning. We never got into trouble, but that was the thing to do. We just hung out…about 20 guys together, all summer long. I had a good high school career as a running back/linebacker and I was about 6′1″ and 195 pounds, which wasn't huge, but it was good size for the early '70s. At that time, I really didn't know where I wanted to play college football, but I had plenty of offers.

I went to Notre Dame to take a visit on a Saturday, and my host turned in that night at 10:00 to go study. So I canned Notre Dame.

Then I went to Penn State, and I loved Joe Paterno. The problem there was that I felt like I was in the middle of the woods. We went out that night and went to a Pizza Hut or something like it. That was it for Penn State.

I went to Nebraska and had a really good time, but it was too far.

Lo and behold, I got to Columbus and knew nothing about Ohio State football, except for what I saw on television, and my host was Glen Mason. Glen had arranged for us to double-date that night.

Glen had it down real simple. We stood outside Papa Joe's on High Street and looked north, and there were kids everywhere. He told me, "On the left side, we go to school and we study and we live. On the right side are the sororities and fraternities and more housing. Down the middle, we party! Welcome to High Street."

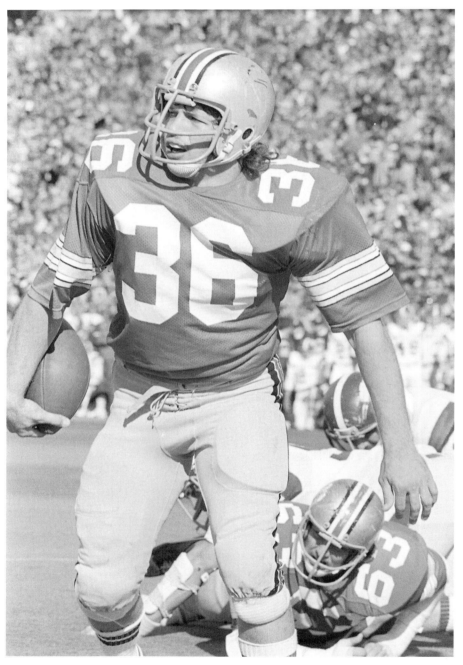

152

At fullback or linebacker, Bruce Elia could star on either side of the football.

I thought, *This is simple—I am going to Ohio State.*

But the truth is that I still hadn't decided after that. My dad was a construction guy, and he didn't say much during the whole process. One night he asked me which way I was leaning. I said, "I am leaning toward Penn State, but I really didn't like it there."

He then said something I'll never forget: "Why don't you go play with the best?"

We never said another word. The next day, I called up Ohio State and said I was coming. I knew then that my dad had challenged me. I was a little scared about it, and I knew Ohio State was loaded with talent. It seemed like a football factory, and I was from a small school in Cliffside Park, New Jersey.

Once I got to Ohio State, I ripped up my ankle right away and was out for a month on crutches. I would put my arm around Steve Myers and Jim Cope, and they would carry me to Papa Joe's. My ankle was the size of my head.

My sophomore year, I was about the fifth-string fullback and I could hardly get any time in practice, and now I was starting to get frustrated. They sent me to some JV games, and I had a couple of 100-yard games, and just when I thought I was doing well at fullback, George Hill, the defensive coordinator, said he wanted me on defense. This was the third game of my sophomore year, and by then I was really mad. I was hurting on the inside, because people had told me Ohio State would make me a linebacker, and sure as shit, that's what they did.

On that first day at linebacker, I intercepted a pass, and coach Hill got so excited. That really inspired me, so I began practicing really hard. I would come out early and stay late to learn more about the position. Little by little, I was getting better. I had [Randy] Gradishar and Rick Middleton—two future first-round picks—in front of me. The one thing I did—I went after all the running backs with a passion and I smashed them. I thought, *If they wouldn't let me be a running back, then I am going to punish the guys who are.* That was my simple Jersey logic.

In the '73 opener against Minnesota, they had just come up with "Buck of the Week" and "Hit of the Week" awards that year, and I was running down on the opening kickoff and I smashed this guy who was blocking for Rick Upchurch. The guy flew into Upchurch, who fumbled, and when I opened my eyes, there was the ball right in front of me. I jumped on it, and when I came to practice that Monday, there was my picture for "Hit of the Week" and "Buck of the Week." I still have those plaques.

One day, after Champ Henson got hurt, I was sitting in the whirlpool and Woody came right up to me and pointed his finger in my face. "You are going to play fullback!"

"I will only play fullback if next year you let me go back to linebacker," I told him.

I ended up starting at fullback and had a pretty good year over those final nine games. In the third game, I went over 100 yards in one game and had four touchdowns in another, but by this time, Pete Johnson, who was behind me, had been getting better and better. By the time we got to the Rose Bowl, Pete and I were switching on and off each series.

The following year, I went back to linebacker, and Pete became the full-time fullback.

That summer before my senior season, Woody had suffered a heart attack, and there were all kinds of rumors about whether he would return. Many of us were outside the building before our first meeting of the season, and we were discussing whether Woody would last the season.

"Woody will never make it."

"He'll probably have another heart attack."

"He probably wants to be buried at the 50-yard line in Ohio Stadium."

"We had better go easy on him, because he's getting too old to coach."

Those were the comments going back and forth.

Well, Woody called us all inside for this first meeting. There were about 120 players in there, including freshmen who never knew Woody aside from being recruited by him. The meeting started in typical fashion. He was talking about past accomplishments, and he was complaining that *Sports Illustrated* ranked us No. 1, and then he started talking about Michigan. "They'll be ready for us at the end of the year," he told us.

At this point, we were a little bored because we had all heard this talk before.

All of a sudden, Woody raised his voice. He said something like he knew he was going to have a heart attack. "I was gonna have it on Tuesday, but I postponed it until Thursday so I could hire a new backfield coach on Wednesday," he said. "I know a bunch of you think that I won't make the season. You think I'll probably have another heart attack and die. Well, fuck my heart, fuck my heart."

Then he beat on his chest in front of everyone to get the point across. Then he spoke the words I'll never forget:

"I'd rather die a winner than live being a loser, because when you are a loser, you die a little bit each day.... Now let's get dressed and start practicing to win a national championship!"

I was ready to run through the wall.

The other classic Woody moment happened after that Michigan State game that year.

We were waiting in the locker room for 45 minutes to find out who won the game, and we still had our uniforms on. I remember at the end, Archie got into the end zone and we thought we had won, but nobody was sure. Woody ranted and raved and walked around the locker room asking everybody, "Did we score? Did we score?" He came up to me and asked me. I said, "I saw the official put his hands up."

Suddenly, Wayne Duke, the Big Ten commissioner, walked in. Now Wayne was a big guy, about 6'4", and everybody gathered around him. He told Woody, "I have to speak to your team." Woody could sense what was coming, and at this point, he started to scream, "Wayne, don't you fuck me! Don't you fuck me!"

Now George Hill had to hold Woody back so he wouldn't punch him. Woody had his arm cocked and his fist clenched and was trying to throw a punch, but he couldn't with George hanging on his arm. He just would not accept that we lost that game. We all wouldn't accept it. I can still see Woody trying to get at the Big Ten commissioner and land a punch. He just hated losing so much.

At the time President Nixon was going through his impeachment troubles, we were at the Rose Bowl, and Woody came into practice one day. He told us, "Now I want to tell you that people need friends. I visited an old friend today, Dick Nixon. Right now, he has no friends. Nobody wants to be friends with him, but I am still Dick's friend. Dick can count on Woody. Woody will be there for Dick Nixon."

Here we were thinking about the Rose Bowl practice, and Woody was telling us about his visit with the president of the United States. He was the type of guy who would help out anyone who needed it, from the president on down.

I believe it was the four best years of my life. I learned the most as a person that I could have anywhere. I had the most fun, and I acquired some of the best friends of my life. I learned what it was like to be down and what it was like to be successful. I certainly learned how to win, and I learned a lot from Woody from his speeches about being a good, moral person, to be respectful and decent and honest. I had learned most of that from my parents, but he reinforced it.

For me, Ohio State was the best place I could have ever chosen.

My family and my son are all big Ohio State fans. When I took him to the Ohio State–Michigan game a few years ago, we went over to the Schottenstein Center, and they have these little TVs where you can select Ohio State highlights from the past. Here I was with my son, and they were announcing my name and some of the big games I had. That was very special for me.

Recently, I was put into my high school hall of fame, and I had to give a little speech. There were a few hundred people there, and I looked out and said, "I want to thank my father for challenging me to go play with the best. I want to thank him for challenging me to go to Ohio State. Thanks, Dad."

Bruce Elia became one of the few Ohio State players in the modern era to ever start on offense and on defense. In 1973 he led OSU in scoring with 14 touchdowns, and in '74 he led the team with 144 tackles.

156

DOUG PLANK

DEFENSIVE BACK

1972–1974

MY EXPERIENCE AT OHIO STATE was dramatic and instantaneous. Let me start by stating that my first day of summer camp was a disaster. After running a two-mile conditioning test in the morning, I coughed up my breakfast for the next 30 minutes. In the afternoon, we practiced at the stadium on AstroTurf, and I had never played on turf and was impressed by the traction. At the time, I was projected as wingback and was running the football that afternoon. On an end run, I was preparing to make a cut when I was hit from the blind side. I immediately went down on the turf and felt a sharp pain in my right knee. I did not realize it at the time, but I had torn meniscus cartilage that would float around in my knee for the next three months. I was constantly injuring the knee due to the damaged cartilage.

Finally, in November, the knee locked in place and it required surgery. During this time, I believed that several coaches and players doubted the commitment and effort I was giving. This obstacle became an opportunity for me. After the surgery, I was determined to rehab my knee and strengthen my body. The surgery convinced me to concentrate on defense because of the reduced stress on the knee. For the next few months, I listened intently to Coach Woody Hayes about his philosophy of life and football. I will never forget two phrases that he constantly mentioned: "You practice the way you will play," and, "The will to win is not as important as the will to prepare to win."

These two ideas became my doctrine for the remainder of my football career. I became a self-motivated player who practiced and played at game tempo every time I stepped on the football field. I was passionate to prove myself and vengeful toward anyone who was not wearing an Ohio State uniform. I treated every game and practice as if it were my last. In my desire for contact, I would hit anyone in my path.

In my career at Ohio State, I played on great teams and played behind great players. I started six games in three years because of other players' injuries. One of those starts was in Evanston, Illinois, against Northwestern during my senior season. Two Chicago Bears scouts attended that game, and I believe now that I must have played pretty well that day. The lessons I learned and the philosophy I adopted from Ohio State enabled me to take advantage when opportunity knocked. In Chicago, I became the first rookie to lead the Bears in tackles in franchise history. Every team needs players who are stars and others who fill specific roles on the team. I feel very lucky to have attended Ohio State. Whatever I gave in effort, I received much more in return with incredible memories and a fantastic wife.

One of those memories happened much later than during my playing career at Ohio State. In my last three seasons as a Buckeye, I played in three Rose Bowls. To play in the Rose Bowl was a tremendous reward for a successful season, as we all know. Many families of the players also attended the Rose Bowl game and other related activities leading up to the game. Due to the financial situation in my family, my parents could not afford the opportunity to see me play in the Rose Bowl in person. My mother was the driving force in my athletic career through high school, and I always realized that I owed her a great deal due to her love and attention to my career.

I had started in the Rose Bowl during my sophomore season against USC, and I played in each of the other two games. If I ever had a chance, I told myself that I was going to take her to a Rose Bowl game. In 1996 Ohio State won the Big Ten title and was to play Arizona State in the Rose Bowl. Because I lived in Phoenix, this was a perfect matchup for a great game as far as I was concerned.

My mom had polio when she was a child, and we struggled getting through the traffic and the crowds. We missed the warm-ups and arrived in time to see the teams take the field. My mother had a wonderful time at several Ohio State events and during the Rose Bowl parade. When she entered the stadium before the game, she was amazed at the immense crowd and anticipation for the game, but when the Ohio State team came out of the tunnel with the band playing, my mom began to cry. I looked at her and asked her if she was okay.

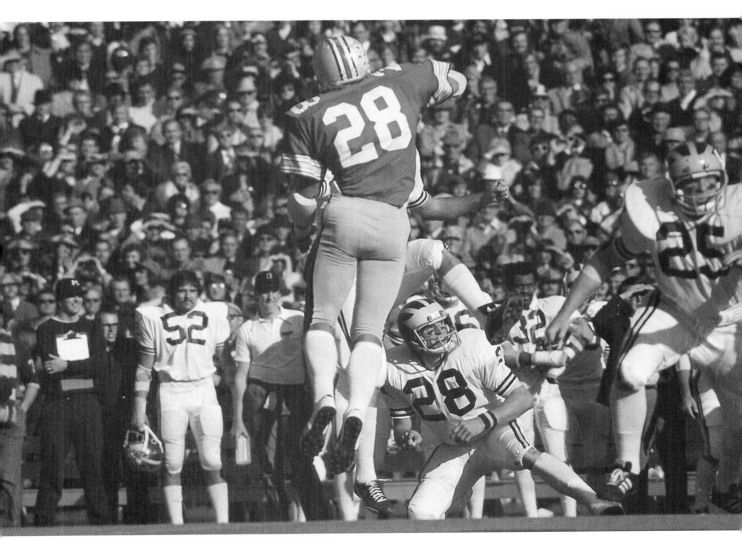

Doug Plank leaps to try to block a field goal during the 12–10 win over Michigan in 1974.

With tears in her eyes, she looked at me and said, "Doug, I wish I would have been here for you 22 years ago when you ran onto this field."

"Mom," I said, "you were here—you were in my heart!"

That day and that game—an Ohio State victory—was one of the best memories in my life.

Doug Plank was drafted in the 12th round of the 1975 draft by the Chicago Bears, for whom he played eight seasons.

BRIAN BASCHNAGEL
WINGBACK
1972–1975

IGUESS YOU COULD SAY I WAS an overachiever. I always worked hard at academics and athletics, because that was my way of fitting in. My family had moved 16 times because my dad worked for the Woolworth Company and would get transferred. He would take over a store, get it back on its feet, and move on. It was our lifestyle, but I spent the final three years of high school in Pittsburgh. All that moving taught me to adapt. As far as college goes, I am Catholic and I adored Notre Dame. I was going to go there, but I also wanted to visit some other schools just to be fair to myself.

[Then–Ohio State assistant coach] Earle Bruce was recruiting me at that time, but during the recruiting process, he was named head coach at Tampa. At that time, it had boiled down to Notre Dame, Penn State, and Ohio State. Coach Bruce called me, and I was really confused, because I thought he was going to try to recruit me to Tampa. He said, "Look, I don't know where you want to go, but I am stepping out of the recruiting process for obvious reasons. I want you to know this: I can honestly tell you Ohio State is the best place for you." That really impressed me.

The first time I met Woody Hayes, he came to my volleyball practice at my high school. We were practicing, and I figured he would want to check out what I looked like on the court, how I moved, and what type of an athlete I was. But he didn't. He was over in the stands reading a book. He never once, not once, looked up from that book. It was *Animal Farm*. Then we went out

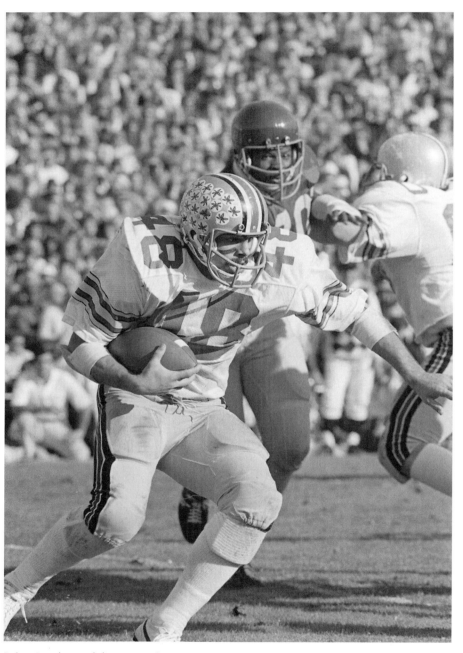

Brian Baschnagel, here carrying against USC in the 1975 Rose Bowl, redefined the wingback position.

to dinner and we talked for three hours at this restaurant. In those three hours, he never once mentioned football. Not once. That impressed me.

You can say he sincerely impressed me from the beginning. I could tell he was really concerned about me and my well-being. I mentioned I wanted to major in business and maybe attend law school later. So he promoted the business school at Ohio State and then he promoted the law school. He cited some examples of people who had graduated from both. Now I was comparing this to other coaches who recruited me. Notre Dame promised me I would go to four bowl games, play right away, and all that. All they seemed to talk about was football.

I was a running back, I liked Woody Hayes already, and I knew he liked to run the football, so I made my choice. I was recruited with another running back from Columbus, and you may have heard of him. His name was Archie Griffin. In 1972—the first year that freshmen became eligible to play—early on in the North Carolina game, we were stumbling around and not very effective. They called Archie's name, he rushed for 239 yards, and he became an overnight hero. I was happy we won the game, but I didn't know where that left me. I have to tell you that I came to hate Archie over the next few days, and then he didn't practice that Monday because of all the bumps and bruises. I wondered what kind of character Archie had. For those few days, I was thinking about transferring or quitting.

Then after that practice, Archie came up to me and looked me right in the eye. "Look, you are from Pittsburgh; I am from Columbus," he told me. "If it were the other way around, they would have asked you to go in the game Saturday and you would have done the same thing."

I wanted to hug him right there. That taught me a lot. I decided on the spot that I would be proud to play behind Archie Griffin for four years. From that beginning, we grew really close. I wasn't going anywhere. I still get chills every time I think of Archie's words to me. Right then and there, I was proud to be a Buckeye.

On the first play I ever played, I went back to return a punt. There were 88,000 people in the stands, and my knees were just shaking. I dropped the punt but jumped on top of it and recovered it. I remember Woody saying something like that was the mature thing to do.

The starting wingback, Rich Galbos, got hurt later in the season, and I moved to the wingback spot. I guess it was a blessing in disguise. It was very much a role-playing position. I learned to block, and they threw me passes, and once in a while they threw me a bone and I ran a counter. I think the most car-ries I ever had in one game was seven, and some games I didn't have any.

Woody was the greatest motivator, but he was extremely fair. It was always very positive. He motivated through intimidation and positive reinforcement, and I learned early on that you have to pay attention to where he was on the practice field. One day, Greg Hare was at quarterback and I was not in the play but I was standing next to Woody. Greg dropped back, scrambled toward Woody, who bumped into me trying to get out of the way, and then Greg threw an interception. I was still looking downfield, watching the play. At the same time, Woody turned and punched me in the stomach. "Get out of the way," he told me. I never saw it coming, and I had nothing to do with the play, but I learned right then to keep an eye on Woody during practice.

He really was a perfectionist, but by the time I became a senior, I learned a lot of his tantrums were fabricated. We had lost to Michigan State twice, in 1972 and '74 when we scored but they disallowed the touchdown. (I don't think we were set on that play, after looking at the film, but Michigan State was holding us down, not letting us get another play off, and we should have been given one more play.)

So before our senior game against them, he called all the captains in and told us he wanted us to give a talk to the team about what this game means to us. He pulled me to the side and said, "Brian, when you talk to them, I want you to swear. That will emphasize what this game means to you."

"But, Coach," I said, "I don't swear." I did promise him I would show plenty of emotion. As we left the room, I heard him ask somebody to make sure there were two pitchers of water in the front of the room before the team came in for the meeting. So the team got in there, he started in on his speech and was getting real emotional in front of the team. He was yelling, raising his voice, talking about how much we wanted to beat Michigan State, and he suddenly picked up this pitcher of water and threw it against the wall. It had to be staged, although I know his emotions were sincere.

We won the game 21–0.

You know, Woody never mentioned the Rose Bowl in motivating us. He always said "the Big Ten." That was our goal every year. We never even talked national championship, because there wasn't the emphasis on it then that there is now. We just said, "We have to win the Big Ten." We would pre-pare for Michigan for half of each week and then prepare for the team we were playing for the second half of the week.

That was our goal, to beat Michigan and win the Big Ten. My biggest regret now is that we never won a national championship, and that '73 team and '75 team were good enough to do it.

Offensively, only two things frustrated me at that time—we never changed our snap count, and when we did, we would jump offside; and in a tough game, we couldn't throw the ball effectively. We did it in practice but never had success passing in a close game.

One time we did, and I'll never forget it. We were at Michigan [in 1975] and trailing 14–7 and down to a fourth-down play on our final drive. Corny just looked at us in the huddle and said, "Hold hands and we're going to say a prayer." It was the first time he had done that. Now I don't think the Lord really cares who wins a football game, but it worked—he threw to me along the sideline for the first down. Then we marched down and scored a touchdown. Ray Griffin picked off a pass to set up the next touchdown, and we won 21–14. That was a great team.

Off the field, Woody always encouraged us to mix in with the regular student body. He wanted us to be students before football players. One professor of mine didn't think that way. She was an economics teacher, and I remember she came flying in the room on the first day, a little late and a lot flustered, and she announced, "If anybody in here is a football player, you might as well leave right now, because you will fail this course." I slouched down in my chair, but her comments motivated me. I got the highest grade on the first midterm and had a 98 on the second. The final exam was at 8:00 AM and I stayed up studying all night. Exhausted, I decided to close my eyes for a few minutes before I left for the test. Sure enough, I fell asleep only to wake up an hour into the test. I ran to the classroom and up to the professor. She handed me the test and said, "You were doing well, but not that well."

My roommate for four years was Garry McCutcheon. He was a quarterback and also from Pennsylvania and still is a close friend to this day. On the day of the NFL Draft, in April 1976, I had a very busy day. I had a test, a paper due, and an 8:00 AM class. I remember walking back to my apartment, just drained from all that, and I thought, *Oops, this was the day of the draft. I wonder if I got drafted.*

So I got back to the apartment, and Garry poured me a beer. We started to play a game of gin, and he said, "By the way, the Steelers called and wanted to know if you would like to play for them. I told them I thought you would." So we played a few more hands, and a few minutes later, he said,

"The Redskins also called and wanted to know if you were available in the fifth round, would you be willing to play for them? I told them that you would." By this time, we had finished our beer. Garry got up, poured me another, and said, "By the way, congratulations, you were drafted by the Chicago Bears in the third round." I could have killed him.

After the draft but before graduation in June, Woody called me into the office. "Brian, what are you going to do?" he asked me. I said, "What do you mean, Coach?" He repeated himself, but louder, "WHAT ARE YOU GOING TO DO?"

"I guess you mean after graduation. I don't know if you heard, but I got drafted by the…" Before I could get the words out, he picked up a book and slammed it on the floor, screaming, "There goes your law degree!" After all those years, he had remembered that conversation we had at that dinner during recruiting.

I told him I could do both, and besides, "I might not even make the team," I told him. We started walking down the hall, and he was yelling at me, "Brian, I know you too well. You'll make that team, play for 10 years, and never get your law degree…."

I went to Chicago, made the team, and after the season, I came back to Columbus and knocked on his door to see him. His desk always faced away from the door. He never turned around. He just said, "Get out of here and don't come back until you are enrolled in law school." He was serious—he wouldn't see me. That really bothered me, so I went down and enrolled in a continuous education program to take some accounting classes. With proof in hand, I went back to see Woody one more time. I realize now that all Woody wanted was for us to prepare ourselves for the day we left the game of football.

The final time I saw him, he was in his hospital bed and was getting released that day. I visited him for about 20 minutes, and as I stood in that room, I was thinking to myself, *This man is a great man…he really cares about people.* I guess I didn't realize what we meant to him as players, but I really felt I touched his life as much as he touched mine. I am grateful for that. Everybody at Ohio State had such an influence on me, and yeah, you can say I made the right decision.

Brian Baschnagel, a two-time Academic All-American and team captain in 1975, played nine seasons for the Chicago Bears.

TIM FOX

DEFENSIVE BACK

1972–1975

I WASN'T VERY HIGHLY RECRUITED coming out of Canton Glenwood High. I think Kent State recruited me, and so did Indiana and Lou Holtz at North Carolina State. I had ruptured a kidney during my senior year in high school and missed the final three games. The Ohio State coaches never saw me play football, but they did come to one of my basketball games, and from that I was surprised when they offered me a scholarship. I was one of the last guys offered, and we had only about 12 freshmen in 1972, which was the first year that freshmen were eligible since the '50s.

My dad was dead set against my going to Ohio State. I guess he thought I would be over my head. On a recruiting trip, we were having a brunch at the golf course, and my mother was going through the buffet line and trying to balance her purse on one arm and hold the plate with the other. That is when Woody Hayes came to her assistance and carried her purse down the buffet line for her. He won her over, and from that day on, my mom loved Woody Hayes, so I had one fan of my going to Ohio State.

My first impression came on the first day—picture day. It was the first time I was in Ohio Stadium. That was great in itself, and then they gave me No. 47 and I was thinking how great this was. Then I looked around and saw two more 47s, and that dampened my enthusiasm [Tim ended up wearing No. 12 throughout his career].

They called for all the freshmen offensive backs to go over there to get their picture taken. They called all the freshmen defensive backs to go over to another spot. I had played both ways in high school, and nobody had told me what position I would be playing. So I went up to [assistant coach] John Mummey and asked him where he wanted me. "Where do you want to go?" he asked me. He just said, "Go where you want to go." I looked over at the offensive picture, and they had Archie Griffin, Brian Baschnagel, Woody Roach, and all these big fullbacks. I weighed about 165 pounds at the time. I looked over at the defensive guys and I saw only one, Craig Cassady, and thought my odds were much better over there. So I went to the defensive side and that's how I ended up as a defensive back at Ohio State. That was how it happened.

I played in every game in 1972 as a freshman and started several at free safety. I remember when we were playing Minnesota; Rick Upchurch was their tailback at the time. I think Tony Dungy was the quarterback. My main job was that I had the pitchman on the option. That was my job for the day. I played pretty well and kept tackling Upchurch, but thank God they didn't pass, because I had no idea what our coverages were at that point.

That freshman class was a tight-knit group. We all got along pretty well, but I was always afraid of the upperclassmen. I remember this big, old defensive tackle, Ed Trepanier, who never played much because he was always yelling at Woody during drills. One day at Steeb Hall, he grabbed Archie and held him out of a window by his ankle. He just had him by one ankle, and it was high off the ground! I know Archie will never forget it. God, if he would have dropped him…

The freshmen had their own locker room in those days, and one time an upperclassman, Chuck Bonica, had been late for practice a few times. Woody said, "That's it. He's off the team." So the seniors got together and decided there would be a work stoppage until he reinstated Chuck. So they came into our locker room and told us, "Look guys, nobody is going to practice today. You just stay in here until we tell you otherwise."

So we did. Next thing we knew, Woody came busting into the room, screaming at the top of his lungs. He had let Chuck back on the team, but we were late for practice.

In my four years, we accomplished so much. We never lost a home game and never lost to Michigan, but we were 1–3 in Rose Bowls and should have been 3–1.

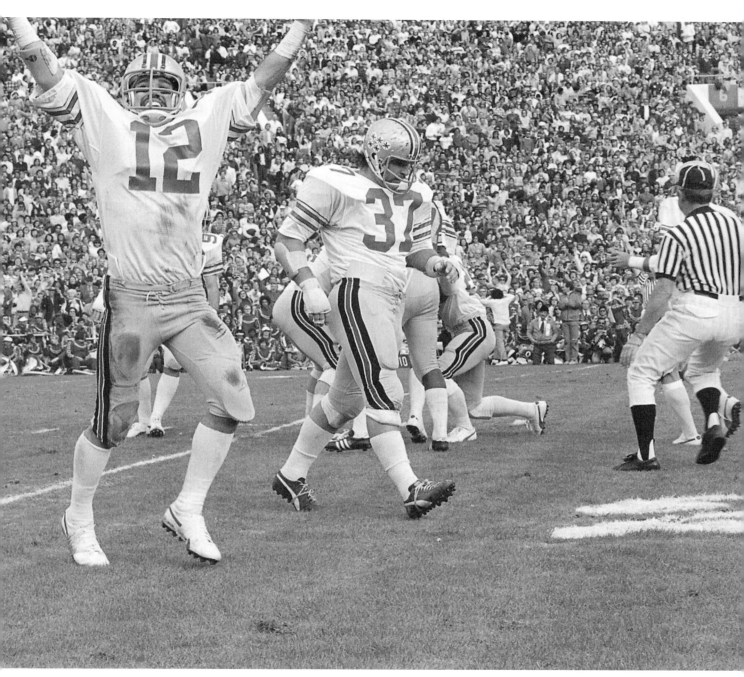

Tim Fox (12) celebrates a big play in the 1975 Rose Bowl against USC.

That 1972 USC team with Sam Cunningham that beat us was simply great. We couldn't have beaten them, but the next year, we really beat them badly in the Rose Bowl. The following year we lost to USC by one point, and that team wasn't that good. J.K. McKay caught that pass near the sideline that still haunts me.

But none of those losses compare to the Rose Bowl at the end of my career. We were undefeated and had really smoked UCLA [41–20] earlier in the season in Los Angeles. I think the coaching staff got a little overconfident because we had beaten them so badly. Woody really liked our senior class, and I really believe he got a little soft on us while preparing for the Rose Bowl that year. He softened on bed check, saying, "Look guys, I keep waking you up during bed check, so I won't be coming by. Just sign in when you come in." Well, that was an open invitation for some guys to stay out way past curfew.

Then we stayed in our regular hotel the night before the game, and we never did that before at the Rose Bowl. We didn't really have a good game plan, either. I think we forgot to work on the things that got us there. It was definitely the toughest loss of my career. It was extremely disappointing. It still hurts. Those are the ones you remember all these years later.

170

We had great teammates at Ohio State. Archie was the consummate team player. He absorbed whatever Woody said. He never felt like going out and having a beer with the guys, because he felt that responsibility that Woody had put on him.

I really wish I would have taken the time to enjoy those years more. Coach Hayes made you focus so much. You really didn't take time to enjoy what you accomplished. The NFL was so much easier than what I went through at Ohio State. I was a young kid. Coach Hayes was a perfectionist, and he would just drive you and drive you. Nobody in pro football motivated like Woody Hayes did. He was the best at it. That work ethic stayed with me in the pros, and it does today in sales. I can thank him for that.

It really was tougher for the offensive players. Woody was in their faces constantly. I wasn't sure he remembered my name since I was on defense, but he would call me "Canton" after my hometown. I can still see him after that loss to Michigan State [in 1974] when we thought we had scored to win the game, but the refs didn't allow it. [Big Ten commissioner] Wayne Duke came into the locker room to tell Woody that the game would not be reversed, and Woody grabbed him by the lapel and lifted him right off the ground. He stood there holding him up—his feet were in the air! Then he wanted to get a bunch of us and go to the Michigan State locker room and finish the thing—men to men. But a few assistants talked him out of it.

Another time Woody let this guy from *Sports Illustrated* come in, and he spent all this time with him and thought there would be a positive story about him and Ohio State. Well, the guy just ripped him in the article. We were at dinner, and there was this big dishwashing container up there. Woody would take a glass out of it, read a quote from the story, and smash the glass on the wall. He would read another quote and smash another glass. He must have smashed 12 glasses.

I definitely love Ohio State, and I have to tell you I was really disappointed when my nephew decided to play at Penn State. My daughter, Haley, was a captain of her field hockey team at Ohio State, and my other nephew, Dustin, is doing well there. I will always be a Buckeye.

Tim Fox, a team captain and All–Big Ten in 1975, was selected in the first round of the 1976 NFL Draft by the New England Patriots, for whom he played six seasons. He also played for the San Diego Chargers and the Los Angeles Rams.

CORNELIUS GREENE
QUARTERBACK
1972–1975

I HAD GROWN UP IN WASHINGTON, D.C., and played at Dunbar High, having had a pretty good senior season as a quarterback. Michigan State was the first big school to recruit me along with all the ACC schools. When Ohio State became interested and Coach Hayes looked at me, he told me that he thought my neck was too small and I might get hurt playing in the Big Ten. While all the other schools were telling me I would start right away, Coach Hayes told me, "If you are good enough to play here, you will. If you are not, you won't."

That put the challenge in front of me, and there was no doubt in my mind. Mom thought he was the most honest coach there was, and I really liked Rudy Hubbard, who was the running backs coach. At the time, some of the people who mentored me in D.C., from coaches to friends and neighbors, didn't think Ohio State would ever play an African American at quarterback. Some people at Michigan State had told me the same thing.

So I had a lot of naysayers who didn't think I should go to Ohio State for one reason or another, and I wanted to prove them wrong.

Woody Roach was a running back from my area, and his father drove us to Columbus that fall. We got there at about midnight. The students weren't there yet, and High Street was empty. Here's this big, old university and nobody was on campus. I thought to myself, *What have I done?* You could say I was pretty homesick right away.

On the second day of practice, we had a 9:00 PM meeting and I was walking down the aisle when the clock struck 9:00. I caught a mouthful from Coach Hayes that night. I knew from that moment not to be a minute late, and that was the last time I was ever late.

That freshman season was a time of doubting myself. I had to learn the whole game all over again. We ran an old-style offense in high school, and I had never run the option before. I had to learn all the plays and the footwork for a quarterback that went with them. George Chaump, the quarterbacks coach, developed me from the beginning.

We were coming right out of the civil rights era at that time, and I was a minority for the first time in my life. Growing up in D.C., I was used to being around African Americans but not many whites. At Ohio State at that time, I think we had 50,000 students and about 500 blacks, but I never once felt any racial tension. It was a learning curve for me, because I was quick to stereotype people, too. That was the best teaching experience I could have had. For the first seven weeks, I roomed with Brian Baschnagel, but Brian was from the opposite—he came from an all-white community. We became best friends.

173

Then once the season started, I roomed with Archie [Griffin], and that led to some lonely times, because he made the travel squad and I didn't. I started to get some serious stomach problems and didn't know what was wrong until Dr. Bob Murphy diagnosed it as an ulcer. He said, "Don't worry, you're only the fifth quarterback that Woody has given an ulcer to." I guess he had given one to Rex [Kern] and to Tom Matte. From that time on, the lady at the cafeteria would never give me fried food—I had to have everything broiled. Well, I would come in, and there were two or three buildings of students eating in our cafeteria, but I would have to go up and get my specially prepared meal, and everybody started thinking I was a prima donna. They didn't know the real story of my health problems.

All of my life I had kept things in when something bothered me. I never talked about my problems, but I was under a lot of pressure at that time and was away from home for the first time. I learned how to open up, and I never had another ulcer again.

Going into spring ball of '73, I was still tied for third-string, but I had a very good spring, and my confidence went up from that point. Heading into that fall camp, Greg Hare, the returning starter, was chosen as a captain. He would be the starter in the morning practice, and then I would be the starter in the afternoon practice. But Greg pulled a hamstring, and I was in there for that first possession in the first game against Minnesota. We drove right down the field, and I scored. We won that day 56–7, and I had a pretty good game, and I was the starter ever since.

Coach Hayes still didn't have much confidence in me as a passer. On some third downs, he would bring Greg in, and I thought, *Who are we fooling now?*

I was really Coach Hayes' whipping boy, and I would get it from him at least three times a day, because if you are a quarterback, you will screw up at least three times a day during practice now matter how good you are. He would leave me in tears, but I knew Coach loved me because his confidence in me grew as I got older. We knew Archie was his favorite, and Archie wouldn't practice until Thursday of each week, because he was so banged up. But it didn't matter how beat up I was; I had to practice. I guess Coach Hayes just figured the more work I got, the better I got.

During the Iowa game, I had jammed my right thumb, and it was hurting during that 10–10 tie with Michigan. I threw one pass that day, and we ran it all day. In the Rose Bowl, I threw an interception on the first play of the game, and I was scared to go by Coach Hayes, but the coaches said, "That one was our fault—we called the wrong formation." We went right back out and threw that pass again and we started clicking. That turned into a great day for us. [Greene was named the game's MVP in a 42–21 win over USC.]

I went back home for a few weeks after that season, and they retired my high school jersey. They gave me the key to the city and called it "Cornelius Greene Day." On that day, the naysayers couldn't recall telling me not to go to Ohio State.

We had a lot of expectations for that '74 team, but the Michigan State loss was just devastating. We had control of the game and then gave up two big touchdowns. We drove down to the half-yard line and had 26 seconds left, but Champ [Henson] misread the hole and ran up the lineman's back. We had time to get off one more play, but they wouldn't let our guys up. After the game, when the Big Ten commissioner came in there and told us the loss was final, Woody ripped him up one side and down the other. Then he said, "Let's go to their locker room and kick their ass." I remember seeing Ray Griffin grab his helmet and head out the door—he was ready to go. It was the only regular season game we ever lost in my four years.

That next year at Michigan, we were undefeated and everything was on the line. We were behind 14–7 and faced a third-and-11 or -12. What I remember

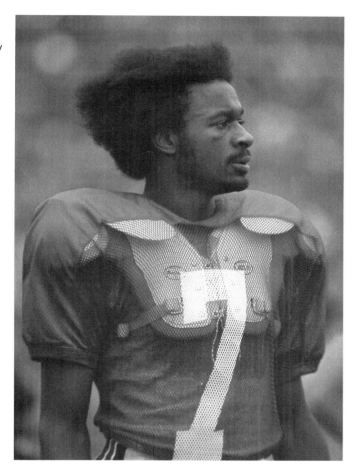

Cornelius Greene was so respected by his teammates that they named him MVP in 1975.

is on the play before, I had scrambled around our own end zone and threw one up deep, and the ball was batted up into the air and finally fell down to the turf. If that pass would have been intercepted, we would have lost.

Before this third-down play, I got the group together and said, "This prayer is for the believers." We got our hands together and prayed. I didn't do it for us to win the ballgame; I did it to bring us back together as a unit. Then I called "84 barb," a play that called for a receiver wide right to run a streak pattern and for Brian to run an out pattern underneath. We got it for the first down, and Brian got the wind knocked out of him. Then we went right down the field and scored. Ray Griffin got the big interception and took it down to the 3, and we scored again to win the game.

I was being interviewed on TV after the game, and I gave all the credit to the Lord, and I couldn't believe the fan mail I got after that. People were telling me that it had changed their lives. That just blew me away.

After that season, we went to vote on the MVP for the team, and Woody started the meeting off by saying, "We will elect Archie again as the MVP, and it will be the first time that anybody has won it three straight years." Then Lenny Willis raised his hand and said he thought Cornelius Greene deserved it, and then somebody else suggested another player, so that forced the vote. It turned out that I had won the team vote by only one vote, and Archie had voted for me because that's the kind of guy he is.

The Big Ten team submitted all of their team MVPs, and the conference MVP was selected from that pool. Anytime you can be the MVP of a team, that is special, but to be the MVP of a team that includes the greatest player in the history of college football is something unbelievable. One thing I always did...I knew what it was like to be a freshman and not play. So when the freshmen came in, I made them feel welcome and helped them out, so I probably got a lot of sympathy votes from the freshmen.

I have no regrets at all. I couldn't have had a better college career or made a better group of friends. I am a die-hard Buckeyes fan, and today when my son mentions Ohio State, he says "we." Ohio State and the state of Ohio mean so much to me because of the love and support they gave me. When I go back for reunions, I am always the next-to-last to be introduced ahead of Archie, and I always receive good applause, and that feels very good. Archie's name and number are up there on that stadium now, and that means a lot to all of his teammates.

I feel our class at Ohio State left a solid legacy there, and I am proud to be part of it.

Cornelius Greene, a three-year starter at quarterback during which Ohio State had a 31–3–1 record, was selected as the Big Ten's Most Valuable Player in 1975.

ARCHIE GRIFFIN
RUNNING BACK
1972–1975

I GREW UP IN COLUMBUS, and I had always liked the Buckeyes, but heading into my senior year of high school at Columbus Eastmoor, I really thought I would attend college at the U.S. Naval Academy or Northwestern. When Ohio State started to recruit me, I admit I was very excited. One day after wrestling practice, my wrestling coach handed me the phone. Woody Hayes was on the other end of the line. He wanted to have dinner and talk, so we went to the Jai Lai restaurant and talked for a long time. I remember being very excited about the opportunity and the possibility of going to The Ohio State University, but after the dinner was over, I wasn't so sure they wanted me. Coach Hayes hadn't said a thing to me about football—he talked only about getting a college education.

I also visited Michigan, and it was right after Bo had his heart attack. He was at home in bed, and I liked him because he was so much like Woody. But once I realized Ohio State was still interested in me, I knew it was the right place for me. Another factor was that I had a brother at Kent State and a brother at Louisville, and I thought I would make it easier on my folks if I stayed closer to home.

It didn't dawn on me until the end of my senior year in high school that, for the first time in a long time, freshmen would become eligible that next season, but my only goal at that time was to make the varsity.

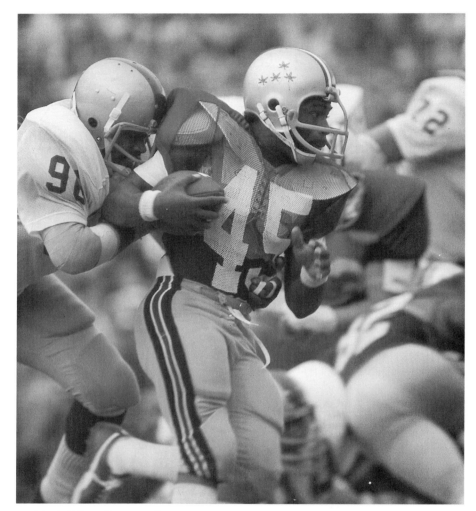

Archie Griffin rolls up yards against Southern Methodist in 1974.

Once I was on campus, I realized how much bigger and faster the guys were than in high school. What I really remember was training that summer for the mile run. The running backs had to do it in five minutes and 45 seconds, and I could never make it. I tried all summer, but shoot, I couldn't get down there. It really troubled me. So we got out there that first day of practice, and I ran a five 30-something. I thought I had really done something, and then the varsity came in, and I saw this big linebacker named Randy Gradishar run it in 5:15. Man alive, I couldn't believe a big guy could run that fast.

I didn't know at all if I was going to play that season. I was on the scout squad, and I did pretty well during that first scrimmage, but I had no idea of where I stood. When the varsity went to the hotel before that first game against Iowa, we stayed in the dorm. So in that first game, we got to beating Iowa pretty good, and some of the freshmen got to play late in the game. I was really excited, knowing this was my shot to show them what I could do. I was thinking about breaking a long run and scoring a touchdown. They called "18 sweep"…to the right side. I had wondered if the holes would be there for me the way they had been all day. As the play developed, I was shocked, because there was this gaping hole in front of me. On that play, I did something fundamentally wrong—I kept my eyes on that hole and never looked back at the football, which hit me right in the hands and bounced off. I had fumbled on my first play.

That was it for me for that day—I got taken out and didn't get another carry. I really felt like I had blown my chance, and I prayed hard just to get another opportunity. I still practiced very hard and did everything I was supposed to do that next week, but I wondered.

In the second game, North Carolina blocked a punt to go ahead of us 7–0 midway through the first quarter. At that point, somebody called my name on the bench, and I knew I was the only Griffin on the team, so I figured that they must have meant me. But I was so shocked that I almost went in the game without my helmet.

I was in a daze that day. I really was. The guys later told me that my eyes were as big as saucers in the huddle. Next thing I knew, they were announcing over the PA system that I had rushed for a record [239 yards on 27 carries, which set an OSU and Ohio Stadium record at the time]. I really had no idea.

Things did change for me somewhat after that game. I heard what they were saying on TV that night, and I heard it on the radio when I went out on a date. I just tried not to let it affect me. I knew I was still a freshman. I was still a student-athlete, and I had my responsibilities to practice hard, go to class, and do the things I was supposed to do.

Off the field, the guys were just great. I lived in Smith Hall at the time, and we had a lot of fun. Everybody has heard that story about Big Ed

Trepanier holding me out of the window there. It was really only the third or fourth floor, not the 10th or 11th as the story goes, and he had me by the ankles when I told him, "Big Ed, whatever you do, don't drop me!"

The following season, I really felt like I was in a flow. I remember walking down the hallway one day after playing Wisconsin, and I had a pretty good game, and Woody was walking the other way toward me. I just said, "Hi, Coach," and he looked at me and said, "Damn it, you are the best damn back in the country. Damn it, yes you are."

And he continued on walking. That really made me feel good. I thought, *Wow, I know this guy really cares about me, and I am going to play my heart out for him.*

It was a great season for us, and we won them all until we got to Michigan. That 10–10 tie really felt like a loss, at least for 24 hours, until they announced they had picked us to go back to the Rose Bowl. The year before, USC had just killed us, and we all wanted another chance at them.

That's why to this day that 1974 Rose Bowl remains one of the most satisfying, if not the most satisfying, games of my career. We redeemed ourselves and put it to them pretty good [42–21].

That season, we had put three players in the top six of the Heisman balloting. John Hicks had finished second, I was fifth, and Randy Gradishar was sixth. So the following year, people continued to remind me that I was a Heisman candidate. I tried to put all that talk aside and tried to do the best I could for our team because I wanted to contribute and win a national championship. They held the Heisman ceremony so much differently than what they do now. After that season, the Downtown Athletic Club called the sports information office on a Monday, and they told me I needed to catch a plane for a Tuesday press conference. I figured all the candidates would be there, but when I got to New York, I found out that I was the only guy there, and they announced me as the Heisman winner. I was very happy and delighted about the whole thing, but I guess it didn't really sink in. I came back home and then had to return that Friday with my family. There was a Sunday night dance and then the presentation on that Monday.

When we got there that weekend, Malcolm McCloud of the Downtown Athletic Club had told me how emotional the presentation can be. John Cappelletti had won the year before, and as everybody knows, he dedicated it to his dying brother, Joey. Everybody was crying. Anyway, Malcolm told me, "Don't worry if you get up there and cry. It will be all right."

Griffin poses with the famed trophy that he won twice.

Well, I wasn't that type. I didn't know what he was talking about. I just couldn't see myself crying up there. So I got up to give my speech, and what did I do? I couldn't get out 10 words before I started crying. I looked out at the audience, and everybody out there was crying. I was sort of embarrassed, but I got through it.

My roommates were Steve Luke and Cornelius Greene, and when I got back home, they really let me have it. One of them said, "Great speech...but did you have to cry?"

The next year, I have to say that I was more prepared and I didn't break down.

That '75 team...now we had a team there. I think we were picked to finish about third in the Big Ten heading into that season, and I remember that was the first spring we didn't prepare for Michigan—we prepared for Michigan State. They had beaten us up there the year before on that controversial finish when we found out the outcome 45 minutes after the game had ended. I still believe we scored on that final play, and I know that they were lying on our center and wouldn't let him up so we could get the snap off.

But we opened against them in '75 and played very well [a 21–0 win at Michigan State]. We rolled through that season, until we came to the Michigan game and fell behind 14–7 late in the game.

I really remember Cornelius calling us together in the huddle before that final series, and he just said, "Let us pray—God, give us the strength to be our best." We knew this was a big series and it was our last shot. He hit that pass to Brian [Baschnagel], then I had a decent run, and we got it down there and scored to tie it up. And Ray [Griffin] picked off that pass to put us in position to go ahead. That was a great, great win for us. In those four years, I am proud to say that we never lost to Michigan.

We had beaten UCLA so badly earlier in the season, so for that '76 Rose Bowl, we were trying to guard against overconfidence. It was the fourth year in a row that we had been out there. We all knew the ropes of the game and what led up to it. That day, we moved the ball up and down the field, but we just didn't score. We let them hang around, and when you do that, they are going to think they can beat you. That's what happened.

That was my final game and the most disappointing loss I ever experienced. Period. We all thought we were good enough to be national champions that year, but we never got one. That game really hurt.

I got my degree in March of '76, a quarter early, and Woody Hayes was there. He really liked it when one of us got our degree, and he always made it known when one of us graduated. I felt I could go in and talk to him about anything, and I stayed close to him over the years. The final time I saw Coach Hayes, we made plans to have lunch, because I wanted him to meet my wife, Bonita. But we never got to do that. I was driving to work on March 12, 1987, when I heard that he had died. I just turned around, went back to my house, and sat down for a while. Then I went into the bathroom and cried.

There isn't a day that goes by—and I mean not *one* day—that I don't think of Woody Hayes or my father. Not one day. He was very, very good to me. He was a very special person.

Being at Ohio State, playing in the state of Ohio for my entire career, and now working here, the tradition we have gets in your blood and remains there. When you see "Script Ohio," or when that band comes down the ramp to enter the stadium, it makes the hair on your back stand up. I was born at University Hospital, I grew up here, and I played my football here. It's unlike any other place in the world—it's such a special place.

I know I was meant to be a Buckeye.

Archie Griffin, the only two-time winner of the Heisman Trophy, finished his Ohio State career with 5,589 rushing yards and an NCAA-record 34 100-yard rushing games. He also was one of eight three-time All-Americans to play at Ohio State. He played seven seasons with the Cincinnati Bengals. A member of the College Football Hall of Fame, he was named president of the Ohio State Alumni Association in June 2003.

BOB BRUDZINSKI
DEFENSIVE END
1973–1976

ICAME FROM FREMONT, OHIO, which was a town with a lot of Michigan alumni, such as Rob Lytle, who was a high school teammate of mine before heading to Michigan. In making my final choice in picking a college, I had narrowed it down to Michigan, Michigan State, and Ohio State when I got a call from Ara Parseghian from Notre Dame. He asked me, "How about a good Catholic Polish boy like you coming to Notre Dame?"

I said, "Well, Coach, I have whittled it down to these three…" and I heard "click"—he hung up on me.

I didn't have a real good visit to Michigan, and the guy who took me around there was a big jerk. I liked Bo [Schembechler], though, but I got bad vibes from the place. Craig Cassady was my host at Ohio State, and he was a really good guy. There were great guys there, it seemed right, and my dad wanted me to go there.

And how could you not be impressed by Woody Hayes? He really never talked about football with me when he recruited me. When he came to the home, he tried to sell the parents on Ohio State, and Dad liked him because he was in World War II, and they talked about the war.

When I got to Ohio State, I roomed with this one guy whose mother had just died, and he was very depressed. It got to be really depressing for me, too. I had an eight-track tape with "Stairway to Heaven" on it, and he played

Bob Brudzinski, shown here against Purdue in 1976, was named MVP of the 1976 team.

it over and over and over. He just stayed in his room and played that song. He never made it—he left school after that.

It was my first time away from home, and all of the freshmen were basically scared, but everybody at Ohio State was so friendly that it didn't take too long to get adjusted and to feel at home. I remember we had to get bused over to West Campus for classes, and I hated that because I was afraid to miss even one class. If the old man found out, you would pay for it, and you didn't want to get on his bad side. He treated everybody pretty well, though. Whenever he saw me in the hallway at the North Facility, he would always say, "Bob, how are you doing today? Things okay?" I knew the best thing to do was to be quiet, keep my mouth shut, work hard, and stay out of his office. I can still see that office—he had a little bed in there.

The funny thing is that we never really had a weight room at the North Facility. They put a little Nautilus in there, because Woody went through a phase where he believed in that, but the year after I left, they built a weight room.

I played behind Van DeCree, who was a two-time All-American defensive end, for those first two years, but I got my share of practice time. Van always had some sort of injury during the week. He would point at his shoulder and say "shoulder" or at his knee and say "knee." He missed a lot of practices, but he played on Saturdays. I practiced all the time, and I really believe that had a lot to do with making me a much better player heading into my junior year, when I got to start.

One of the few times I saw Woody get really upset with one of his players during a game was in the Rose Bowl after Neal Colzie spiked the ball, which took us out of field-goal range [in an 18–17 loss to USC in the 1975 Rose Bowl]. He made a great interception and then he did that. When he came off the field, Woody got in his face and really let him have it.

The next year, there is no question in my mind that we should have been national champs. We just kicked UCLA's ass earlier in the year, and I remember what Esco [Sarkkinen] said when he scouted them before that game. He said, "They are young and good, and you have got to watch out for this team. They will be getting better and better, and I hope we don't have to play them again [in the Rose Bowl]."

I admit that I don't remember much about [the Rose Bowl], or I choose to forget it, but I do remember that their linemen were huge. As my career went, it was one of the first times I could have won a championship. I never really won the big championship game. We lost that one at Ohio State, and then I played on three Super Bowl–losing teams [one with the Los Angeles Rams and two with the Miami Dolphins]. I never won the big one.

My senior year [1976] was a very frustrating year. It was considered a down year. We lost to Missouri when they went for two points and got it, and then we tied UCLA 10–10. And we were beaten badly by Michigan, but the Orange Bowl against Colorado was one of our best games and a great way to go out.

We were getting our ass kicked early in that game, 10–0, and we came back. We were loose for that game, though, and that's why we played so well. We went to the beach and had a really good time in Miami. Plus, it was just great not being cooped up in that Sheraton in Pasadena, as we had been the three previous years. It seemed that we had a loose curfew at the Orange Bowl. I remember saying hi to "Sark," signing in at the hotel for bed check, and going right out the back door a few times. A lot of guys were doing that.

Ironically, I live in South Florida now, and one of my sports bars hosts the Broward County OSU Alumni Association when the games are on TV. We play "Across the Field" and all the other school songs, and everybody gets into it. We pack the place with Buckeyes fans.

187

I never regretted choosing Ohio State. The fans were great, and I can say it was the best four years I could have ever asked for. I got to meet a lot of great people, people I am still friends with. I live in Florida, but I still get back to see a game once in a while. I took my two boys to Phoenix for the Fiesta Bowl, and I have never seen them get that excited about a football game. They are real Buckeyes fans. It was an awesome experience. And we won the championship game, something that got away from me during my playing days.

Bob Brudzinski was twice All–Big Ten and an All-American in 1976. He played four seasons with the Los Angeles Rams and nine with the Miami Dolphins.

BRUCE RUHL

DEFENSIVE BACK

1973–1976

A S I WAS SITTING IN THE STANDS in Tempe, Arizona, for the Fiesta Bowl, all those memories of why I became a Buckeye came flooding back to me. They seemed to instantly bridge the gap of those 30 years. I was from Michigan, and people always asked me, "Why did you choose Ohio State?" There were no Michigan players on the Buckeyes roster at that time, and I was the first player Woody Hayes successfully recruited out of Michigan—and it was in the middle of the well-known "10-Year War" between the two schools. I became a Buckeye and a traitor.

I had established three priorities when deciding where to attend college. First, I was determined to be the first in my family to receive a college diploma. I knew that the Ohio State coaches fully supported classroom achievements, since Woody consistently graduated more than 80 percent of his players.

Second, I wanted an opportunity to play. Woody played freshmen during this era; Bo Schembechler did not. As it turned out, I was fortunate to start in a few games during my freshman year, and I played in the 1974 Rose Bowl, enjoying the big win over USC.

My third concern was to experience a quality social life. Columbus, Ohio, offered all of that. Over the years, it has proved to be a great place to live and raise a family. The standard and quality of living in Columbus exceeded my expectations as I learned how the community embraces the program. I met good people and developed relationships that eventually helped me establish a career after football.

Only OSU football alumni or current players can describe the experience of running through that tunnel and onto that field for the first time. To me, it was as if I were floating on a magic carpet out to the field, while the band and the roar of the fans were our fuel. I don't recall feeling my feet hit the turf.

I have so many great memories on the field, but I will share just a few. I had three interceptions in the 1974 Wisconsin game that still stands as a school record shared with many other players. I guess it was my 15 minutes of fame. On the other side, I was the safety on the play when Michigan State's Levi Jackson ran 80 yards for the game-winning touchdown in 1974. That following season, Michigan State's plastic stadium cups featured a photo of Levi running down the sideline and OSU's No. 43 chasing. That was me.

One of my favorite assistants was Esco Sarkkinen. He had played at Ohio State in the '30s and was part of the coaching staff for decades. Esco would hold daily trivia contests on the team bus when we were bussed down to the stadium for practices. He would say, "Anyone with the right answers wins my orange drink." Esco also was a traditionalist. He once interrupted our ring committee meeting comprised of juniors and seniors who were engaged in designing the ring to commemorate the 1975 season. We were breaking tradition by having a gold rose on the top of the stone instead of the "O" or "Ohio" that was usually inscribed. Esco yelled at us for messing with tradition.

Years later at Anne Hayes' funeral, I looked down at Esco's hand. He was wearing two rings—the 1968 national championship ring and the '76 Rose Bowl ring that we had designed and had broken tradition. "It was one of my favorites," he said. During his funeral, he was received while wearing those two rings and a pair of gold pants on his lapel.

Those gold pants were and still are a favorite tradition of mine. As most Buckeyes know, a player receives a gold charm when the team defeats Michigan. This tradition originated in the '30s, and being from Michigan, beating Michigan was always special for me. But defeating Michigan in 1975 at Ann Arbor for the Big Ten championship—earning another Rose Bowl berth and finishing 11–0—made that win particularly satisfying.

Everyone knows it was to Woody, too. He was somewhere between a father and grandfather figure to me. He consistently expressed his beliefs and values to his team with passion, and although I did not always agree with him, I always respected him. I grew closer to him after he was finished coaching. I think I became more than a former player; I became a friend. We met regularly, and I enjoyed going over to his home to visit.

As everyone knows, Woody loved military history, and the personalities of war and the battles were often subjects of speeches on practice and game days. He took advantage of impromptu situations to embellish evil in opponents to help get us psyched up for a game. One time during a trip for an Indiana game, the Bloomington Chamber of Commerce welcomed us with a token desktop paperweight as we exited the bus. Woody encouraged us to throw the gift away. He told us to beware of smiling faces and those bearing gifts. "They are only trying to take your minds off the game and soften us up," he said.

Another time I saw him get riled up at Joe Paterno. The 1975 Penn State game was a big game, because we were undefeated and the schools had not faced each other in more than a decade. I believe Woody respected Joe Paterno because he ran a clean and honorable program. But before the game, he stormed into the locker room and repeated a conversation that he just had with Paterno. "Do you know what Joe Paterno just said to me?" he yelled. "He said, 'Woody, you're coming off that heart attack and you're working too hard; you had better take it easy.'"

"I had a notion to slap him," Woody told us. "How dare he try to soften me up!" He then went into a 15-minute unplanned speech that was one of his best. We beat Penn State 17–9.

Woody truly wanted us to be educated, and he also exposed us to great thinkers. My introduction to the writings of Rudyard Kipling came at the expense of a teammate who had snapped a wet towel at an opposing fan during a game. The fan probably deserved it, but our teammate was quarantined for the weekend to learn and consequently recite the poem "If" ["If you can keep your head when all about you are losing theirs and blaming it on you…"].

The player had to recite all four verses, without notes, to the team before practice on that Monday after the game. Woody was right there to help him as he stumbled to remember the next line, and Woody didn't need any notes. I framed a copy of the poem and hung it on my oldest son's wall as he grew from an infant into a teenager.

A native of Michigan, Bruce Ruhl loved being part of the "10-Year War."

Woody often talked about paying forward. You know, don't pay back, pay forward. I experienced his conviction over and over again with his endless charitable and humanitarian actions, and many were done quietly without public notice. He often visited Children's Hospital in Columbus. We knew this because he would apologize for leaving study table early to go downtown to visit a sick child. After our 1974 Rose Bowl victory, we returned to Columbus during the night, and there were thousands of fans at the airport to greet us. Someone gave him a huge bouquet of roses. Woody decided to make a special trip to Riverside Hospital, and he asked the registration desk for names of patients who did not have any visitors that day. He passed out those roses to all those patients in the various wards. That was his way of paying forward. He was such a great man.

It went so fast. I remember my final game at the 1977 Orange Bowl. When your senior season starts to wind down, there is a realization that the clock is ticking. I was on the field during the last play as an incomplete pass fell toward my direction. We celebrated the win, but I walked off the field very slowly, taking in the smell, sounds, and sights of the moment. I knew I would not play in another game as a Buckeye. I just wanted to remember that instant forever.

From that moment forward, I knew I would become a fan of Buckeyes teams to come. In the locker room after the game, the coaches went around to the seniors and thanked us for our careers and wished us good luck. I knew their sentiments were sincere. I waited until the very end to take my uniform off, because I knew I would never wear those pads and colors again. As it turned out, it was the last time I wore a football uniform.

I have no regrets. It's always been great to be a Buckeye.

Bruce Ruhl was Academic All–Big Ten in 1974 and '75.

TOM SKLADANY
KICKER/PUNTER
1973–1976

GROWING UP IN BETHEL PARK, Pennsylvania, I didn't even know where Ohio State was. All I knew then was Pitt football or Notre Dame because they were on TV all the time. *What's a Buckeye?* I thought. I remember when George Chaump recruited me. He said, "Woody doesn't want you. I want you, but they don't want to give you a scholarship because there's never been a scholarship given to a punter at Ohio State."

So I took my visit to Ohio State, and there were 88,000 fans at the game. I thought, *Wow!* But Woody told me this: "Now, we're probably not going to give you a scholarship, but I hear you kick pretty good, and if you come up here and if you do what Coach Chaump says you can do, you may end up getting a scholarship."

At the same time, Notre Dame, Michigan, and Penn State were offering me full rides. So I told Coach Chaump I wasn't coming, because I had offers with full scholarships. Finally, Woody told him, "If you think he can do it, then go ahead and give him our last scholarship."

Woody called up and told me, "Now, son, we're going to give you a scholarship. Are you coming or not?" I told him I had one last visit to take, to Penn State. "You don't want to come here, son?" Woody asked me. "You better make up your mind."

I ended up signing the scholarship to become a Buckeye, and I was the first kicker to ever get one to Ohio State.

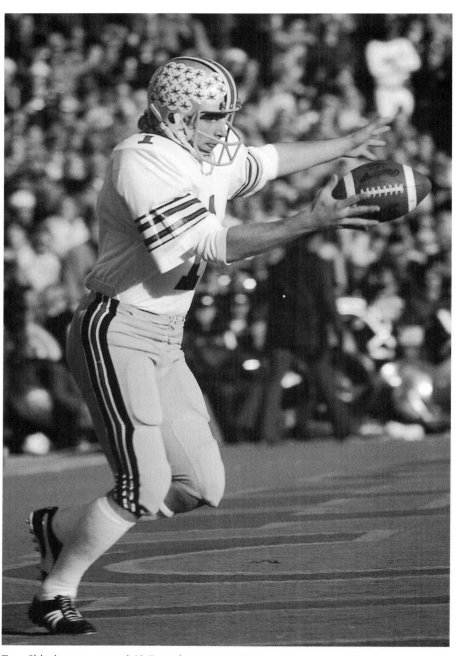

Tom Skladany averaged 42.7 yards per punt during his career and holds the school record with a 59-yard field goal.

The first guy I met up there when I was getting recruited was Ken Kuhn. We were sitting at this bar near campus, and someone introduced me to him. He reached over, and I thought he was going to shake my hand, but he took my glass of beer. He drained it, bit it, and chewed the glass. Blood was coming out of his mouth. That's my first impression of Ohio State—Ken Kuhn ate glass!

When I went out on that field for that first practice, there were seven punters and eight kickers. They were all walk-ons. I was thinking, *What did I get myself into?* Here I am the first scholarship punter, and these senior walk-ons are pounding the ball past me. I knew I could punt, but it's different punting in front of Woody Hayes, Randy Gradishar, and John Hicks. I had the scholarship, but these other guys deserved it, I thought then.

It went down to the final week of camp, and Woody named me the starting punter, as a freshman. So I went out there for the first punt, in front of eighty-eight thousand people in the Horseshoe, and I got a 41-yard fair catch. I ended up that year with 35 punts, 35 yards returned, and a 35-yard average. Everything was 35. I was last in the Big Ten, and I broke my leg in the Michigan game when I got clipped. I did lead in tackles on the kickoff team. When I didn't bomb it out of the end zone, I made the tackle. But Michigan sent a guy after me, and he clipped me from behind, broke my leg, and dislocated my ankle.

195

I remember Woody came up and asked, "Well, how is he?"

The trainers told him, "Coach, it's bad."

He said, "Well, check him out over there," meaning on the sideline.

I missed the Rose Bowl and had a cast up to my hip for two and a half months. I really think that's what made my leg stronger. My thigh grew an inch and three-quarters carrying that cast around campus. My leg got hard as a rock. That, and I worked my ass off that summer.

The next season, my first punt went off the side of my foot, but it rolled and ended up 61 yards. On the very next one, it was a 55-yard spiral for a fair catch. I led the nation in punting with a 46.7-yard average. From then on, I don't know if it was mental, all that work, or my leg, but I hit spirals the rest of my life. I made All-America as a sophomore and was on top of the world.

Until then, Woody didn't call me by name. He just called me "Punter"— as in, "Punter, get back here!" After I made All-America, it was "Tom."

I remember I hit a 59-yard field goal, which was the Big Ten record at that time [it remains the OSU record], and averaged 56 yards a punt—in the same game [at Illinois in 1975]. But Woody never really said, "Nice game." He was like my father that way: he never really complimented me, but it motivated me. And I noticed he would do it in the papers. He would say, "Archie Griffin is the best running back in the history of college football," or, "That Skladany…you won't find a better punter." He'd tell you after your playing days—in front of other people, too. I guess he didn't want you to get fat-headed.

The guy was hilarious. He was the most intense, honest, hardworking guy there could ever be. Here's what I always told people about Woody Hayes: you were afraid of him as a freshman, you hated him as a sophomore, you liked him as a junior, and you loved him as a senior. He took you on an emotional roller coaster. Nobody would outwork him. You'd go in to work out for the summer at 7:00 AM, and he'd still be on his couch from falling asleep at night with the projector on and he would have the same clothes on. He'd burn out four projectors a year.

I remember one time I went to be on *The Woody Hayes Show*. The image I have of that time is he was passed out between a Pepsi machine and a Coke machine in the lobby. I mean, he was sleeping with his tongue out, drooling on his tie. He was absolutely beat. They had to wake him up five minutes before the show. He just wouldn't stop working.

And that's what he wanted us to do. Before my junior year, I developed a new practice routine. I went home and punted around a nine-hole golf course. I punted from the side of the No. 1 tee; I would jog, pick it up, stop, and punt again. I would punt it to the green, go pick it up, and jog to the next tee. For 300 yards, I would have six punts, and all that running in between.

I always had fun before, during, or after practice at Ohio State. I made up these games, such as throwing golf balls out of the stadium. I could throw a golf ball from the block "O" at midfield right out of the stadium. All of the other guys thought it must not have been that hard, but nobody else could do it. I'd bet five bucks a man and get all warmed up, throw it out of there, and take the cash.

When it was cold, I led the punters and kickers into the locker room, and we would be eating jelly doughnuts and drinking hot chocolate because they didn't need us until the final 15 minutes of practice. At times, we were in there either studying, playing cards, gambling, or eating. This one time the trainer ran in and was yelling my name. "Woody can't find you!" he said.

I went out of there running as fast as I could. I could hear Woody: "Where the hell is the punter?" Everybody was laughing because I had jelly all over my face. I stayed outside after that.

I was the goof-off, but that's how I got through it.

I remember we had this little party for Woody the year after he was fired. He didn't like that, but we all wanted it. Everybody put up 50 bucks and guys came from California, Texas, Kansas, everywhere. Bo came back and talked. I remember Woody telling Rex Kern, "Rex, I don't like the idea that you're spending money flying all the way from California for this party."

Woody was always worried about his guys.

If only I could bring back that time. It was the best four years you could ask for. I should have paid Ohio State. I had more fun than anyone could have. I went to three Rose Bowls, the Orange Bowl, the Japan Bowl, and the Hula Bowl. I've got six rings and six watches from Ohio State. I had the time of my life. And to think, while I was a senior in high school, I didn't even know where Ohio State was.

I wish all the fans could experience the feeling of running out of the tunnel in the 'Shoe after hearing the band come into the field before a game. You can't explain it with words. It is magical, intense, and overwhelming, and that is the exact moment when you know what being a Buckeye is all about.

Tom Skladany, team captain in 1976, became only the sixth Ohio State player to be named a three-time All-American. He played six seasons in the NFL with the Detroit Lions and the Philadelphia Eagles.

CHRIS WARD
OFFENSIVE LINEMAN
1974–1977

IN 1969 I WAS JUST A VERY LARGE eighth grader who held no great hope of ever really pursuing an athletic career of any type. Most of my coaches' reports were negative at best, but I improved as the years went on at Dayton's John H. Patterson High School, thanks to the coaching of Ken Amlin. And I developed dreams of playing college football.

I'll never forget the day that Wayne Woodrow Hayes visited my house to recruit me. He was so polite and demure that he just won my parents over right from the start. "We would really love to have Chris at Ohio State," he told them. "We will take care of him like our son. He's a fine young man, and he is exactly the type of young man we want at Ohio State. Can you get a commitment from him?"

My father said something like, "It's his decision," but I already knew I was going to Ohio State, anyway. All I did that day was commit to visit. I didn't want my dad to have to go more than 70 miles to see me play college football.

Anyway, because of Woody Hayes' visit, I became an instant celebrity at school. He was the greatest coach from the greatest school, The Ohio State University, visiting me!

When I arrived at Ohio State, it was a few years after freshmen became eligible, so my mind was on playing right away. And it was working out that way, too. I played in every game but didn't start until we had several tackles go down with injuries before the Michigan State game. I was going to get

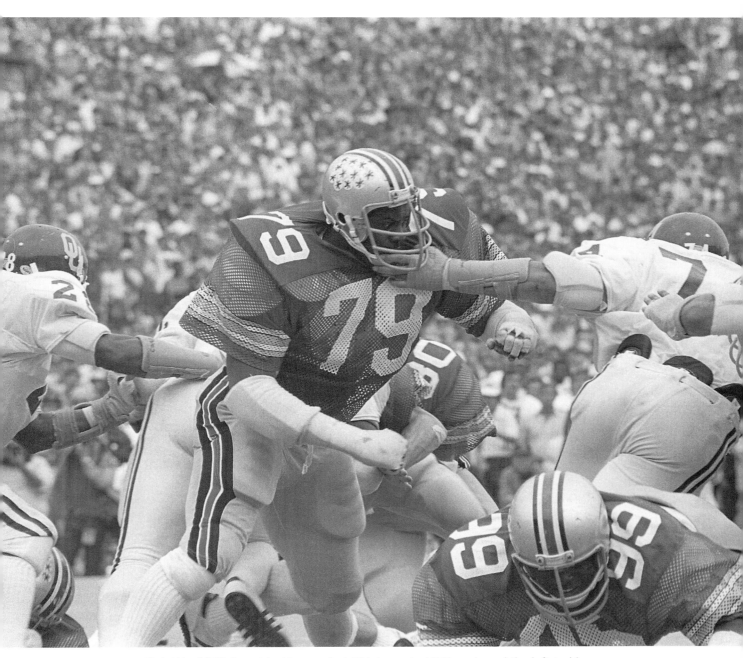

Chris Ward (79), here blocking against Oklahoma in 1977, anchored the left tackle position for three seasons.

my first start. They were ranked high, and we were ranked No. 1 and unde-feated, and I was all pumped up for my first start. Then in practice, disaster struck—I hurt my knee. It turned out to be an injury that was between oper-able and nonoperable.

So we beat Michigan and were headed to the Rose Bowl, but I had this mobile cast on my knee and was hobbling around. We were practicing in Columbus before the Rose Bowl, and it was raining so hard, and then it turned to ice. It was one of the worst ice storms we had ever had. Coach Hayes called me in and asked me, "Chris, how's that knee?" I said, "I don't know, Coach, I don't know, but it hurts."

We were leaving for California in three days, and the doctors didn't know what to do with me. "Chris, we think a lot of you, you know that," Woody told me. "But we're about to go to the Rose Bowl; do you want to go?"

Well, of course I did.

So Coach Hayes got all excited and just said, "I'll tell you what the hell we are going to do, son. You are going to take that cast off right now. We are going to take you outside, and you are going to run. If you can't run, we are operating first thing in the morning. If you can run, you are going to the Rose Bowl."

I said, "Coach, there's ice out there on the field and it's cold."

It didn't matter to Coach Hayes—so I took the cast off and ran like a gazelle.

Woody came in and told the doctors, "Chris is going to the Rose Bowl with us."

The man was a psychological genius. He really was. Anyway, I was fine after that.

I ended up having a great career at Ohio State and having the distinct pleasure of playing with the greatest athletes in my career—which spanned 10 pro training camps, four different teams, and 20 years—right there as a Buckeye. There were no finer teammates, talent, or players anywhere than what we had at Ohio State.

I would have been a four-year starter if it wasn't for that knee injury, and that's something I really take pride in. In four years, we were about 10 points from winning a couple of national championships. That 1975 team that lost to UCLA in the Rose Bowl could have beaten some pro teams. We had the very best players at every position. But it wasn't to be.

During my senior year, I was a finalist for the Heisman Trophy, and during my trip to New York, the president of the Downtown Athletic Club took me to lunch and told me, "We lobbied for you to be the first nonskilled player to win the Heisman Trophy. We really think you deserve it." Well, the Heisman went to Earl Campbell, and I never won the Outland Trophy or Lombardi Award either, but I was an All-American. And I was and always will be a Buckeye.

As long as I live, I will always remember "Script Ohio" on a Saturday afternoon at Ohio Stadium. I love Ohio State, and I would do anything for that school. My heart will bleed scarlet and gray forever.

Chris Ward, a two-time All-American, played for the New York Jets, New Orleans Saints, and Miami Dolphins.

JEFF LOGAN
RUNNING BACK
1974–1977

IBELIEVE THAT THE EXPERIENCE of playing football at Ohio State, while eas-ily documented by wins and losses, statistics, bowl games, and rings, is an ever-growing one. Life experiences today continue to magnify the lessons we learned while playing football at the highest level in college, so this is not something that has yet been achieved but something that continues to grow in each of us.

My experience is unique in that my father played for Woody Hayes in his first year of coaching at Ohio State in 1951. From the very first moment of being considered by Ohio State, I wanted to become a Buckeye.

I was concerned whether I was good enough to be part of the very best, and that led me to look at football programs all over the country. I wanted to play the game I loved, and if at all possible I wanted to do it with the very best. And that was Ohio State.

During recruiting, it became obvious to me that I probably belonged in Division I football due to the interest I was receiving. I eventually convinced myself that all of these coaches could not be wrong, even though most peo-ple in my community were concerned that I would get lost at a big school.

Immediate playing opportunities at other Division I schools were tempt-ing, and the emergence of Archie Griffin as the best to ever play the college game was daunting for a guy who played the same position. Was I willing to

Jeff Logan, here before the Michigan State game in 1976, succeeded Archie Griffin at tailback.

sit back and learn for two years until Archie graduated? I was not even giving consideration to the other excellent running backs already at Ohio State.

In the end, it was the desire to play in the Rose Bowl that was my determining factor in choosing Ohio State. I would have loved to play for Joe Paterno at Penn State, or Lee Corso at Indiana, or even Pepper Rodgers at Georgia Tech, but I could not suppress my intense desire to do it with the very best.

Fortunately, I made the right decision, not because I later became a starter and cocaptain, but because I was given the gift of the great tradition at Ohio State.

One of our greatest traditions unique to Ohio State is the awarding of the gold pants to players on a team that beats Michigan. In my time, we were 2–2 against Michigan, and therefore I own two pairs of gold pants that I consider irreplaceable.

One year I was asked to speak to the team during the week before the Michigan game, and I recall having my son, Critter, join me at the podium. When I completed my speech, I hoisted Critter to the top of the podium and asked him to show them what they were playing for. He reached into his shirt and showed off a pair of gold pants that were hanging from a necklace. Since that day, Critter has worn that necklace each year during Michigan week.

I maintain that we have something very special here, something only those who have been on the inside can know and understand. My guess is that most players who played for Michigan, Nebraska, USC, and the like have had similar experiences, but I will never know for sure.

What I do know is that they do not have what I have, and that is the gift of the great tradition that is Ohio State football.

You see, we at Ohio State realize we live under the shade of trees that we did not plant and we drink from wells that we did not dig. Our opportunity, however, is our responsibility. We must recognize the gift and carry it on for the future generations of recruits who come to Ohio State.

Many people confuse tradition with the bricks and mortar that make up the buildings at this great institution we call Ohio State. While there are landmarks such as Ohio Stadium on the banks of the Olentangy River and the Oval, those serve only as points of reference to me when I look back on the experience of attending Ohio State and being a member of four Big Ten championship teams.

The memories of running out onto the field at Ohio Stadium for the first and last times are memories that no one else can own, unless they were one of the lucky few to wear that scarlet and gray uniform. The fans will always be remembered for their immense loyalty, and they are a big part of our tradition.

Woody Hayes always told us that the best friends and friendships that we would make would be our teammates, and he could not have been more accurate. While each of us has moved on to new lives after Ohio State football, the camaraderie of seeing a teammate at homecoming, at a reunion, or in the Varsity "O" Club room before a game is priceless. This is bigger than the concrete of Ohio Stadium and 100,000-plus screaming fans. I think we who were there to play the game and those lucky enough to get there in the future understand that this tradition of being a Buckeye is not something that you can kick or carry. This is what makes it so priceless.

Jeff Logan rushed for 1,248 yards in 1976 and was named a team captain in '77.

TOM COUSINEAU

LINEBACKER

1975–1978

BACK WHEN I WAS RECRUITED, I had a big advantage because my dad was a high school coach, and he had sent several players on to college football. Two of them were Pete Cusick and Tommy Marendt, who each went to Ohio State. At that time, you could take as many recruiting visits as you wanted. But my dad was familiar with the recruiting process and he told me right off the bat, "Don't waste anybody's time. You can't be serious about more than four schools anyway. If you visit a place and you have no notion of going there, you are taking a spot that somebody else may need."

My four schools were Ohio State, Michigan, Notre Dame, and Penn State. It became pretty simple for me the day Ara [Parseghian] left Notre Dame. I had visited the campus up there and was very impressed, and being from Saint Edward's High, there was some awful strong pressure for me to go to Notre Dame. But if Ara wasn't going to be there, I didn't want to go there. I liked Joe Paterno, but I didn't want to play in a 4–4 defensive scheme, which is what Penn State used.

The first time I met Coach Hayes, he came to our school and I was running a little late. As I walked into the foyer of the building, the place was packed with people. There was this huge crowd around him, and there he was, holding court. He was holding court as only he could do. Nobody was in class—everybody was listening to him. I remember the sea of kids parted as we met.

I was excused from my class, and we went down to the athletic offices and talked about everything—everything but football. That was his way. Sometimes, he gave you the impression he wasn't interested in you for football, because he never talked about it. He left that more to the assistants. For a young guy like me, it was hard to relax around him, and he knew that. He worked really hard to make you feel comfortable, but the man was a legend. He asked a lot of questions, and I think I gave a lot of one-word answers. His way was to recruit parents. When he talked to my parents later at the house, I was like a passenger in the car of my own life.

On the evening before signing day, Woody was at the house in our basement with Joe Paterno and Gary Moeller [then the defensive coordinator at Michigan]. Now there were some high-profile coaches in the same place at the same time. We all sat there and talked, but it was very uncomfortable. Thank God my mom and dad were down there with me. Coach Hayes was the first to leave. He went to the door, and I followed him. He turned around and told me, "I'll be back at 7:00. You tell Mom that I like bacon and eggs, and pancakes would be nice."

Then he stuck out his hand out and asked, "Are you ready to be a Buckeye?"

"Yes, sir," I said.

I want it to be clear—I didn't settle on Ohio State. That was the first really big decision of my life.

207

On the first day of practice, I remember Teddy Smith came off the line and hit me so hard. My face mask was crushed, and I just went, "Wow." I called Dad and said something like I might be over my head here, and he said, "Don't worry, everything will come to you. Give it a little time." By the end of the first week, the offense was running the isolation in 7-on-7 drills. Pete Johnson was the type of runner that you knew where he was headed once he got the handoff and started. He would get that can up in the air and head for the hole. On this day, I just headed to the spot with a full head of steam and blew it up. Coach Hayes was all upset and screaming, and he was the type of coach who would come right back with the same play. So they gave it to Pete again, and I did it again…I just hit Pete as hard as I could for a loss in the backfield. Now Coach Hayes was really upset. He came running over and grabbed my face mask and started screaming at me. George Hill, our defensive coordinator, came over and smiled. "Great job," he told me. "Great job."

Woody was a big believer in hitting during practice. We just banged the crap out of each other. Anyway, the upperclassmen seemed to accept me from

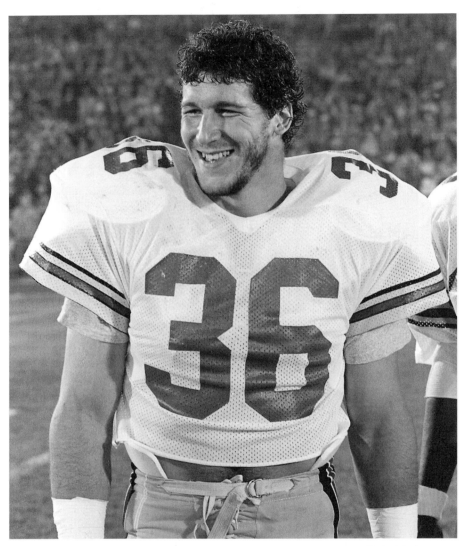

Tom Cousineau, shown here in his final game (the 1978 Gator Bowl), holds five Ohio State tackling records.

that point. I remember one night I was dead in bed, sleeping, and six of them came in and gathered around me. Somebody said, "You ready? You with us? We're going out, and you're coming with us. Ready to hit High Street? Let's rock and roll." That was their way of accepting me, I guess.

But that's the way it was at Ohio State. The seniors helped the freshmen, and that was the great thing about it. That freshman year on the road, I roomed with Timmy Fox, because I think Coach Hayes wanted me to be around a leader. Woody really believed in having older players mentor younger ones.

One of the first plays I remember in an Ohio State uniform—we were at UCLA early in the '75 season, and I was the wedge buster on kickoffs and punts. I was headed down there on one, and Wendell Tyler was just getting ready to catch the ball. I was timing it just right to be there at the same time, and, all of a sudden, I got crushed high and low from each side. It turned me over, and I ended up face down on the ground. I hit so hard that my face mask dug out this big chunk of grass, and it became stuck in my face mask. I was semi out of it; I couldn't see anything and I couldn't feel anything. I thought I was blinded. What a humbling experience, but we just crushed them that day.

Kenny Kuhn had meningitis, and I got thrown in there awfully early and started most games my freshman year. Being around the guys I was playing with, I just didn't want to let anybody down. It was a great group of guys and great players. Eddie Beamon was always talking. Aaron Brown had a great year. Tim Fox was a leader on that defense. Nick Buonamici was quiet and would lead by example. Bob Brudzinski was a great player.

209

To end that season, we played UCLA again in the Rose Bowl for the national championship. What an awful memory. That one still hurts.

A few years ago, my wife and I were test-driving a car in Los Angeles, and we got off the freeway. This guy was in the car with us and he said, "I know a great road we can drive on," but I didn't know where we were. It turned out that this road went around the Rose Bowl. So we were driving around it, and I got such a bad feeling in my stomach. I told this guy, "I can't be here. I am sorry, but this brings back really bad memories. Let's get out of here."

We had such a great team in '75, but we lost all those seniors before that next season, and we had to forge a new identity, I guess. We worked really hard at trying to do that. I remember that Missouri game; we were beating them so badly that I came out of the game and had taken my tape off. We dominated them, but the next thing you know, they came roaring back. They scored and went for two on play-action to go ahead, and I was covering the guy out of the backfield. I saw a flag and thought it was on me, but it was on the other side of the field. They got another chance and got the two-point conversion to beat us by one point. That was a hard one to take. My family had some friends who were huge Missouri fans down for the game, and they got a little obnoxious after that.

The one thing that stands out through those years is how much we all got along. We would go out and have a lot of fun, and there was just tremendous camaraderie. We were in New Orleans at the Sugar Bowl my junior year, and a bunch of us went to Pat O'Brien's. We were sitting around this big, round table and were pretty smacked because we all had hurricanes in front of us. Woody had walked in there, but I never noticed him until he sat down at our table. He was talking to us like there was no big deal, because he figured those hurricanes were just fruit punch. Then he reached over and took a sip of one, and he finally figured out that the juice was just for coloring. He got up, threw this hurricane against the wall, and the race was on. I fell out of my chair and was crawling around on the ground, going from table to table to get out of there without him seeing me. I got away. I knew that whoever he got his hands on, he would put his eyes right on them. He wanted to remember who was there. So he grabbed somebody and he ended up remembering about four faces. They had to run some extra laps or something like that.

He wouldn't openly condone drinking, but I think he liked the camaraderie we had socially.

Before my senior year, 1978, I was a captain, and I have to admit that I was really disappointed with what happened. I thought [quarterback] Rod Gerald had earned the opportunity to keep playing. My belief to this day is that Woody gave Art Schlichter his word that he would start from the beginning, and Woody was a man of his word. But I was surprised he would make that promise. We were an option team, and we couldn't become a drop-back team in a couple of weeks of summer camp. I had no problem with freshmen playing, but it was a mistake for Art right out of the shoot.

We opened with Penn State, and how many interceptions did we throw that day? [Five.] I remember after the third, Art was running off the field, and I was running on, and I grabbed his face mask and I just got all over him. A lot of guys did that day. I know Art wanted to play better, but he wasn't ready and we were frustrated. Had he been phased in slowly, our year would have been different. It wasn't all Art's fault. We dropped the ball on both sides. It was a really tough year. We wanted to finish strong and go out doing some big things, but it just didn't work out that way. We underachieved that year [7–4–1 record]. I had played pretty well, but I would have traded it for winning.

My class had played in the Rose, Orange, and Sugar Bowls, and now we were at the Gator Bowl. At that time, Jacksonville was a crappy town. It was a terrible stadium. It was hard to live with that trip. We tried to look at it as an opportunity to play a good team in Clemson, but I don't know if we did that—from the administration to the coaching staff to the players.

We paid for it in the end.

We didn't know much about them and got into a bigger fight than we had anticipated. They came to play that night, because it was a chance for them to make a statement. The reputation of Ohio State—regardless of what our record was—was something other teams shoot for.

People always ask me where I was when it happened. We had called a time-out, and as a captain, I was very interested in what the play was going to be, so I was right there when they called it. We were in field position where we could kick a field goal to win the game. The instructions were very clear to Art: "If the play is not there, throw it away or sit down in the middle of the field, and we can still kick it." I can still remember that conversation like it was yesterday. Well, not only was it not there, but it was pretty much double-covered. But that's why Art became a tremendous quarterback later on. He had a confidence in himself that he could make the play, and as he matured, he made plays like that.

After the interception, I was thinking, "I can't believe we blew this chance." Then all hell broke loose. I didn't think much about what Woody did at the time. It looked like a small forearm and a push to me. He didn't hurt him. We had seen him do a lot worse a hundred times in practice. I was just thinking about how we could get the ball back one more time. When [the game] was over, I ran over to shake their hands and then sprinted into the locker room. I changed and was out of there in about five minutes. All I was thinking about was that we lost my final game. Woody came in and was out of control, and I wanted no part of it. I couldn't get out of there fast enough.

I was disconnected from the aftermath. I was done. I got on a plane the next day and headed to Hawaii for the Hula Bowl. When we landed, I heard the news [of Coach Hayes' firing], and suddenly everybody wanted to talk to me about it.

As I think back, he hit me only one time in four years. It was in the spring game after my junior year. As we always did, we were playing for steaks and beans, and Rod [Gerald] had the yellow jersey on—meaning we weren't allowed to hit him. The referees were always scared to death of Woody anyway, and they were spotting the ball to benefit the offense. Finally, I got in the huddle and said, "No more of this. Let's hit him. I'll take the heat." Finally, I had a shot at him and I just decleated him. I really let him have it. I remember the crowd went "Oooh…" All of a sudden, I hear, "YOU GODDAMN DUMB SON OF A BITCH!" and Woody was coming at me with that half run, half waddle. When he got to me, he hit me right in the solar plexus. I saw it coming and tightened up. I looked around, and everybody was laughing. George Hill was just howling. George came over and said, "Don't worry about it."

In the end, I loved the guy and I loved Ohio State and I always wanted to tell him that.

Years later, I had been carrying this large picture of him around in my trunk and wanted to get him to sign it. His secretary called me when he was in town, and I stopped in at his office over there in the ROTC building. He was going somewhere on campus to make a speech, and he asked me to go with him. We came back, and he signed this photo, and I finally got to express my feelings to him. I told him how much I cared about him, respected him, and how much he and Ohio State meant to me.

The next day, my wife called me and asked, "What did you say to Woody Hayes yesterday?" I said, "Why?"

"Well, he died today," she told me. I couldn't believe it. I was crushed. I believe I was the last player ever to see Woody Hayes alive.

Ohio State has been a big part of my life. The traditions, the people, the coaches, and my teammates were the best I could ever ask for. I will always be proud to say that I am a Buckeye.

Tom Cousineau, who finished his career with 569 tackles, became the first player from Ohio State to be taken with the first pick of the NFL Draft (Buffalo Bills in 1979). After playing in the Canadian Football League, he played four seasons with the Cleveland Browns and two with the San Francisco 49ers.

KEN FRITZ
OFFENSIVE LINEMAN
1976–1979

I AM AN OLD-SCHOOL TYPE OF GUY, and I wanted to play for Woody Hayes. If I would have been a basketball player, I would have wanted to play for Bobby Knight because he believed in the same things Woody did. I have always been a big believer in discipline, and there was nobody better at it than Woody Hayes.

I remember they shut down my high school when he came to visit me. Fran Curci was speaking that night, but kids trampled over him to get to Woody. Fran understood because he said he was always used to following Woody, but that shows what magnetism the man had.

A lot of the lessons I learned in life, I learned from Woody. That's why I went there in the first place. I knew that you learned more on the football field about life's lessons than you did in the classroom. And you could say Woody Hayes was our professor. You know what he said about getting knocked down and getting back up? That is so true. Woody taught us all to be honest and straightforward with people. He demanded respect, and we gave it to him because he earned it.

I remember how Woody used to nickname us when he got mad at us. He would call us by our hometowns if he didn't remember our names. He would call Tom Waugh "Norwalk," and he called me "Ironton." Yeah, he would punch us in the stomach, but it didn't hurt us. We would just laugh about it.

You know that coaches couldn't do that today, because all the players' parents would be suing them. Hey, if he didn't punch you, he didn't want to make you better and he didn't care about you.

I skipped class one day, and one of the professors called him. The next day, Woody woke me up and went to class with me—all day. Can you imagine the kids' reactions to see Woody Hayes walking in and sitting down in their classroom? I told him that I would never miss another class. Coaches today wouldn't do that for you.

It really saddens me to think how it ended for him. I wouldn't ever say anything negative about the man, and if you are in war, those things happen. That Gator Bowl was the most ridiculous bowl game we ever played in, and we probably shouldn't have been there in the first place. It was a fifty-five-thousand-seat stadium, and I think Clemson got fifty thousand seats. It turned into a fiasco. Those fans were very rough on us. We were spit on, and it seemed that everybody there hated us. As the week went on, the resentment just built up and built up.

Then the kid made the interception and got in Woody's face. He was a fierce competitor, and it happened. Everybody asks me if I was the one in the picture with him, and yes, that was me. I was trying to hold him. I'll never forget that plane ride home. It was very quiet, and Woody wasn't going to apologize. But at the end, he told us he wouldn't be the coach of Ohio State anymore.

Earle came in the next season and wanted to run everybody out of town. I think the reason we had a good football team is the fact that most of us got pissed off at him. We had a lot of unity because we all stuck together. Don't get me wrong, I like Earle, and he reminded me a lot of Woody. I would play for him again. He didn't have all the pizzazz Woody had, but who did?

That Michigan game [in 1979] is the memory for me. We went up there and won 18–15, and I finally got a pair of gold pants. I really think that team should have been national champs, but we had so many injuries in the late part of that Rose Bowl against USC, we sort of ran out of gas. But I will always believe we were the better team. The greatest talent I ever saw was Art Schlichter. He could do about anything on the football field, but that day we could have used another touchdown. That Rose Bowl still is one of the greatest moments of my life. It was huge, and because of it I could understand what the 2002 team went through at the Fiesta Bowl. We all had to be tickled to death that they brought home the championship.

Ken Fritz (56) prepares to make a block against USC in the 1980 Rose Bowl.

I really have no regrets, and I would I do it again if I could, but my body wouldn't be able to take it. My hips and lower back are a big problem these days, because we played on turf in those days and we took a lot of pounding.

The first time I went back to Ohio Stadium later, I stood in the stands and just soaked everything in. You know, when you are playing, you really don't hear anything. But I stood there and listened as the band came out of the tunnel and realized what a magnificent thing that is. It gets you so fired up.

The memories I have of Ohio State and Woody Hayes will never leave me. It was a great time in my life, and I am very proud to have played football for the Buckeyes.

Ken Fritz, who started three seasons at guard, was All–Big Ten in 1978 and 1979 and an All-American in '79.

DOUG DONLEY
WIDE RECEIVER
1977–1980

I HAVE TO TELL YOU ABOUT THE DINNER that made me a Buckeye. It was the time Woody Hayes came to my house to have dinner and to recruit me. He came with assistant coach Alex Gibbs. All Coach Hayes talked about was what a great school OSU was and what a great education I would get. He told many war stories, too, but he never talked about football. I could tell my parents were loving everything they were hearing, while I wanted to hear about football, playing time, the national championships, etc.

All of a sudden the phone rang; my mom answered it and told me that I may want to take the call in the back room. I picked up the phone, and it was Bo Schembechler from Michigan calling, reiterating their interest in me coming to Michigan. I went back out to the dinner table, and Coach Hayes immediately asked me who was on the phone. Very nervously, I answered, "Coach Schembechler." Coach Hayes immediately stood up, came down to my end of the table, stood over me, stuck out his hand, and said, "I want a handshake and verbal commitment that you are coming to Ohio State."

At that time, I was still considering Notre Dame and Michigan, but I was scared to death so I shook his hand and that was the end of that.

It was the best decision I was ever forced to make.

Woody always said, "You win with people, good people." And we were surrounded by class people. The coaches were the best in the business. The training staff and doctors were the best. They took care of our every need;

218

Doug Donley (47) led the Buckeyes in receiving for three consecutive seasons.

they all cared about the players and were proud to be Buckeyes. The equipment guys were incredible—[John] Bozick and his staff bled scarlet and gray. I remember that the coaches' secretaries were people you wanted to go visit with. They were all first class.

Then you had your teammates. Woody always told us, "The relationships you develop here the next four years will last forever." He was right! The leader sets the tone. Look at what Coach Tressel has done now. He instilled discipline, a sense of purpose, a pride for the program, and team unity. That's the same thing Coach Hayes did.

When I think of Ohio State, I think of all the first-class, quality people, and I am proud to be a part of that. It is hard to appreciate all of these things while you are there, but when you step away and look back at the memories, the relationships, the entire experience, it truly is a great feeling.

You learned very quickly playing under Woody Hayes that beating Michigan was the top priority. We started from day one with Michigan on the mind. Every practice during the season was intense, but practices during Michigan week were incredibly gut-wrenching. Any fumble, interception, or missed assignment caused an eruption of large magnitude. Players and coaches were on pins and needles all week. You didn't talk or laugh during the week. It was war.

I remember Coach Hayes giving his pregame talk in the Michigan locker room, and the last thing he said was, "We are going to come out fighting." Well, he led us down the tunnel at Ann Arbor, and you are supposed to take a hard left and go to your sideline, but Coach Hayes made a detour with us following him and ran into the "Go Blue" section of their student body waiting on the field. A small fight erupted, but like he said, we came out fighting. Michigan games were like no other—the crowd, the intensity on each side, the national exposure, and the feeling afterward. It was the ultimate joy if you won and the ultimate agony of defeat, that lasts forever, if you lost. Getting those gold pants was quite an honor!

My freshman year…it is a very intimidating time for any freshman coming into Ohio State. I played behind Jimmy Harrell, who was a great guy. He took me under his wing and taught me the ropes. He was the consummate professional. My first roommate, Calvin Murray, had a tremendous faith in God and was instrumental in helping me grow as a Christian. He was an inspiration to me. That first year is hard, and we endured it together. I could name more than 100 guys whom I share a special bond with. The most unfortunate thing is that we all went different ways after it was over, and you do not get to see them very often.

If I could give any advice to recruits today, I would tell them to look at the head coach. He is the leader of the football program, and its success will mirror the head coach. His values, character, and leadership abilities will be a determining factor in your success as an individual and as a team. Look at the players—these are the guys you are going to battle with. Surround yourself with quality people. And this is very important: look at the school, because your education is a must. Football does not last forever. For most, it ends after your college career, and if you are lucky enough to play pro ball, your career is short.

An education lasts a lifetime. Do not take it lightly!

I would tell the current players to enjoy this time and make the most of it. Give it your best both on and off the field. Don't look back with regrets and say, "I wish I had," but say, "I'm glad I did." You are a part of one of the best traditions in the world. Do not take it for granted. Appreciate it, respect it, and enjoy it! Keep the tradition alive by holding your teammates accountable to the standards set before you. Set a good example for the young guys coming in; they are watching you. Play the game and win or lose with class.

Ohio State football is all about commitment, excellence, character, pride, and teamwork.

When I got drafted to play in the NFL, I was two classes short of graduating. After some pressing from Coach Hayes and a call from Coach Tressel, who was an assistant some time after I left, I came back and finished to get my bachelor of arts.

I am very proud of that. And I am very proud that I played for Ohio State.

Doug Donley, who had 106 receptions for 2,252 yards and 16 touchdowns in his career, was Ohio State's first wide receiver to be named All–Big Ten (1979 and '80). He played four seasons with the Dallas Cowboys.

CALVIN MURRAY

RUNNING BACK

1977–1980

I BELIEVE THAT EVERY DIVISION I SCHOOL in the nation recruited me, but I chose Ohio State because Coach Hayes recruited my whole family. Ohio State was the only school to put me in the dorms and not a five-star hotel during recruiting, and that impressed me. Plus, the seniors had four Big Ten championship rings on their fingers, and I wanted one of those. They told me, "If you want one of these rings, you come to OSU."

So I chose the Buckeyes over Tennessee and Notre Dame.

Playing football at Ohio State changed my life in so many ways.

For example, I will never forget when it was a very hot day and we were complaining about our legs hurting. After practice, Coach Hayes told us to get on the bus, and he took us to Children's Hospital. There, we saw many children with serious burns and incurable diseases, and yet many of them had smiles on their faces. It taught us that we needed to be thankful that God has given us the opportunity to play sports and to appreciate the things we did have.

Another example of how Ohio State changed my life is that I realized when you go to college, you get two educations—one with books and one with people. If you fail with people, you will fail in getting your education. Coach Hayes was the best at teaching that.

I remember in one team meeting, all the black athletes sat on one side and all the whites sat on the other side. Coach Hayes did not say a word, but for the next meeting, we all had assigned seats—black, white, black, white. Then he told us that we were divided and that no team could go to war if they were not united as one.

Coach Hayes did not believe in racism, and he knew that we had to be a family to succeed.

My favorite teammates were a lot of players, but the ones who were above the rest were Leon Ellison and Vince Skillings. I could tell so many stories about all the good times we had together. Because of Leon and Vince, my years at Ohio were some of the best times in my life. We all had one thing in common: Yeshua [Hebrew for Jesus] as Lord of our lives.

We went to the movies, played basketball, watched TV, made fun of each other, studied the word of God together, did Word Power together [this was Coach Hayes' so-called freshman English class, which started at 6:00 AM], did study table, and cried and laughed together. We were the three musketeers, and no one could break our friendship. We still get together and keep in touch today.

Coach Hayes believed in team unity and that all of us [players and coaches] had to take showers together. It was a game to see who was going to wash Coach Hayes' back. If we knew when he was coming, we wouldn't tell the last few guys in the shower, so that one of them would end up washing his back.

The game that I remember the most was the Rose Bowl against USC— January 1, 1980. If we had won this game, we would have been national champs. Everyone figured USC would whip us because of all the All-Americans they had—guys like Marcus Allen, Charles White, Anthony Munoz, Joey Browner, Chip Banks, and Ronnie Lott. As everyone knows, it ended in a 17–16 loss.

Another game I will never forget was when we beat the team up North in '79. I beat them only one time, and it was one the best times of my life. I remember sitting in the locker room at Michigan Stadium, and Coach Bruce was getting us ready. I could hear the best band in the land marching down through the tunnel onto the field. They got my spirits so high I couldn't wait to get at the Wolverines. It was the first game in which we scored a touch-down in their stadium in four years. What a great feeling!

The play I remember the most was my 86-yard reception from Art Schlichter against Washington State in '79. It remains the longest pass play in OSU history.

Calvin Murray slashes through a hole during the 1979 season opener, against Syracuse—Earle Bruce's first game as head coach.

Watching the 2002 team win the national title brought back some bitter-sweet feelings, only because of our lost chance to be national champs. It still hurts today.

We have the greatest fan support, band, and city—Columbus bleeds scarlet and gray. I am proud of where the football program has been and where it is headed, and I hope that the young men who wear the scarlet and gray will keep our family name clean.

I realize that when you travel to other states, there are true Buckeyes fans everywhere, and I am proud to this day that I was the captain of the 1980 team and to realize that Ohioans always love you no matter how long ago you played at Ohio State.

I made the right decision to be a Buckeye!

Calvin Murray rushed for 2,576 yards in his career, 11th on Ohio State's all-time list. He was a captain and the MVP of the 1980 team.

VINCE SKILLINGS
DEFENSIVE BACK
1977–1980

O N THE DAY FOLLOWING A huge snowstorm, I was walking down the street in the little town of Brenizer, Pennsylvania, where I lived, wearing only a pair of shorts and slippers when a car with an old man in the passenger seat pulled up beside me. "You want a ride?" came a voice. I pointed to my home, which was only about 70 yards away, and declined the offer. Then George Chaump greeted me and said that he would like to introduce Coach Woody Hayes to me. Maaaann! Was I surprised and embarrassed. Coach Hayes must have thought I was a fool to be outside dressed the way I was.

My mother, Gladys Louise Skillings Dukes, had met Coach Chaump before, but not Coach Hayes. After introducing everyone, including my cousin, Curtis Clayton, back at the house, I began to settle down. However, to my immense surprise, Coach Hayes asked, "Don't you have something to do, young man?" I told him that I was going to work out with Curtis but that it could wait.

"Well, go do your workout, because I didn't come here to talk to you, anyway. I came here to talk to your mother," he said. Still recovering from the shock of Coach Hayes' bluntness, I reluctantly went to my workout.

Four hours later, I got home just as Mom and Coach Hayes were finishing their conversation. He then turned to me and said, "You have a beautiful mother, son. Would you like to attend Ohio State University?"

226

Vince Skillings was a three-year starter in the secondary.

With my mouth hanging to the floor, I answered, "Yeah, sure, of course." He then went on to say, "I won't promise you that you will start or even play at Ohio State, but I will promise you a fair chance to do so. I also guarantee that if you listen to me and our staff, you will get your degree."

Right there and then, I was sold on Ohio State, and I hadn't even talked to Coach Hayes for more than three minutes total. I could have chosen from Syracuse, Boston College (which almost persuaded me to change my mind), Penn State, West Virginia, Pittsburgh, UCLA, and more, but Coach Hayes was the only coach who seemed more interested in me as a person and not just another cog in the machinery of big-time college football.

Once on campus, Leon Ellison, Cal Murray, and I became known as the "Three Musketeers." Rarely did anyone see one of us without the other two somewhere close by. I will never forget the day the three of us were really depressed during preseason camp as freshmen. We were really homesick, so we went for a walk and ended up downtown at some hole-in-the-wall church. We all decided to give our life to Christ right then and there. We came back all fired up and elated with a new outlook on things.

Leon became like a brother to me. Leon felt he was not getting the playing time he deserved at defensive end, and we would always talk about it at our apartment. He would be so frustrated and disappointed, and yet he never complained. He just kept practicing hard, trying to crack the starting lineup, and I really admired him for that.

Our families are very close to this day. He was the stabilizing force for me during my years at OSU. Ron Springs, my host during my official visit to Ohio State, also became a close friend. One day, Ron took me to his uncle's home, Spencer "Shade Tree" Brown. That is where I would meet his cousin Joyce. I immediately became enamored with Joyce, and we dated for the next three years before I foolishly ended our relationship. That became one of my biggest regrets.

On the field, Ron really carried us with his running ability. He was just one of those guys whom everyone looked up to.

Everyone who played for Coach Hayes has some good stories, and one of mine is the funniest moment I remember. It was prior to a homecoming game. Coach Hayes called the second-team defense to go against the first-team offense. Well, all the defensive starters went to the visitors' sideline and sat down on these folding chairs that were set up. Man, why did we do that?

227

I didn't even notice Coach Hayes leave the middle of the field. I just saw players falling over chairs and beating feet toward the open end of the stadium. There was Coach Hayes, running down the sideline, kicking over chairs, screaming, "Get up! Get up! This ain't no goddamn country club!" Then he saw Al Washington still seated, and he picked up a chair and began chasing Al with it. Al's eyes nearly popped out of his head as he jumped up and took off running. Coach Hayes started throwing all the chairs into the stands, repeatedly screaming, "This is not a country club!" We were falling all over ourselves with laughter. Later, I often wondered how he didn't suffer a heart attack.

The 1980 Rose Bowl will be in my memory forever. The national championship was on the line, and USC had such greats as Charles White, Anthony Munoz, Roy Foster, Ronnie Lott, Dennis Smith, and Marcus Allen. USC was supposed to crush us by 35 points, but we had them on the ropes until the final two minutes of the game. They scored on that final drive to beat us 17–16, and it just tore us apart. It was the first time that I had ever cried following a loss. Everyone was crying, from coaches to players. We knew we had that game. It was truly the toughest loss I ever experienced.

I've had a few regrets, like Coach Hayes getting fired, the run-ins I had with Coach Bruce, for which I apologized years later, and breaking up with Joyce. It was a prayer and dream of my mother's that at least one of her children graduate from college. I thank God that I did.

Coach Hayes was right—I earned my degree in 1982, and I discovered that when I did listen to him and the staff's advice (a lot of times I didn't), things went very well for me. Often during interviews with potential employers over the years, the fact that I played football at Ohio State for Woody Hayes would break the ice. That and my degree opened doors for me that I otherwise would have never had the chance to enter.

As I look back on it, we were all one big happy family.

Vince Skillings, who had 13 career interceptions, was drafted in the sixth round by the Dallas Cowboys in 1981. He was named All–Big Ten in 1979 and '80.

The
EIGHTIES

GLEN COBB

LINEBACKER

1979–1982

AS IT TURNED OUT, I didn't get to play for Coach Hayes, but I have a story that I love to tell about him. During my senior year in high school, I was invited to watch the team practice in preparation for the Gator Bowl versus Clemson. It was a cold, wet December day, and the team was still in Ohio. The practice was being held in the Horseshoe, and not many recruits were there that day. Anyhow, I was standing along the sideline when Coach Hayes motioned for me to come over to him. At the time, the team was broken out into individual position groups doing drills.

When I reached Coach Hayes, he asked, "Son, do you see those linebackers over there?"

I replied, "Yeah."

"No, you will respond by saying, 'Yes, sir.'"

I corrected myself: "Yes, sir."

"Son, I want you to watch those linebackers today. You watch them. If after the end of practice you think you can play alongside them, then I'll give you a scholarship. If you don't, then get back on I-71 South, and go back down to the farm and stay there!"

"Yes, sir."

I trotted off, and my thoughts turned to farm life. It's a pretty good life, really. *I can do that*, I thought. Understand, the mind-set I had was that it was very intimidating. I didn't think I could compete academically or athletically.

Glen Cobb was at his best running sideline to sideline.

I remember that during that same visit, I watched a tape of the previous season's highlights and said to myself, *There is no way you can compete at this level.* The whole Ohio State thing was out of my league. However, I really believe that if God wants a person somewhere, He will provide a way.

As you know, that Gator Bowl would turn out to be Coach Hayes' final game, and I never got to play for him. But I did become a Buckeye the following season.

My first year, the freshmen came in early prior to two-a-days. We had three practices without pads. I remember thinking, *This isn't so bad.* Then came the upperclassmen. We put the pads on and went full contact. Dennis Fryzel was our linebackers coach, and you will not find a more colorful and excitable man. The very first contact drill he put us through was a tackling drill. One player ran the ball, the other tackled. Nothing fancy, but good old-fashioned smash-mouth football. To ensure that contact will occur, the runner must run straight ahead inside of two cones spread a few yards apart. This doesn't allow for much deviation east or west. Well, I had a crack at it both ways. First, I ran the ball and was tackled. No big deal. Then I tackled one of my fellow linebackers. It wasn't pretty, but I got him down somehow. Then we started on the second round. This time I faced Al Washington, who was 6'5″ and weighed about 260 pounds. I was considerably smaller and weighed 210 pounds soaking wet. I took off with the ball, of course running straight up not knowing any better. Al, I would say, put a pasting on me the likes of which I had never seen nor felt before. When I got up, my face mask was broken in three places.

232

I can say that it never happened before, and it never happened again. Keep in mind, this was my very first contact drill at Ohio State. This was very entertaining to the upperclassmen, and I think it accomplished the initiation that Coach Fryzel wanted. "Welcome to the Big Ten," he said.

Who was the toughest player I ever played with? No doubt here, it was Art Schlichter. I saw him time and again take substantial poundings as a freshman, especially in the Penn State game [a 19–0 loss in 1978] played in the 'Shoe. Penn State All-Americans Matt Millen and Bruce Clark firmly planted their helmets in his chest all day long. Although he wavered, he still got up. Coach Bruce was fond of saying, "When you get knocked down, get up." Art carried this to the max in that game. During our high school days at Miami Trace and later at Ohio State, I saw him get hit with the best of them. He was one tough amigo on the field.

I have to say that Coach Bruce was a man of integrity. Yes, he wanted to win with the best of them. However, he parted ways with coaches at some other institutions in this: he wanted to win the right way—without cheating. He spoke of integrity and its importance often. He spoke often about how a man is known by his friends, so be careful with whom you associate. He spoke about life after football, and the need to grasp the bigger picture. He had a passion for football and he was tireless in his work habits and very committed to the process. He was always mindful of the need to outwork your opponent and the values of hard work. I have the greatest respect for the man. He was a father figure to me at Ohio State and helped me even beyond my days on the gridiron. He took a personal interest in his players. Coach Tressel is fond of saying, "People don't care how much you know, until they know how much you care." To me, Earle Bruce demonstrated the right balance of compassion and competition. I am grateful to have played for the man and know that The Ohio State University was a better place with him during his time as head coach.

You need friends to go through college, and some of my teammates were my best friends—guys like Joe Berner, Dave Medich, and Ray Myers. You won't find them in the record books or in the OSU Hall of Fame. However, they will always be in my memories because they made a big, sometimes impersonal institution such as Ohio State feel more like home. In reality, it is not the institution that you remember the most, it's the people. Without friends, this world is a lonely place. But Ohio State felt like home because of them and many others.

233

It is natural to thank your coaches and teammates for getting you through, but my adviser, Neil Andrew, was truly an inspiration to me. I can recall first meeting Neil on my official visit as a senior in high school. I have to say that Neil helped me for four years and was instrumental in helping me graduate on time with a degree in park and recreation management. I am just glad I didn't go back to the farm and stay there. I went to Ohio State, played football, learned countless valuable lessons about life, and earned my degree.

Glen Cobb, who recorded 336 tackles in his career, which is eighth on Ohio State's all-time list, was a two-time team captain (1981 and '82).

MARCUS MAREK

LINEBACKER

1979–1982

AT FIRST, I WAS RECRUITED BY WOODY HAYES, but that was December of 1978, three weeks before the Gator Bowl incident. He pulled his chair up to mine, and he was about three inches from my face when he told me, "You are an Ohio boy and you are coming to Ohio State!" I grew up in Masury, Ohio, near Youngstown and the Pennsylvania border. Once Earle Bruce was named head coach, he and two assistants—Dennis Fryzel and Glen Mason— came to see me. I was playing a pickup basketball game, and I didn't talk to them until the game was over. I guess that didn't sit well with Earle. He told the other coaches that showed a lack of respect on my part, but it was a close game and we were playing to 15 and I didn't want to lose.

Fortunately, it didn't end up costing me the chance to go to Ohio State.

I can still picture the day my dad dropped me off. I had reservations about whether I could even play there. I weighed 198 pounds soaking wet, and when Dad drove me down there, we didn't say much in the car. Dad was a no-nonsense guy who had dropped out of school in the ninth or 10th grade to help support his family by working at the mill. We got to campus that day, and he got my bags and put them down on the curb. He shook my hand and said, "Good luck and do your best," and he drove away. I think I had tears in my eyes as he drove away.

I was in awe of the university, and I was ready to pack up and come home in those first few days on campus. Everybody was a high school star, and you felt you were just a number. Jeff Gottron was a walk-on, and he and I would play backgammon in between practices in that first camp. We both had sweethearts back home, and we both were homesick. But they gave me [Tom] Cousineau's No. 36 and Jeff had "B-147," so it could have been worse. I remember the coach at Youngstown State once told me, "If it doesn't work out down there, you'll always have a place here." I thought about that a little.

We had our first scrimmage, and I just ran around and made tackles, trying as hard as I could.

In that first game against Syracuse, I played on special teams, and in the second quarter, Tony Megaro went down with a knee injury. I was behind him on the depth chart, but I really thought I was the third-team linebacker until I heard my name called. As I ran onto the field, it was almost as if I could hear eighty-eight thousand people turning the page in their programs to see who the hell this kid was. On that first play, they ran right at me, but somebody forgot to block me, and I tackled the guy for a one-yard loss.

The great thing was the fact that as Tony rehabbed his knee for three or four weeks, he was right there helping me out. He was teaching me, standing right behind me. That year was pretty special because we had a real good team. I went into every game nervous, but it wasn't because I was afraid of the guy across from me. I just didn't want to look bad or get beat and have it show up on film in front of my teammates. I always had that fear of somebody making me look bad.

235

As a freshman, I made three tackles on that goal-line stand we had up at Michigan. It was their first drive, and they went right down the field, but they went for it on fourth down, running an option, and I made the tackle. I'll never forget that day [an 18–15 OSU victory], because it was so loud we couldn't hear each other in the huddle.

At the Rose Bowl, it was a business trip for us. We were out there to accomplish one thing, and we were totally focused on it. We actually were just a few minutes away from being national champs [leading USC 16–10]. I remember that I couldn't even see Charles White in the backfield behind those linemen because he was shorter than everybody else. All these years later, I may think, *If I could have made one more play, or stopped the ball...* What I remember is how close we were.

During my sophomore year, I remember walking across the campus, and Woody Hayes and I were on the same path. I was thinking, *He won't remember who I am.* Not only did he remember, he remembered my parents' names and

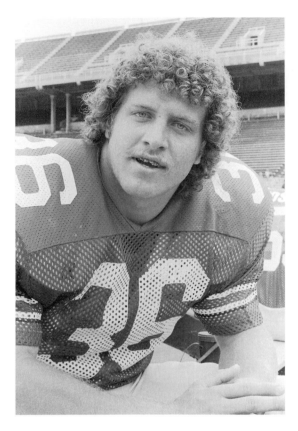

Marcus Marek ranks third in unassisted tackles, first in assisted tackles, and first in total tackles on the Ohio State career list.

one of my friends from high school. "Didn't you have a friend who was going to Allegheny College?" he asked. He never forgot people.

It is an honor today to hold the career tackling record. Records are made to be broken, but somebody would have to average about 12 tackles per game for four years. I was just fortunate that I never got injured.

I have no regrets. I made the best of what talent I had, and playing at Ohio State those four years was like a dream come true for me. That Ohio State atmosphere drove me to play. It drove me to want to be a good player. When I went back to a game for the first time, I gave my ticket to someone else and just tailgated and watched the band come across the street from St. John Arena. I loved the festivities of it all, and it really was the first time I got to experience it. Those were all things I never saw before.

Ohio State is unlike any other school. It is an amazing place, and game day at Ohio Stadium is an amazing day. Everybody is wearing scarlet and gray. Everybody is there to support the Buckeyes. When I took my wife back the first time, we stayed at the Holiday Inn on Lane Avenue. An hour before the game, I said, "We had better get walking." She said, "What do you mean? The stadium is right there. It won't take that long." We started to walk, and I left with one beer in my hand. By the time I got over past St. John Arena, I had guys shoving beers at me and telling me how much I meant to them. I think I ended up with a 12-pack, but it really gave me an idea of how great the fans are.

I look back now and I can really sense how important being a Buckeye is to me.

Marcus Marek, Ohio State's all-time leader in tackles with 572 and an Academic All-American in 1980, played three seasons in the United States Football League and one in the Canadian Football League.

237

VAUGHN BROADNAX
FULLBACK
1980–1983

WHEN I MADE THE DECISION to attend The Ohio State University, choosing the Buckeyes over Notre Dame, I had no idea what the future would bring. But I have never regretted that decision for even one day since.

I played with many great players and have so many fond memories and stories. You'll laugh at this one. Jay Holland was one of the finest athletes I have ever seen, but he just never seemed motivated. During a game against Northwestern, I noticed Jay was asleep on the bench. It was not uncommon for a player who doesn't play regularly to retreat to the bench, don a helmet, and catch some z's. Well, on this day, we were up by about 50 or 60 points, so everyone was getting an opportunity to play. After a change of possession, Jay's number was called.

After someone woke him up, he immediately ran on the field and lined up at safety. Northwestern fired a pass downfield, and Jay intercepted it and returned it for a long gain. He then came off the field, and everyone was congratulating him, and he promptly found his seat on the bench. He went right back to sleep. True story.

I remember seeing Keith Byars showing up at camp as a freshman. I was amazed at how big he was and at some of the things he could do. A classmate of his was Pepper Johnson. I can honestly say that Pepper was the hardest-hitting and best linebacker I played against. I didn't like it because we had collisions on nearly every play in practice. William Roberts was the most graceful big

Vaughn Broadnax, here carrying against Northwestern in 1983, was one of the most bruising blockers in Ohio State history.

guy I ever saw. My roommate my freshman year was Rowland Tatum. We called him the "Nicknamer" because he had a name for everyone.

Here's an example: "Misleading"—this player had huge biceps, but when he took off his shirt, it was quite apparent sit-ups were not his priority.

I guess I will be known for "the Block" in 1981 at Michigan. We were behind 9-7 late in the game, and we drove down the field with several key plays by Tim Spencer and Art Schlichter. When we got inside the 20, we knew Bobby Atha would nail the field goal, but we knew a touchdown would eliminate Michigan's winning with a field goal. In the huddle, Art called "Play Pass 28." The play is designed to attack the outside and force the defense to either stop the run or defend the pass. Michigan chose to defend the pass. I was blocking Carlton Rose; I just held my block, and Carlton went down and tripped up two other defenders, allowing Art to scamper into the end zone. At that time, I didn't realize the impact of the play, but I do now all these years later. It was the result—a victory over Michigan.

The worst defeat I can recall didn't involve Michigan. In 1982 we played against a Stanford team that we had beaten a year earlier at Stanford. I had left that game unimpressed by John Elway. But a year later, we were leading and driving with about three minutes remaining and turned the ball over. Elway then drove Stanford down the field to beat us in the final seconds. When I think of Elway and "the Drive," I don't think of the Browns versus the Broncos but of that drive that beat us in 1982. That year we started 2–3, and there was some dissension and finger-pointing. Then we upset a heavily favored Illinois team and won the rest of the games. We beat an arrogant BYU team led by Steve Young, 47–17 in the Holiday Bowl, and I truly believe we were the best team in the country at season's end.

I can't begin to describe the range of emotions I experienced while sitting in the stands during that Fiesta Bowl for the 2002 national championship. To see the look of joy and pride in the faces of several of my ex-teammates brought tears to my eyes.

Everyone knows that The Ohio State University is my alma mater, and I still get so emotional when our alma mater is played at the end of each game. How much does my alma mater mean to me? We named our daughter Carmen.

Vaughn Broadnax, who started at fullback (1981–1983), made one of the most famous blocks in school history, leading to the 14–9 win at Michigan in 1981.

KIRK LOWDERMILK
OFFENSIVE LINEMAN
1981–1984

IT WAS A GOOD THING THAT I WAS a pretty fair wrestler, or I don't think I would have ended up at Ohio State. I was from Salem, Ohio, and I didn't get recruited by the big schools—just Toledo and Cincinnati. I was kind of what they call a potluck guy, but I went down to the state wrestling tournament and beat two guys who were headed to play football at big schools. Mike Golic would go on to Notre Dame, and Dave Crecelius would head to Ohio State.

I won the heavyweight division, and the next day I met with Coach Bruce. He offered me a scholarship and said, "Go home and think about it."

I told him, "What's there to think about? I will sign it right now." There was no question where I wanted to go. I always wanted to play at Ohio State.

Once I was there, I remember getting to play just one play at our first scrimmage, and it motivated me. I was really broken-hearted. I just decided that was it—I was not going to sit on the bench for four years. I would do anything to get on that field, and that's how I got my letter as a freshman—I was on the kickoff team.

You'll never forget that first time you run onto that field in front of ninety thousand fans. Really, it's a cliché, but your feet don't touch the ground. On my very first play as a Buckeye, I hurt my knee. My foot just got stuck on the artificial turf, but I didn't want to tell anybody, because I didn't want them taking me out of the game.

Kirk Lowdermilk, here blocking against Purdue in 1982, was All–Big Ten in 1984.

The Michigan game of my freshman year was one of the most exciting games [a 14–9 OSU victory] of my whole career. I can still see Vaughn Broadnax making that block for Art Schlichter. That was just an awesome game.

My sophomore year, they moved me to defense. I was too slow to play defense, but I was getting playing time and that is what mattered to me. I backed up Spencer Nelms at nose guard. I remember during that Florida State game [a 34–17 loss], I got a deep thigh bruise, and Dr. Murphy gave me a shot right on the bruise. I walked out of the locker room and passed out. The following spring, they moved me back to left guard. Hey, I just wanted on the field. Then I played center for my senior year.

The game everybody remembers in 1984 was the Illinois game when Keith [Byars] turned it on. We got down 24–0, and I could tell from looking at Keith in the huddle that he was ready to do something. He scored, came back to the bench, and the TV cameras were on him, and he said, "We're coming back, baby, we're coming back!" I was standing right next to him when he said it.

He brought us back, and everybody remembers him losing his shoe on that long run. That was such an amazing game [a 45–38 Ohio State victory].

I have to say that Keith, John Frank, and Pepper Johnson were my favorite players, and it wasn't so much because they were good, it was because they were tough, they practiced hard, and they were physical each and every day. They were first-class people.

Later, at Wisconsin, I broke my fibula in my left leg, making the rest of the season very disappointing. We beat Michigan, and I got in for a charity play just to say I played, but it hurt so much to be injured when I wanted to be on the field with my teammates. It was my senior year and I couldn't play against Michigan…that hurt more than any broken leg.

We were 3–1 against Michigan, which means I have three pairs of gold pants. I gave them to my mom, my sister, and my wife. They wear them on chains.

Once we went to the Rose Bowl, nothing was going to keep me out of that game. I knew I couldn't do any more damage, so I played the whole game. We drove it right down the field on that first drive, missed a field goal, and ended up losing to USC 20–17. I really believe that we were the better team and that is one game we never should have lost. Plus, it was my final game, and it was tough leaving the field. I loved being a Buckeye, and I can

243

still remember sitting in that locker room, in no big hurry to take off the uniform. I remember Coach [Fred] Pagac coming over and giving me a hug. It's very sad when it all ends.

I will never have a bad word to say about Coach Bruce. I think back to what he used to preach to us and how it all makes sense now. I remember how he used to get fired up and would pound his index finger on the desk. I don't know how he didn't dislocate it. The guy loved his players. The time Curt Curtis put his foot through the glass door at the French Field House, nearly slicing his calf off, Coach Bruce was crushed. It ruined the guy's career, and Coach Bruce was crying for him. I don't think President Ed Jennings ever understood what that man did for the university. His firing a few years later was a black eye for the university, and I really believe he deserved better.

I told my daughter, who's a good athlete, that she will like college ball so much better than high school for one big reason—everybody is there for the same reason. They are there to get better and compete. The intensity in our practices was unreal. The game was the easy part, but the part I really liked was the work in practice. We would work hard in practice, compete against each other, and then go have a beer together.

We ended up with two Big Ten titles and a Rose Bowl trip, but I would have liked to win a national championship.

Because of my NFL career, I didn't get to go to a Buckeyes game in Ohio Stadium until 1998, and I was just mesmerized when the band came down the tunnel. You know, that's something you don't get to see when you are a player. Man, I almost got emotional. I was just stunned. It really makes the hair on your neck stand up. It never gets old. Those are the things that make Ohio State really special.

Kirk Lowdermilk, a team captain in 1984, became one of the NFL's best centers in eight seasons with the Minnesota Vikings.

MIKE TOMCZAK

QUARTERBACK

1981–1984

I'LL NEVER FORGET THE FIRST DAY I had set foot on campus as an Ohio State freshman. We were in training camp, and Jim Lachey and I were walking down Woody Hayes Drive toward High Street. Who's coming the other way? It was Woody himself. He stopped us, and the thing that shocked us was that he knew everything about us—our parents' names and about our coaches. He told us how important an education was, and we listened intently. It was a unique experience.

I started to learn the tradition at Ohio State from the previous summer when I attended the football camp there. Growing up south of Chicago, I was named Player of the Year in the state of Illinois, and I was being recruited by Michigan, Notre Dame, UCLA, and Wake Forest. But I was sold on Ohio State for so many reasons, and I couldn't wait to become a Buckeye.

When I got on campus, there were six quarterbacks in my class, and of course, Art Schlichter had one more season as the starter.

But I wasn't afraid of competition, and I didn't take a redshirt season. I ended up as the third-string quarterback that season, and I traveled to all of the games. I will never forget that Michigan game of my freshman season when Vaughn Broadnax made the big block and Art worked his way into the end zone. Those guys, along with Marcus Marek, Glen Cobb, Gary Williams, and all the upperclassmen, were larger than life to me. Art was like

Mike Tomczak rebounded from a broken leg to lead the 1984 Buckeyes to the Rose Bowl.

246

an icon, more so then than anybody is right now. He just looked like a quarterback, on and off the field.

I learned about adversity right away as a sophomore. We started pretty well and beat Baylor and Michigan State, and we had Stanford beat in the third game. We were ahead and moving down to about their 35 late in the game. I threw a pass I shouldn't have thrown, and it got intercepted. John Elway then led Stanford to the winning score in the final seconds, and we had a lot of upset people after that game. We lost to Florida State and got beat by Wisconsin 6–0. I was benched. Everyone is affected by an Ohio State loss, but when you lose three in a row…it got really bad.

That whole thing put me into a shell. I was still a young kid and I wanted to prove people wrong, and as everybody knows, the media can be pretty tough in Columbus. We went to Illinois, and that was my home-state team. I wanted to go back and prove that I could do the job. I give Coach Bruce credit because he threw me back in there and gave me another chance like he said he would. We beat Illinois 26–21 and won the rest of our games.

Earle was old school. He was very prepared, very disciplined, and very organized. I remember that during my sophomore year, we would have breakfast together twice a week at the Holiday Inn just to get to know each other and get on the same page.

The next year, in the season's second game, we beat Oklahoma on the road in one of the most physical games I ever played. I remember the big talk all week would be whether John Frank would play because of the Jewish holiday, but John played and had a huge game. We were the underdog that day, and we just physically dominated them. Our defense beat up Marcus Dupree so badly that he didn't play in the second half. I cramped up and spent the night in the hospital. Emotionally and physically, we were drained, and I think that is one reason we lost to Iowa the next week.

I went through my share of adversity the next year. In the spring game after my junior season, I was running the option when I got hit high by Pepper Johnson and low by Dave Morrill. I knew my leg was broken right away. It was just one of those things. Some doctors said that was the end of my career, and Coach Bruce wanted me to redshirt my senior year, but I said, "No, I am going out with my class."

It was a long road to recovery. I didn't start the opener my senior year, but that was the last game I missed.

247

At the end of my career, I had three pairs of gold pants from beating Michigan, and I have to say that beating them up there was the ultimate. They were always very clean, hard-hitting football games. We used to stay outside of Ann Arbor in some little dumpy hotel, and our locker room there would have a single nail sticking out of the wall with your number above it. Those are the types of things you remember.

I thoroughly believed it was a privilege to play at Ohio State. In turn, I tried to do my best to uphold the rich tradition we have, on and off the field. I care about that school, and I do bleed scarlet and gray. A lot of people mature during adolescence, but I grew up between the ages of 17 and 21, and Ohio State allowed me to do that.

After my second year in the NFL, I decided to endow a scholarship. Jim Lachey did the same thing, and our goal was to get many others to do it, too. I decided I wanted to pay forward, since I couldn't pay back.

At the Fiesta Bowl in 2002, I was watching practice on the Wednesday before the game, and as a past captain, I almost felt a sense of duty to address the team. I just told them, "The world is betting against you. Write down your goal. Write down 'national champions.'"

Before the game that night, four or five players came up to me on the sideline and said they had written it down, and I thought it would have been neat if my speech touched just one guy. But that's what Ohio State is all about. The most wonderful guys I ever met in my life were my teammates at Ohio State. What you come to understand is that the people who played before you, and after you, are all part of the family.

Mike Tomczak, who passed for 5,569 yards and 32 touchdowns in his career, played 17 seasons in the NFL—with the Chicago Bears, Green Bay Packers, Cleveland Browns, Pittsburgh Steelers, and Detroit Lions.

KEITH BYARS
RUNNING BACK
1982–1985

I WANT TO SAY IT WAS AN EASY DECISION to come to Ohio State, because when I was a young boy I watched all of the games on TV and I knew I wanted to play for Woody Hayes. But once I grew up and all the schools in the country started to recruit me, it was easy for me to get confused. I know I hated Michigan with a passion, but I actually went up there on a recruiting visit, met Bo, and thought, *This is not as bad as I thought it was.* In the summer before my senior year, I went to Wilmington, Ohio, during the Bengals' summer camp and met with Archie Griffin. He told me, "If you are looking for a challenge and you want to be the best you can be and go against the topflight competition every week, you need to be at Ohio State." And I was from Dayton, so he told me, "All of the top running backs in Ohio stay in Ohio."

Pittsburgh was recruiting me pretty hard at the time, and Dan Marino was there, but I told Dan, "You have only one more year left when I get there." I wanted a great running back tradition, and when I added everything up, I knew I was making the right decision to come to Ohio State.

I also knew then that no one player was bigger than Ohio State, and that's a part of it that I really liked. I wanted to be a part of something big and something important.

Once I committed, during the OSU spring game prior to my freshman year, the coaches told me I would be rooming with a guy named Thomas Johnson. When we met that day, we really didn't need an introduction. We just walked up and started talking to each other like we had known each other for all of our lives—"What are you going to bring? You bring the TV, I'll bring the radio…"—and that's how it went for Pepper Johnson and me. We bonded right away, and he's been my best friend since.

When coaches put roommates together, it is a crapshoot of whether it will work out, but in all these years, we've never had a cross word between us. We thought an awful lot alike, and we had so many great conversations in that dorm room. When the going got tough, we wouldn't let each other quit. When he was down, I picked him up, and when I was down, he picked me up. And we still do that to this day. It really was like meeting a brother I never knew I had.

When I got to campus for summer camp, I was amazed at how fast the game was. Everybody was bigger and faster than what I was used to.

I remember this linebacker, Clarence "Curt" Curtis. On one of the first days of training camp we had to do weight testing, and he couldn't bench 225 pounds. A lot of the guys were standing around laughing. He jumped off the bench and got mad at them. He said something like, "It doesn't matter what you can lift, it matters how big your heart is." So we got out to practice, and I saw him pick up this 300-pound offensive lineman and toss him into the quarterback's lap. I thought, *He's got a point.*

250

Then in the first scrimmage, I was supposed to block the inside linebacker, and I thought I knew where he was coming from. All of a sudden, Curt came rushing in from the outside and gave me a forearm shiver in the head. Now after this play, I was thinking I was really sweating pretty badly, but somebody came up to me and said, "Are you all right? Because you are bleeding." I had this big cut over my eye, and that was the first time I ever needed stitches.

I thought to myself, *Welcome to college football.*

The first time I ever went to a college football game was the day I played in one. It was a dream come true. We were playing Baylor, and I was playing on the punt team. In camp, guys had told me what it would be like to run onto the field at the Horseshoe in front of ninety thousand fans: "You wait, it will be unbelievable—your feet don't hit the ground." They were right—it was exactly that way.

Tim Spencer was All–Big Ten that year and a great back, so I played mostly on special teams as a freshman. I couldn't wait for my sophomore year. I wasn't nervous at all, just excited to get my opportunity. I worked hard and tried to

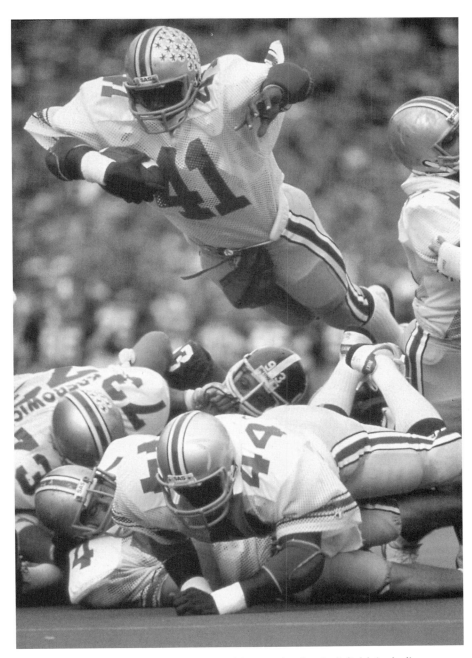

It seemed as if Keith Byars could do anything on the football field, including defying gravity against Michigan State in 1984.

be the best I could be, and I took it very seriously. I had a really good sophomore year [1,199 yards rushing, 22 touchdowns] and made some All-America teams, but my goal in college was to be better than the year before each and every year. I wasn't shy about it—I wanted to win two Heisman Trophies.

Everybody always asks me about that Illinois game my junior year and the run without my shoe. Over the years, I figured there must have been more than one hundred thousand fans who were there that day, because more than that have claimed to be there to see it. I remember we got down 24–0, and I had fumbled. But when I scored, we all felt we were coming back, and that's when I told the TV cameras exactly that. I just said what the whole team believed.

On the [67-yard] run without my shoe, it was a simple draw designed to go left, but I saw a big hole on my right. I saw an opportunity to go for the home run. As I was going upfield, I made my last cut to the left, and my shoe started to come loose. I was about to lose it anyway, so I just kicked it off [at Illinois' 35-yard line]. Then I thought, *Now I had better run faster, because I don't want anybody to step on my foot.* People still bring that play up when they meet me.

As a junior, it came together [1,764 yards, 24 touchdowns] for me, and I thought I really should have won the Heisman Trophy [Byars finished as the runner-up to Boston College's Doug Flutie].

252

Later in the NFL, I would ask Doug Flutie, "How's my trophy doing?" I should have won it, but things don't always work out the way you want them to.

Then I thought I would get another chance as a senior, but during camp before the season started, I was running when I made a cut, and I didn't hear anything, but I felt it. Something in my right foot wasn't right. I limped over to the trainer and told him we needed an X ray.

It was something doctors had never seen before, but in plain terms, I broke my foot. At that time, the doctors didn't feel it would keep me out all that long, and I tried to gut it out later, but I wasn't the same. Otherwise, I would have considered redshirting and coming back the next year.

It was very disappointing, but it really was a freak thing.

I didn't get the chance to go back to Ohio Stadium until I retired from the NFL, and I always told my wife, whom I didn't know in college, "You have got to go back to Ohio State with me. It is totally different from pro football." When I was inducted into the [OSU Athletic] Hall of Fame in 2000, my wife and kids went back with me. My kids got to come out onto the field with me, and it was a special moment. We took some pictures of everybody over by my tree at the Buckeye Grove.

You know, when you are 17 or 18 years old and you have to make the biggest decision of your life, it is very difficult to do. I believe I did it well, and I am so glad I came to Ohio State. I just think about all of the friends I have from my days there, and that is very special by itself. I knew back then it would impact me for the rest of my life, and it did. I made the right decision, and I enjoyed every minute of my college career.

Despite missing most of his senior season, Keith Byars finished his OSU career with 3,200 rushing yards—fifth on the all-time list. He scored 46 touchdowns—second all-time behind Pete Johnson. Byars, who was the Big Ten MVP in 1984, played 14 seasons in the NFL.

THOMAS "PEPPER" JOHNSON

LINEBACKER

1982–1985

I'LL BE HONEST—OHIO STATE really didn't do a good job of recruiting me. In fact, it was kind of a bad recruiting process and the worst visit I had out of any of them. I was considering Arizona State, Minnesota, Michigan, and Michigan State, but I had always loved the tradition of Ohio State, even while growing up in Detroit.

When I visited, Earle Bruce was visiting with other recruits and then had to go somewhere, and I never even got to meet him. My hosts that day were William Roberts and Doug Hill. They just told me, "It is best to see Ohio State for yourself. So go walk around campus, get a feel for the place, and we'll be here if you have any questions." They really thought that this place would sell itself. But it sort of made me mad that Coach Bruce didn't see me, and I started thinking I had a point to prove. But when I visited Michigan, it seemed there was a lot of animosity among the players. They just didn't seem to get along that well, and I think they may have been recruiting me as a tight end.

Despite the foul-up on my visit, I started thinking Ohio State was the best place for me. It wasn't so far that my family couldn't come see me play. So I signed without ever meeting the head coach, and anybody will tell you that

Pepper Johnson was one of the hardest-hitting linebackers in Buckeyes history.

is very unusual. My life changed during the spring Scarlet and Gray Game in 1982. Not only was that the first time I met Coach Bruce, but Coach [Bill] Miles told me I would be rooming with some guy named Keith Byars. The first time I saw him that day, he was wading through a lot of people, and I knew that must be Keith. He saw me, too, and he knew his roommate was named Thomas Johnson, but he thought that must be a white guy. He walked up to me and asked, "Thomas?" I said, "Yeah, just call me Pepper."

From that day forward, we became very close. We really became just like brothers. As I write this, I know he's somewhere in South Florida on the golf course.

I remember the day my mother and sister dropped me off that fall in Columbus. They were about to cry, but I felt very comfortable at Ohio State from the beginning.

We had to pass a 12-minute run where the linebackers had to finish seven laps. I had trained all summer for that thing. That's all I thought about, but I misunderstood what we had to do. I thought you just had to finish the seven laps within that time and that would be that. I didn't realize you had to fin-ish the 12 minutes no matter what. All anybody talked about back then when it came to the 12-minute run was Glen Cobb. They talked about how nobody could beat him. They said he was half human, half horse when it came to that run. So I heard Earle's whistle and I took off like a bat out of hell. I could even hear the trainers standing around the track, saying, "He'll never keep up that pace." I was leading this thing and was beating Glen by about half of a lap, and I finished my seventh lap, sprinting to the finish. I broke it down and stopped but everybody started screaming. I was waving, accepting what I thought was their congratulations. I even got a quick drink of water. But they were screaming because I had stopped. I didn't know you had to run the whole 12 minutes. Earle was going crazy, hollering at me. There went Glen, running right by me. Have you ever tried to restart running after you had stopped? It's not easy, but I took off and tried to catch Glen. Finally, they blew the whistle as Glen made his eight laps and I was about 10 or 15 yards from the line. I was so disappointed.

That very first practice, I experienced a real eye-opener. Shaun Gayle was one of our hardest hitters on defense, and the offense ran a toss play with Tim Spencer. Shaun came up for support to make the tackle, and Vaughn Broad-nax led the blocking ahead of Tim. Vaughn and Shaun met head-on and wow!...the collision was huge. They hit each other so hard, I could feel it. They got up, patted each other on the back, and went back to the huddle. I tightened my chin strap and told myself, *Welcome to college football.*

I came from a Detroit public school where we would be happy if we had 250 people in the crowd for one of our games. All the stories I had heard about running out of that tunnel before a game for the first time were true. That is a highlight of the 'Shoe for everyone who has ever played there. Still today, after all these years, it remains my ultimate feeling. I just can't imagine anyone not enjoying it. I was near the front and I sprinted over to the bench. I really don't remember my feet touching the ground that first time. I got over there, and I remember seeing guys flipping over from the top and then winding up on the bottom of the pile.

My first game action came on kickoff returns and coverage. Keith and I both got our first action that way. The thing that was important to me was getting Buckeye leaves, and if you made a tackle on the kickoff team inside the other team's 20-yard line, you got a leaf. I played behind Marcus Marek at linebacker, so that was the only way for me to get a Buckeye leaf my freshman year. That's what I took pride in, and I think we led the nation in kickoff return average that season. Keith returned kickoffs, and we still take pride in that. In my first game against Michigan, I tackled Anthony Carter on a kickoff inside the 20. That was huge.

The next few years, it didn't really matter to me when I was named All–Big Ten and All-American. It really didn't. I never really liked individual honors like that. I took more pride in receiving Buckeye leaves and being named the team's "Defensive Player of the Week." I had been voted captain for my junior and senior years, and to be recognized by your peers like that, no All-America team can match that. It's how you play in the eyes of your peers and what type of person you are for them…that's the stuff that matters and that's what sticks with me now.

257

As a captain, I felt responsibility, too. I remember when two of our starters, Rory Graves and Terry White, got suspended before my final home game for doing something really stupid. We lost to Wisconsin 12–7, and the next day we had a team meeting. They had to hold me back from putting my hands around one of those guys' necks. I was about as mad as I could get. Who wanted to lose their final home game? Either one of them could have made the plays to make the difference to win that game.

Before the Michigan game my junior year, Woody Hayes came to the captain's table, and I got to sit next to him. Woody and I were sitting there talking, and he was telling me all about how good these cinnamon rolls were. He always loved those cinnamon rolls from the golf course, and he was telling me how to put a little butter on them and how to eat them. The next year, he sat next to me again, and we had the same conversation. Now I looked out and saw 100 guys looking up at me and Woody talking together. They were all wondering what we were talking about, because it was an intense conversation. But they had no idea that it was all about cinnamon rolls. That was one of those "Call Mom and tell her what you did today" type of deals.

I remember when he walked in to give us a talk before a Michigan game. You know, we respected Coach Bruce and listened to Coach Bruce, but when Woody came into the room, every set of eyes looked straight at him. People sat up in their chairs. You could just feel it. He was just awesome, and people knew it. Nobody even looked off to the side. Nobody fiddled with a watch or pen or anything. I thought, *Man, why wasn't I born four or five years earlier so I could have played for this man?*

The thing Woody told us was how to be a real football player. He told us he hated to see a guy miss an interception and then pound his fist on the ground or look at his hands like his hands let him down. Just because of what Woody said, I never did that after that, even in the NFL. I never looked at my hands if I dropped a pass. I tell my son that today. There's no need to do it.

258

One thing Keith and I never did in all those practices was hit each other. I never tackled him, he never blocked me, and it drove Coach Bruce crazy. Finally, in our final spring game, he put us on opposite sides, and Keith cut off the tackle on one play. I just blew him up. So that night at dinner, Coach Bruce must have played that 10 times on the film. (Keith got me back later in the NFL during a Giants-Eagles game when I was chasing Randall Cunningham.)

I am coaching today, and I tell everybody about what I experienced at Ohio State. If I had to do it all over again, I would. Not a doubt about it. Not a hesitation. I loved every moment I was there, the good times and bad times. It was a great experience.

Pepper Johnson, who recorded 379 tackles in his Ohio State career, played on two Super Bowl championship teams in his seven seasons with the New York Giants. He also played with the Cleveland Browns, Detroit Lions, and New York Jets. He has been an assistant coach with the New England Patriots since 2000.

MIKE LANESE
WIDE RECEIVER
1982–1985

I WOULD LIKE TO SAY I HAD a really good reason for selecting Ohio State over Michigan. I didn't. Several schools recruited me, but from the beginning I knew it would be a toss-up between spending the next four years in Columbus or Ann Arbor. I researched each school's academics, football program, and a category I just called "intangibles." No matter how I examined the data, I couldn't distinguish between the two. Michigan had been stealing guys from the Cleveland area for a few years, and several of my friends in high school were big Wolverines fans. So early on, I probably leaned toward Michigan.

I struggled with the decision for a few weeks. But as the signing date drew near, I woke up one cold February morning from a fitful sleep and, almost unconsciously, I said aloud, "I am going to Ohio State." Call it an epiphany. Call it an attack of prospective common sense. Call it what you will, but then and there I committed to be a Buckeye for the rest of my life.

It was the most important decision I ever made, and it was clearly one of the best.

That's not to say my Ohio State career started out all peaches and cream. I was an all-state tailback at Mayfield High School and wanted to play tailback in college. Coach Bruce promised that I would get a shot at playing tailback. He kept his word. The problem was that he also recruited four other all-state tailbacks, three from Ohio and one from Tennessee.

Mike Lanese was a winner on the field and a champion in the classroom.

One of the three from Ohio was a guy named Keith Byars. He looked like a fullback to me, but Coach Bruce promised him a shot at tailback, too. As summer camp began for freshmen, it was pretty obvious that Keith was a man among boys. Keith saw playing time as a freshman while I rode the bench. During the week, I played scout-team tailback, with my 6', 185-pound frame getting beaten up on a regular basis by the likes of Marcus Marek. At the end of my freshman year, Coach Bruce asked if I wanted to make the switch to flanker. The hardhead that I was, I said no. But midway through my sophomore year I had another one of those epiphanies. Barring a pretty significant growth spurt, I concluded that if I wanted to play, I would have to find a different position. So I made the switch to flanker.

I could always catch the ball pretty well, so the transition to flanker was pretty natural athletically. But emotionally, I felt as if I should be watching the game from the stands. A tailback, especially at Ohio State, is a large part of the game. Sometimes he is the whole game. Wide receivers can go a whole game without getting so much as a grass stain. I struggled and played little my sophomore year. I never lost confidence in my ability, but something was missing. Little did I know that something was Cris Carter.

In the summer before my junior year, I decided to take a summer class and stay in Columbus to work out. The quarterbacks/receivers coach at the time, Jim Tressel (whatever happened to him?), asked if I would consider taking on a roommate. I had a feeling I was being set up, and I really liked living alone. So I said no. But Coach Tress persisted, and I wound up with Cris as a roommate. He was, in a word, unique. He is one of those guys who just lights up a room. When Coach Tress asked me how things were going, I just shook my head and asked, "Who is this guy?" Even John Bozick, our equipment manager, liked him. And he hated all freshmen.

I think Coach Tress thought I would be able to become something of a moderating influence on Cris, but it was Cris who ended up influencing me. When summer camp started in 1984, things just clicked for me as a receiver. No more doubt, no more second thoughts. I enjoyed playing wide receiver. I enjoyed playing, period. After being written off in the preseason, the Ohio State receiving corps ended up making a pretty respectable contribution to the 1984 Big Ten championship season.

Despite the success I had as a receiver, people remember me for one catch. During the Michigan game in 1984, I fumbled a punt just before the half. But I came back in the fourth quarter to make a big catch on a third-and-long that kept a drive alive. We went on to win 21–6, and I was named the Chevrolet MVP for the game. To this day, little old ladies come up to me and say, "I remember that catch you made against Michigan...." I guess there are worse things to be remembered for.

Ohio State fans are, literally, everywhere. I've had the good fortune to travel around the world, and whether it's Singapore or Shanghai, Mombassa or Mexico City, I've run into people who love Ohio State. It's pretty humbling, really. They don't always know the names or faces of the legends, and some have never actually seen a game, but many can hum the fight song or "Carmen Ohio" as well as anyone in Ohio Stadium.

Three things distinguish the Ohio State program from the rest: first, Ohio State is a world-class university. It's one of the few universities in the country that offers a truly overwhelming array of opportunities and challenges. Ohio State is a place where you can be intellectually curious, where you can think about yourself and your place in the world. Given Ohio State's size, comprehensiveness, and diversity, I can think of no better place for a young student-athlete to define the parameters of his or her intellectual experience.

Second, the Ohio State program embodies the no-nonsense, Midwestern work ethic. No frills. No glitz or glamour. Just a bunch of tough coaches, players, equipment guys, and trainers. It's no surprise that a guy like Earle Bruce would find success at Ohio State. Earle was a football coach. He didn't care about image. He just wanted to line his team up against our opponent and play clean, hard football. He treated his players fairly and made sure that we kept our perspective. During one practice, for example, after returning from my first Rhodes Scholarship interview, he wanted to make sure I was still thinking about football. We were running passing drills, and I ran the wrong route on a play. As I jogged back to the huddle, he yelled to the rest of the offense, "He has to be the dumbest guy I ever coached!" That was Earle. No slack. Just do the right thing all the time.

Third, the Ohio State program is about winning. Win fairly. Win with class. But win. We had a team full of guys who wanted to win, but I can't think of anyone who wanted to win more than Keith Byars. I've never met anyone with a more competitive spirit. There were games where he would just wear down the defense with his combination of speed and strength. And I saw him play with pain, too. During one game, I saw him come back to the huddle a little wobbly. He was bleeding from his mouth and nose. I told him to take a blow for a play so he could gather himself. But he wouldn't leave the field. During another, he knocked a linebacker from Purdue out cold. The biggest frustration of my career was seeing him robbed of the Heisman in 1984.

As the years go by, I forget the scores and statistics. I even forget a few of the names and faces. But I take a piece of Ohio State with me wherever I go. Whether it was as a naval officer 10 years ago or now as a banker, I often think back to that cold day in February when I made a commitment to become a Buckeye. It made all the difference in my life.

Tradition is the glue that keeps the Ohio State program together. Despite the coaching changes, despite the player transition, through the good times and bad times, it is the tradition built over the past 100 years that remains and sustains the program. I am honored to be a part of it.

Mike Lanese, who had 73 receptions for 1,175 yards in his career, was a team captain in 1985. He was a two-time Academic All-American and the only player in Ohio State history to earn a Rhodes Scholarship.

CRIS CARTER
WIDE RECEIVER
1984–1986

I HAD SO MANY CHOICES COMING OUT of high school in Middletown, Ohio—I could have gone almost anywhere to play basketball and anywhere to play football. I had always considered basketball my first love, and my brother Butch played basketball at Indiana and had played with Isiah Thomas. My brother George played at Illinois State, and my brother John played at West Liberty. But one of my football coaches, Bill Conley, who's now at Ohio State, told me: "Cris, there are a lot of Isiah Thomases out there playing basketball, but there are not many tall receivers like you!"

I had decided to narrow it to five basketball schools and five football schools. Butch used to tell me, "Don't go to Ohio State. They never have thrown the football, and they never will."

Then one day, I came home and was worn out from people asking me where I was headed to college. I sat down in the living room and told Mom, "Everybody is asking me where I am going and what I am going to do, but nobody ever asks you what you think. So, what do you think, Mom?"

She looked at me and said, "Son, I always had a dream that one of my boys would play football for the Buckeyes."

I also figured this out: there is a tremendous benefit to being an Ohio State alum and being in Ohio.

I knew right then what I had to do: I committed early—but part of the deal was that I could play basketball at Ohio State, too.

Chris Spielman committed early, too, and he and I helped recruit the rest of the class. We had the No. 1 recruiting class in the country, and we had plans to win a national championship. There was Chris, Alex Higdon, William White, Tom Tupa, Greg Rogan…we knew we had an awesome class.

I remember when I first got to campus, Lenny Willis was finishing up his degree and he was playing in the NFL. I was basically a basketball player playing wide receiver, and he helped me out on my routes, but I almost left Ohio State a few days after I got there.

When I got there, there was the first team, the second team, and the scout team. All the freshmen were on the scout team. I told Coach Bruce, "I am leaving school. You promised me a chance to make the varsity, and this is not what you had told me while you were recruiting me." He had told me, "If you don't start as a freshman, I would be surprised."

The next day, they moved Chris Spielman and me up to the third-string on the varsity. Now there really wasn't any third-string, just two spots—for me and Chris. I have to say that Jay Holland, Doug Smith, and Mike Lanese were guys who really helped me. They were receivers who were fighting for the same jobs, but they were very, very helpful. So was Mike Tomczak, who was a senior and the starting quarterback.

Now, I had seen the team come out of that tunnel a dozen times…with Coach Bruce standing there in front and the police holding the team back. I just didn't know what it would be like to run onto that field. Literally, my feet didn't touch the ground that first time in my freshman season. It was so exciting. When I got into pro football, that feeling made me love Ohio State even more.

You wind up chasing that feeling again for the rest of your life.

I didn't start those first two games in '84, but I started against Iowa in the third game, and I was in there ever since.

That whole experience of playing in the Rose Bowl that year was very special. I had a pretty good game [nine receptions, a Rose Bowl–record 172 yards], and that was the first day I became convinced I would never play basketball again. I would just stick to football.

In practice, Keith Byars and I used to play these games to challenge me to do something no one else had ever done. We used to play catch near the sideline, and I would try to make one-handed catches and still keep my feet inbounds. So when people mention that one-handed catch I made along the

264

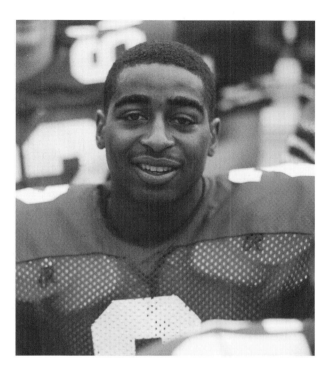

Cris Carter, an All-American in 1986, amazed opponents and his teammates with acrobatic receptions.

sideline of the Citrus Bowl my sophomore year against BYU, that's where that comes from. I had made up my mind that is the type of player I wanted to be. I didn't want to be average, or even good—I wanted to be great.

Still, I admit there were many times I was frustrated with our offense. It seemed it was always a struggle with the coaches to open it up a little and throw more. We would run on first down, run on second, and then try to throw to me on third-and-long. We didn't have the most sophisticated passing game in the world. It was frustrating for me.

I was close to most all of my teammates and especially those in my class, and that's why what happened before the 1987 season made it so tough. I was ruled ineligible [for dealing with an agent], and it crushed me. We were pointing everything toward that senior year, and we were all coming back. We were going to be good, and we knew we were going to be good. Everybody else knew it, too.

When the ruling came down from the NCAA, and then [OSU athletics director] Rick Bay said, "Cris Carter will never wear an Ohio State uniform again," I had only one option, and that was to apply for the NFL Draft. I didn't want to leave; I wanted to file that appeal, but Ohio State did not want to do that. I was upset at myself. Given what I knew about athletics, I didn't have to do what I did to get into that predicament.

I admit that initially I was a little bitter, and of course, my teammates were mad at me. The most vocal one of all was Chris Spielman. He is a no-nonsense kind of guy who does the right thing. He had a few choice words for me, and I understood that. I really did. I respected him so much.

After that, I just had to withdraw from school and leave Columbus. It was on every TV station, every radio station, wherever I went in town. Then all of those things just wore that '87 team out. We didn't have an offensive leader, who [quarterback] Tom Tupa needed. I faced the question that if that wouldn't have happened to me, we wouldn't have had a bad year, and Earle wouldn't have been fired. I had to live with that, but I do know something about Ohio State, and Bill Myles told me, "Hey, every coach who ever worked here has been fired."

I still have to say that playing at Ohio State was a great experience.

I feel some relief that people have forgotten what happened as the years go by. Earlier in my pro career, I still caught flak for it, and I had stayed away from Ohio State for a few years because of the emotion and frustration people showed to me. I always wanted to make those fans cheer for me, and if they did, I enjoyed it so much.

It is the truth to say that I always have been in pursuit of making all Buckeyes proud of me. Not everyone has that opportunity to put on that helmet and wear those Buckeye leaves. I have no regrets about my choice to play for Ohio State, and I will always have a deep fondness for the Buckeyes.

Cris Carter, who recorded 168 receptions in his three-year Ohio State career, played for the Philadelphia Eagles, Minnesota Vikings, and Miami Dolphins. He ranks third in NFL history in receptions behind Jerry Rice and Marvin Harrison and fourth in touchdown receptions, behind Rice, Terrell Owens, and Randy Moss.

CHRIS SPIELMAN
LINEBACKER
1984–1987

WHEN I WAS A KID AND I PLAYED with my G.I. Joes, I didn't play army like all the other kids. I lined them up on each side and played a football game with them. I was a coach's son, and from an early age, I loved the game and studied the game so that I could be the best I could be.

In deciding where to attend college, I was torn between Ohio State and Michigan. I thought the two schools mirrored each other, but I was an Ohio kid, and once I got through all the fluff of everybody telling me how much they wanted me and how much they loved me, I knew where I had to go. At that time, the governor was calling my house. I came home from a recruiting trip to Miami, and I went through Dayton, and there were a bunch of people there with Buckeyes signs for me to see. I always tried to keep it all in perspective and enjoy the process, and I look back on it with fondness now. I remember meeting with Coach Hayes in his office, and we talked about history some. Here's one thing he told me: "Learn to speak a foreign language—it will help you later." When I first met him, I was eight or nine years old, and we were in a Bob Evans in Canton. He was recruiting Ray Ellis at the time, and they were there. My dad was a high school coach and he knew Ray, so we went over and met him.

People have asked me if I wish I had been born earlier so I could have played for him, but I don't. That wasn't my time or my destiny. When I signed with Ohio State, I knew Coach Bruce was like what I try to be: what you see

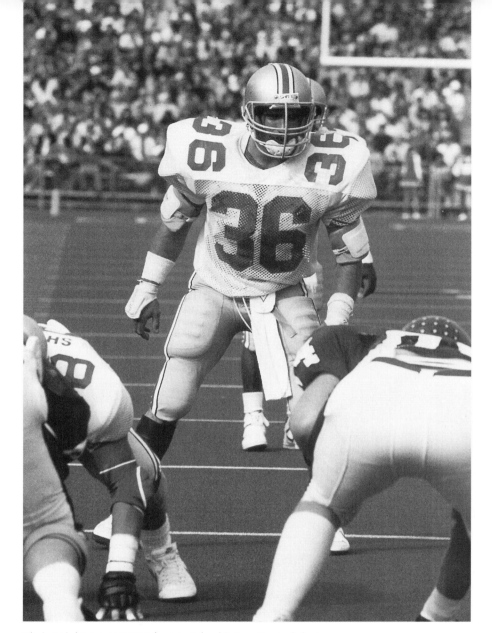

Chris Spielman possessed unmatched intensity and desire.

is what you get. He was passionate about Ohio State, too. He told me I would have a chance to earn a starting job as a freshman, and he was true to his word.

On that first day we were in pads, I just tried running around and making a lot of plays. After the scrimmage, I was named the starting linebacker. Then I hurt my ankle and wasn't able to start the first game against Oregon State.

Now that drove me crazy. I had a goal to start for Ohio State as a freshman, and I was frustrated. But I got in the game in the second half, and I started after that.

Being new to college, football was the easy part for me. Being a coach's son, I always connected with the mental part of the game. I saw the advantage I would get if I learned what everybody's job was on the field—knowing where they were and what they were doing. As I got older, I just elevated that to college. I know I was focused about it.

My wife was my high school sweetheart, and she went to Ohio State, too. She was in a sorority, and when they had their functions, other guys would ask me, "Don't you want to be over there with her?" I said, "Hey, I trust her. She has her thing and I have mine." Mine was to focus on my goals—going to school, playing football, and maybe going to the NFL later. Let me put it this way, they didn't let me host many recruits because they didn't want them hosted by a hermit.

Anyway, in that second half of the Oregon State game, I made plays, and it validated that I could play at this level. We went on to beat Michigan to go to the Rose Bowl my freshman year. I was 18 and playing in the Rose Bowl, and we should have beaten USC that day. You always have that sense that you will get back there, but it didn't work out for us.

The next year, losing to Wisconsin at home irks me still. Losing at Michigan doesn't sit well, either. Then we had a great game plan in the Citrus Bowl, and we played a 3–5 defense against Robbie Bosco and BYU. To start my junior year, we lost the Kickoff Classic, lost at Washington, and then we ran off nine wins in a row. We had a chance to beat Michigan, and that was a bitter loss. The best overall game I had been a part of was the Cotton Bowl against Texas A&M. They had three or four No. 1 draft picks on that team, and everybody in Texas thought they were going to blow us out. I remember sitting in a press conference before the game and asking, "What are we? I mean, hey, we're Ohio State." It seemed nobody gave us a chance, but we won that game quite handily [28–12]. I remember that Coach Bruce almost went to Arizona after that game.

Before my senior season, things didn't go right. We lost Cris Carter [ruled ineligible by the NCAA], and we never overcame that. Without him, we lost a lot of our offense. When I look back at that whole ordeal now, the great thing that came from it is how Cris turned his life around. He is a team guy, he learned from it, and he paid his consequences. He was the ultimate

269

competitor, and he would be the first guy I would take if I were choosing sides. I do respect him very much.

In the end, I feel responsible for what happened to Coach Bruce. Losing to Iowa in our last home game was the toughest loss. We had the game won, but they hit Marv Cook on a pass and scored to beat us [29–27]. It was unprecedented for a coach to get fired before the Michigan game, and it was disturbing to me to say the least, but I was in awe of the way Coach Bruce handled himself throughout that last week. He put his feelings of rejection aside and got us ready to play. One of my fondest memories was from Senior Tackle on that Thursday. He had broken his leg in college and never got to do Senior Tackle. I introduced him that night, and he was the last guy to do Senior Tackle. He went down there and hit the sled, and I realized how much it meant to him. Then before the game, we broke out those "Earle" head-bands, and he was surprised at that. After we won [23–20], we carried him off the field, but I didn't participate in the team celebration much. I just sat back and watched him.

270

When I look back on it, I am really privileged and honored to have played football at Ohio State. All I wanted to do was represent the tradition before me and after me in the best way possible. Ohio State is a living, breathing entity. It becomes a part of you. I am humbled by my experiences there. I have this radio show in Columbus, and I once said, "Our goal is not to be good, it is to be great" and fans called in questioning me, saying, "You expect too much from these kids. You put too much pressure on them."

Pressure is your friend. Being a former player, I believe this is the standard that was set before us, and this is the standard we must uphold. That will never change. We must keep our standards high. That is what Ohio State is all about. I can honestly say that I am very glad I was able to represent this university, and I worked hard to represent it in the right way.

Chris Spielman, who finished his career with 546 tackles, made a school-record 29 tackles (tying Tom Cousineau for a single-game high) against Michigan in 1986. He was named All–Big Ten three times and was an All-American in 1986 and '87 and a team captain in '87. He also won the Lombardi Award in '87. He played 12 seasons in the NFL. He was inducted into the College Football Hall of Fame in 2009.

JEFF UHLENHAKE
OFFENSIVE LINEMAN
1985–1988

PLAYING FOOTBALL AT OSU has had a profound effect on my life through the connections I've made. Everyone knows that Ohio State football is always a topic of conversation at any Ohio workplace, and when people know you played football at Ohio State, they want to know all about it.

The games I remember most, of course, are the Michigan games. I am proud to say they also were my very best. The Michigan loss in 1986 when we missed a field goal with a minute left to go, and we would have gone to the Rose Bowl, would have to be the most disappointing game I played in.

A year later, the Michigan win in Earle Bruce's last game was the most enjoyable. It was a great way to send off most of the coaching staff that recruited me.

Being a captain in 1988, I had the honor to give a rousing speech at the pregame meal before the Michigan game. It worked so well—we were behind 20–0 at halftime. But we came back to lose a close one 34–31. That was the last of my pregame speeches.

The bowl games were great—no school, gifts, spending money, almost like playing in the pros. The one I remember most was beating heavily favored Texas A&M in the 1987 Cotton Bowl. That was an awesome experience because they were supposed to drill us in their home state.

That reminds me of the greatest players I played with: Chris Spielman and Cris Carter. Chris Spielman's hard work and dedication was second to none.

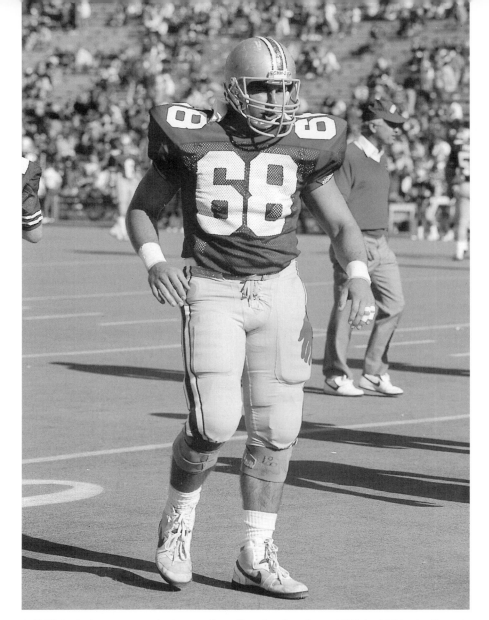

Jeff Uhlenhake was a mainstay on the offensive line from 1985 to 1988, starting at guard and center for four seasons.

I remember Chris, as a freshman in the Rose Bowl game against USC, flipping over a blocker and making the tackle. It was an awesome play. Cris Carter made a one-handed catch against BYU in the Citrus Bowl, and he managed to keep one foot in bounds (of course, everyone saw him make many one-handed catches and get two feet in bounds in the NFL). They were two of the greatest players making great plays.

Maybe you've heard of my favorite coach at OSU. His name was Jim Tressel [an assistant in 1983–1985]. Steve Devine, Bob Palcic, and Fred Pagac were great to be around, too. Steve was very funny and always made meetings enjoyable. I roomed with Fred Pagac's nephew, and we would visit his house, and his wife, Bernie, treated us like her own.

One funny moment with Bob Palcic was in 1986 when we played at Washington. We came in at halftime and we were getting our butts kicked. We were sitting there waiting for our ass-chewing when a loud shriek shot throughout the locker room. We thought someone had broken their leg or something, but Coach Palcic got his finger stuck in the door. You would have thought someone would had to have died from that yelp.

Anyway, it gave us something to laugh about on the five-hour airplane ride home after getting drilled by the Huskies.

All three children in my family have graduated from OSU. I feel as though everyone in Ohio and all the alumni throughout the world can take pride in Ohio State.

The pride exhibited in Arizona during the Fiesta Bowl game against Miami—I do not believe has ever been matched by any school, including Notre Dame. Sitting in the upper deck at the Fiesta Bowl with many players I played with, and who played before and after me, as well, brought so much satisfaction and pride.

Any Ohio State recruit will know they are part of a loving, supportive family. With that family comes responsibility and accountability. The returns from practice, study, social life, and especially the games will be your rewards for everything you are willing to invest.

The bonds made between football players are made great by the brutal nature of the sport. Just know that all Buckeyes past and present are fighting the battles along with you.

I chose Ohio State because they offered me a scholarship, but I became and I am a Buckeye!

Jeff Uhlenhake, a guard, was All–Big Ten in 1986 and the MVP of the '88 team. He played 10 seasons in the NFL.

CARLOS SNOW
RUNNING BACK
1987–1989, 1991

I CAME FROM A SMALL HIGH SCHOOL in Cincinnati by the name of C.A.P.E.—Cincinnati Academy of Physical Education. We were playing in our most intense rivalry game against Ironton, and even though we lost on the scoreboard, I knew I had left everything on the field that day. All that summer conditioning, spring ball, weight lifting, determination, heart, and soul were left on the field in that game. I was lying on the ground after the game and I asked God, "Where did I go wrong? What could I have done better to help our team win?"

A voice spoke over me and said, "Your grade was 99 percent. It would have been 100, but I never give perfect scores, little man." That voice was Earle Bruce's. He then said, "You are the kind of athlete we would love to have at The Ohio State University."

From that moment, I knew I was a Buckeye!

I was 5'7" and 190 pounds, and because of my size, the odds were against me. But Coach Bruce realized the size of my heart. I got the starting job during my freshman season, beating out guys I had looked up to for years, but fumbling was a big problem for me in college because of the tight-fitting jerseys. I can honestly say that, because I never fumbled in high school.

During one hot summer practice, we were doing live goal-line hitting, and I was introduced to the difference between high school and college football.

Carlos Snow bursts upfield during the Indiana game in 1989.

The play called was "22 sprint draw." As I got the ball and saw the hole open up, I went through it and suddenly ran into a brick wall. I had never been hit so hard in my entire sports life. To this day, I can still say that. The hit was so hard that I still have visions of it in my sleep. Mr. Chris Spielman was on the other end of that hit. His helmet hit smack in the middle of my chest, snot flew from my nose, and the pads came out of my helmet. My shoulder pads came undone, and my shoulder popped out of place. To add insult to my injuries, he spit tobacco juice right between my eyes.

"Welcome to Ohio State football," he said.

That man was a great, great player.

The greatest game we ever played in was against Michigan at the Big House in 1987. I think we were down by three points, and Chris was playing the game of his life—he must have had 18 solo tackles at the half. I heard Earle calling for the "little guy." He said. "Put him in right now!"

When I got that call, I almost threw up my breakfast. He put me in the biggest game of the year, and here I was a freshman. He didn't know if I would hold onto the ball or fumble and let the whole team down. Tom Tupa called the play, and it was a pass. I was the No. 3 read on the play, so I figured I wasn't going to get the ball. I ran my route to about four yards from the sideline, and I turned and saw the ball coming. It was coming in a hurry, and I was thinking, "Don't drop it!" Seventy yards later, I was in the end zone. It was the greatest feeling in the world to me.

We went on to win that game, which was Coach Bruce's final game.

At the Columbus Touchdown Club's award banquet, I met Woody Hayes the year before he died. He had told me, "Run tough and run fast!" and that's what I was thinking about on that long run to the end zone in the Big House.

When you walk into my mother's house today, the first picture you see is that of Woody and me shaking hands.

I was always proud to wear the scarlet and gray. My one regret is that I didn't finish school because I put all my eggs into one basket. That would be the advice I would give to all the current and future Buckeyes: whatever you do on the field—finish, finish, finish school, so that life after football can be what you want it to be. I will always love the Buckeyes!

Carlos Snow led Ohio State in rushing in 1988, '89, and '91. He finished with 2,974 rushing yards—seventh on OSU's all-time list.

The
NINETIES

JASON SIMMONS

DEFENSIVE END

1990–1993

WHEN I WAS IN HIGH SCHOOL at St. Vincent St. Mary's in Akron, Ohio State was slow to recruit me. When they did, and they finally offered me a scholarship, it was one of the best days of my life—behind only the marriage to my wife and the births of our kids and, let me not forget, the day I received my diploma from The Ohio State University.

The experience of being a Buckeye will stay with me forever and will always be considered as the best years of my life. It has changed my life in so many ways that it is difficult to describe and to measure. I know I will forever be known as an Ohio State Buckeye and a former team captain. For that, people recognize me wherever I go in this great state. At Ohio State, I learned the importance of teamwork and leadership. I learned the value of hard work and having the will to never give up. How could you give up in front of the Ohio State fans—the best and most demanding fans in the country? I learned early to do whatever it took to make those fans happy.

The campus life was definitely one of the reasons I had such an enjoyable time at OSU. Some people always asked me, "Isn't it hard going to a big school?" To me, that was part of the fun, because I got a chance to meet new people every quarter.

I have so many great memories and funny stories. One time, during a road game at Iowa, the visitors' locker room was painted bubble-gum pink. As many people know, Iowa coach Hayden Fry was very much into gaining

Jason Simmons celebrates a sack against Louisville in the 1992 season opener.

psychological edges any way he could. As we entered the locker room, there was a huge commotion a few lockers away. Suddenly, a bat came swooping down on our heads. People were diving for cover as this bat tried to find a quiet place to hide. Eventually, several players wielding their cleats chased it into the bathroom, where it landed above one of the stalls. We pushed the stall door open to finish off that poor bat, and there was Dave Monnot, sitting there listening to his headphones. He was reading the game day program and trying to get some peace and quiet.

The thing that you take from your playing days is the friendships with your teammates. I could mention dozens of them, but I want to mention Greg Smith and Brian Stablein. They both were deemed too small when they came out of high school, but that didn't stop them from accomplishing their goals. They entered as walk-ons, and the work ethic they displayed became contagious. They eventually earned scholarships and landed immense respect from their teammates.

I was one of Coach Cooper's players, and I know that people find it easy to take shots at him now. Some of it may be deserved, but we need to keep in mind that he helped build the program into a national powerhouse. Although he never got us to the Promised Land, the players he recruited are the source of pride to thousands of Buckeyes everywhere.

I will never forget my position coaches—Bill Young, Fred Pagac, Bob Palcic, and Bill Conley. These men taught me as much about life and what it means to be a man as they taught me about football. Ohio State will always have great assistant coaches, and they fit in that category.

I am thankful for Coach Tressel. He has brought back the pride and many of the traditions to Ohio State. I know that our ship will maintain its present course for greatness because Coach Tressel is a winner, and I am glad he is a Buckeye.

Although playing football was a tremendous experience, it would have been for naught if not for getting my degree. That piece of paper validates everything I worked for while at Ohio State. I would not be as successful after Ohio State without it.

As I look back, I am truly thankful. I am thankful to all the coaches, trainers, equipment managers, and everybody else affiliated with the program. I am thankful for my teammates. And I am thankful for the Best Damn Band in the Land. Most of all, I want to thank the fans. Without them, the 'Shoe would be like any other stadium, and game day would be like any other day.

Now, I am just a fan, too. And like most Buckeyes, I bleed scarlet and gray. I live and die each Saturday afternoon during the fall. We past players regard the current players as part of our extended family. It is a brotherhood that we understand and treasure. I gained another family while playing at Ohio State, and there is no better surrogate family to have than the Buckeye family!

Jason Simmons was named All–Big Ten in 1991 and a team captain in '93. He holds the single-game sack record with four (at Washington State in 1991) and finished his career with 56.5 tackles for loss—third on Ohio State's all-time list.

EDDIE GEORGE

RUNNING BACK

1992–1995

I WASN'T RECRUITED MUCH DURING my senior year of high school. As a matter of fact, no big schools were interested in me. I had a good year at Fork
Union Military in Virginia, and all of a sudden I started to gain the attention
of schools like Louisville, BYU, Virginia, and Virginia Tech. I had a friend
who was on the Ohio State training staff, and he had told the coaches,
"Here's a guy you need to look at."

They told him to have me send a tape. I did. They liked what they saw and
wanted another one. I sent it. The next thing I knew, I was coming out to
Columbus for a visit.

Right away, I was very impressed by the environment. The tradition at
Ohio State just blew me away. It was all I had ever wanted. Coach Cooper,
my mom, and I were standing by the Buckeye Grove, where the trees are
planted for the All-Americans, and I committed right there on the spot.

It is not a stretch to say that I dreamed of becoming an All-American and
having my own tree in the Buckeye Grove.

I got there in time for spring practice in '92, and my first thought was, *I've
never seen linebackers, running backs, and defensive backs this big.* I was overwhelmed.

There were ups and downs right away. I scored three touchdowns against
Syracuse [a 35–12 win] on national television. Then two weeks later, I fum-
bled twice, and we lost a close game to Illinois [18–16] at Ohio Stadium.
Those fumbles…that is what I became known for. I was just finding my niche

Eddie George cuts through a hole during the Buckeyes' 45–26 win over Notre Dame in 1995.

as a short-yardage specialist, and then that happened. It really set me back. I was embarrassed by the fumbles, and we lost the game, really because of my fumbles. At that time, I was very disappointed and frustrated.

That was the crossroads for me. I could have let it get me down and not bounced back, but I decided to work harder and never let it happen again. Raymont Harris told me at the time, "It happens. Fumbles are part of the game, but your character will be revealed by how you respond to it."

He also told me what I needed to work on—I was running right away and not letting the play develop in front of me, and I needed to work on my speed. Still, I never got another real opportunity until my junior year, but it was bittersweet because Raymont was having an outstanding season in '93. I wanted to play, but he was my best friend. I had just had to step back and support him.

I felt I had a very good junior season [1,442 yards], but nobody around the country really knew anything about me. I wasn't breaking off the big runs, but I did have a 76-yard run that season. We were 9–4 and sort of rebuilding.

That next summer, my thought process was that we had the components to compete for a national championship. I thought I had the opportunity to be mentioned for an All-America team, and we were motivated as a team to do something special. We had gotten beat 63–14 at Penn State the year before, and that lingered with all of us. I pretty much worked nonstop and had extra workouts after practice. I had dotted every *i* and crossed every *t*.

We really had a hell of a camp. On offense we had Bobby Hoying, Terry Glenn, and Orlando Pace, and our defense was improving every day.

When we played Boston College at the Meadowlands in the Kickoff Classic of '95, we visited the Downtown Athletic Club, and I noticed all the pictures of Heisman winners, like Billy Sims, O.J. Simpson, Hopalong Cassady, and Archie Griffin. I felt it was an honor just to be in that room. Then somebody took a picture of me with the Heisman Trophy. I thought to myself, *I'll be back to pick this up later in the season.* Of course, I didn't say that out loud, but I did think that.

A few weeks later, we played Washington at home, and they had beaten us in a physical game up there the year before. They really let us know about it, too. I remember that this time around, I was getting into the secondary quite a bit, and it was my first 200-yard game [212 yards]. That is the first time I heard the chant, "Eddie, Eddie!" at the stadium. It was overwhelming…just quite a thrill for me.

Another game I certainly remember was facing Illinois. They had beaten us in '92 and in '94, and they started to say they owned us in our house. I just felt a personal challenge to take it to them. The weather wasn't very good, and I knew we would run the ball that day. I remember looking up at the scoreboard, and I had 188 yards at the half and thought, *Whoa, this is getting out of control now.* I broke the [OSU single-game rushing] record sometime in the fourth quarter on a simple draw for 13 or 14 yards. I really had no idea how many yards I had [314 on 36 carries]. It was that night that I had heard people talk about me and the Heisman Trophy in the same sentence.

A month later, I headed to New York for the presentation and really didn't know what would happen. I figured it came down to me, [Florida's] Danny Wuerffel, and [Nebraska's] Tommie Frazier. Archie had told me just to enjoy the moment, and that's what I planned to do, but when they announced the winner, my life really changed at that point.

I studied the Heisman history and its history at Ohio State, and I understand the fraternity that you join when you win it. It is such an honor, and I am happy I get to represent the Buckeyes in that manner.

As I look back at my entire career, it is an amazing story—how it started and how it ended.

Recently, they retired my No. 27, and it was the greatest honor of all. A lot of people told me I would never reach this level, but I did it. It's funny, but when I came to Ohio State, I wanted to wear No. 20 or No. 6, but they both were taken, so they asked me to choose between 38 and 27, and now that number is retired. It really put a closure to my career.

Being part of the Buckeyes family is very, very special to me. The guys who played in the '50s support the guys who played in the '90s and so on. I can't walk through an airport anywhere without seeing somebody wearing an Ohio State hat. The support is everywhere, and I can say that Ohio State ranks supreme in my mind.

Eddie George, who gained a school-record 1,927 yards and scored 24 TDs in 1995, fulfilled his dream of being named All-America en route to becoming Ohio State's sixth Heisman Trophy winner. He was taken in the first round of the 1996 NFL Draft by the Houston Oilers/Tennessee Titans, rushed for 10,441 yards, scored 78 TDs, and was named to four Pro Bowls before retiring from football in 2004. He was elected to the College Football Hall of Fame in 2011.

BOBBY HOYING

QUARTERBACK

1992–1995

As most kids grow up in Ohio, I'm not sure there is another position in all of sports that boys dream about playing more than being a quarterback at The Ohio State University. It was my dream while growing up in St. Henry, Ohio.

I am the oldest grandchild of Wally Post (my mom's father), who played 15 seasons in Major League Baseball, 12 of those with the Cincinnati Reds. As a child, I had an extreme sense of pride for my grandfather and dreamed of following his footsteps down the path to play professional sports.

Another person I looked up to, and loved to watch play sports at St. Henry High School, was Jim Lachey. Jim was a high school standout who went on to become an All-America lineman at Ohio State. He was drafted in the first round and had a successful career in the NFL, winning Super Bowl rings with the Washington Redskins.

And, of course, I always looked up to my parents and dreamed of becoming a star like my grandfather.

St. Henry did not have a football program when my father attended high school there, but one was eventually started in 1974, so it was a relatively young program.

I was fortunate to play with an incredible group of players there and won three state championships [one for football and two for basketball]. I believe we were only the second school in Ohio history to win football and basketball state titles in the same year. Since then, St. Henry has become a powerhouse, winning six state titles in football, and is regarded as one of the best small-school programs in the state.

There have been seven players who hail from St.Henry—eight, if you include Jeff Uhlenhake, who was born in St. Henry and moved to Newark (we claim him as one of ours, by the way)—who have gone on to play for the Buckeyes.

The bottom line is that I love my hometown and think there is something very special about how and where I grew up.

I have a picture of when I was a little boy lifting weights in an Ohio State football jersey with the No. 14 on it. That, amazingly, became my number when I played college football. The fact that I went on to wear that same number on my scarlet-and-gray jersey in college so many years later shows you how dreams can come true. When I see that picture, it reminds me of those days when becoming the quarterback at Ohio State was truly "the dream."

I realized that it is something that thousands of little boys fantasize about doing, but only few get the opportunity.

And I knew Ohio State is where I wanted to be, if given the opportunity.

After visiting UCLA, Louisville [coached by Howard Schnellenberger], and Illinois [John Mackovic], I was visiting Ohio State when Coach John Cooper got me alone at the Woody Hayes Athletic Center. In that southern drawl of his, he said something like, "Heck, Bobby…you are a Buckeye. Let's get you all signed up!" I can do a great impression of him today.

And he was right—I was a Buckeye. I committed right there and then. I loved Ohio State from the start, so I saw no sense in waiting. This was during my senior season of basketball.

My very first snaps as a quarterback at Ohio State occurred early in my redshirt freshman year. I backed up Kirk Herbstreit, and he had been banged up early against Bowling Green. I didn't have much time to warm up, and I was called on to make an audible on my very first snap. The moment was so big for me that all I could say was color-number about four times—"blue 42, blue 42…(pause)…blue 42, blue 42." I couldn't complete the audible because my heart was coming out of my chest, and my mouth was so dry that I could not speak at the line of scrimmage.

I eventually just called a timeout, which calmed me down. Kirk later came back into the game and played the rest of the year, but those were my

288

Bobby Hoying had a 30–7–1 record as a starting quarterback from 1993 to 1995. He was named All–Big Ten in 1995.

first quality snaps at quarterback and a moment that each player remembers forever.

It was awesome playing football with my brother, Tommy. He came in as a quarterback and went on to play tight end and some special teams as his career progressed. Playing football together as kids and throughout both of our careers as we grew up was a special thing for brothers to share.

Being a Buckeye is being part of an elite family, and sharing that with my brother made it an even stronger sense of the word. We have two younger cousins who have experienced the same family ties as a Buckeye—Ross and Adam Homan. To this day, being a football player at Ohio State is something that the extended Hoying family will always identify with.

If you ask most players what they miss most about the game, you will get a mix of answers, perhaps the great games or great plays someone made. But for me, it was the experiences that surrounded those games: the training, the practices, the locker room banter between teammates, the anxious moments just before a big game, singing "Across the Field" after a victory, and the camaraderie. Those are the things that I most miss about the game of football.

289

And one of the sweetest times was our 22–6 win over Michigan in my junior season. It was special to us because we were the first team to win that game in a while [since 1987], and I was especially happy for Coach Cooper since it was his first win over Michigan. One highlight was my touchdown run against them. It is such a great feeling as a quarterback when you score a touchdown, but even more so against them. There is just something about that game. I played in the NFL with Tyrone Wheatley and Steve Everitt, along with a number of other former Michigan players. You think you are going to hate them (or are supposed to hate them) and that they would be bad, evil guys—but you find out they are very similar to us. They have a great tradition, as well, and work extremely hard. Looking back, every Michigan player I had as a teammate in the NFL was one who had a good work ethic, was unselfish, and was fun to play with. This was odd to me at first because I grew up hating them, and it took a while to get used to.

Some of my most memorable experiences occurred during my senior year of 1995. It was a special year for us. We beat Boston College 38–6 in the Kick-off Classic in the Meadowlands. The next day, the team was to travel to see the New York Stock Exchange. During the off-season, we installed a new five-man protection scheme in the offensive line and were still working out the kinks. Although I didn't get sacked too much that day, I got hit a lot, and the old Meadowlands turf was not too forgiving. To this day, it is the worst I have ever felt after a football game, and I couldn't get out of bed to see the Stock Exchange.

That same year, we were undefeated and playing Notre Dame in what was one of the most hyped non-conference games to be played at Ohio Stadium. A week earlier, I passed for five touchdowns as we easily won at Pittsburgh. After a slow start against Notre Dame, we won 45–26, and I had one of my best games—throwing for four touchdowns and 272 yards in that victory. Terry Glenn had a famous catch and run for an 82-yard touchdown. He had beaten both the corner [Allen Rossum] and safety on the play and out-sprinted them to the end zone. Rossum was known as a national track star for Notre Dame, so he was hard to outrun. (Two years later, we were teammates in the NFL for the Philadelphia Eagles, and I would call Allen "toast" for that play, just so he would never forget that game.)

The game at Penn State that year was extra special. We were down late in the game and facing a third-and-long situation when I hit tight end Ricky Dudley long down the middle with a very tight throw that continued the drive. It is the play that I am most reminded of when people talk of that game. Eddie George ran in the winning touchdown a few plays later that gave us a 28–25 win. I will never forget the joy we experienced after that game. Assistant coach Fred Pagac almost tackled me in the locker room after the game. He was so happy he was crying.

We won 30 games over my last three years as a starting quarterback, we had Coach Cooper's first win against Michigan and pulled off big victories over Notre Dame, Washington, Penn State, and Wisconsin. If our group could have had one more victory over Michigan those years, we could have played for a national championship for Coach Cooper. It didn't happen, and to this day, the 31–23 loss at Michigan my senior year probably hurts the most.

Instead of heading to the Rose Bowl, we headed to Florida to play Tennessee in the Citrus Bowl. Back then, Peyton was just Archie Manning's son to us. He was tremendous to meet, and we talked a number of times during the bowl week. I got a sense as soon as I met him that he was someone who would be extremely successful. He was very confident yet humble. The game was not a fun one for any quarterback—it was a monsoon, and I think it rained three inches during the game. I didn't play that poorly, but we ended up losing 20–14. One of my lasting memories is sitting in my locker in Orlando after my final game and being overcome with great sadness that my time as an Ohio State player was over. I just sat there along with other seniors, cried, and reflected. It is very hard at that moment to comprehend everything coming to an end.

At the end of my senior season, I was awarded the Draddy Award, regarded as the "Academic Heisman" of college football. I traveled to New York for the dinner and was seated right next to Jim Brown! I visited with what I consider the greatest football player in history for almost three hours. It was a surprise when I won the award that night, and then I had to address a crowd of 1,200 in the grand ballroom of the Waldorf Astoria Hotel. I was very proud of winning this award and representing the best of The Ohio State University. Larry Romanoff, my first academic advisor, had told me exactly what I needed to do to win the award early in my freshman year and guided me along the way. I want to give many thanks to Larry.

The history and tradition of Ohio State football are what I am so proud to be a part of. I was elected captain of the 1995 team [along with Eddie George and Matt Bonhaus] and felt a great sense of pride each time I walked onto the field to represent that team and my university.

291

In 2008 I was inducted into the Ohio State Athletics Hall of Fame—one of the best honors I have had in my life. I still hold several school passing records, all of which I am sure one day will be broken, but to be a part of that list will always be an honor for me.

I think being a part of this rich history and tradition is what is so meaningful for former players. My son, Jake, is so proud to have a dad who played for the Buckeyes, and I see so much of myself as a little boy growing up when I see him cheering on the Buckeyes each Saturday.

I am not sure what it *exactly* means to be a Buckeye for everyone, but I know not many are lucky enough to experience everything that goes with it, such as playing in the 'Shoe, earning gold pants for beating Michigan, and working alongside incredible football players and coaches. During my three years as a starter, I was able to play alongside amazing teammates like Korey Stringer, Orlando Pace, Eddie George, Terry Glenn, Joey Galloway, and Ricky Dudley—and that was just on offense.

Shortly after one of our first spring practices during my senior year, our quarterbacks coach, Walt Harris, who was in his first year here and fresh off a stint in the NFL with the New York Jets, and I were having a casual conversation just outside the weight room. I commented about one of Terry Glenn's great catches in practice that day, when Coach Harris simply said,

"Bobby, do you realize that Eddie George, Ricky Dudley, and Terry all would have started for the Jets? Each is better than anyone Boomer [Esiason] played with last year."

I thought he was just trying to pump us up, but he was right on with his judgment of talent. To play with the best is one of the many reasons I chose to play for Ohio State. Eddie won the Heisman Trophy my senior season. I finished 10th.

Those are the types of experiences, rewards, and exposure that comes with playing at Ohio State. And you, in turn, have a duty to represent your university in the very best way you can. I think that carries on throughout the rest of your life and in every aspect of your life. This is what it means to be a Buckeye, which remains in your heart, and you carry that honor and respect forever.

Bobby Hoying passed for 7,232 yards and set Ohio State career records with 498 completions and 57 touchdown passes. He made 38 starts and had a 30–7–1 record. He was named All–Big Ten in 1995. That year, Hoying also became the first Big Ten player ever to win the Vincent DePaul Draddy Award, given to the top senior scholar-athlete in college football. He played five seasons in the NFL for the Philadelphia Eagles and Oakland Raiders, starting 13 games.

LUKE FICKELL
DEFENSIVE LINEMAN
1992–1996

I GREW UP IN COLUMBUS, and I guess I was always a little daredevil because Mom told me later that I always wanted to be the next Evel Knievel when I grew up. My father is a Vietnam veteran who worked on the railroad for Conrail, and Mom was a beautician. I was the oldest of three kids, with a sister just a year and a half younger and a brother four years younger.

Dad always was a big sports fan, and my uncle was the high school wrestling coach. So once I got into sports, it was natural that wrestling became my first love. I started going to watch matches when I was only eight years old and started wrestling when I was 10.

My first athletic dreams centered on becoming an Olympic wrestling champion.

Then one day in the middle of the winter when I was about nine years old, there was a knock on the door at our home in Westerville, and I opened it. It was John Hicks, all 6'4", 295 pounds of him—the guy was huge. His car had broken down, and I hollered for Dad to come help him. They later became best friends. A year after that, John became one of the assistant coaches for my Pop Warner football team.

My grandfather was the police chief and always sold french fries at the Ohio State football games, and he started taking me with him. I would be underneath the stadium, working the concession stands near the rotunda.

Then John took me to an Ohio State–Michigan game when I was 10, and we got to stand on the sideline when the teams ran out onto the field.

I thought right then, *This is what I want to do someday.*

Our football league was for fourth-, fifth-, and sixth-graders, but I started playing when I was in the third grade, since I was bigger than most of the kids my age. So it was no big deal to me. I was an offensive lineman, and then they moved me to fullback during my final year. I remember coming through the hole too high one day during a demonstration drill, and John lit me up with a blocking dummy, just about knocking me out. I learned real fast that day that you don't come through the hole high.

I eventually moved to tight end as a sophomore. I wasn't real fast, but I had pretty good hands.

As a wrestler, I lost four times as a freshman, but never lost another match from my sophomore through my senior seasons, winning three state championships. Bobby Douglas, the well-known Arizona State wrestling coach, was the first coach to visit me at home. Then Ohio State and Michigan started recruiting me, and I knew I wanted to play both sports in college, but I did not want to go too far from home.

294

When I visited Michigan, I just didn't fit. I tell high school kids all the time these days, "I hope it becomes as easy for you to decide as it was for me."

I came to Ohio State and was hosted by Bobby Hoying. I knew right away that I fit in with the guys at Ohio State. It felt natural to me. It felt right. I was supposed to visit Notre Dame and Penn State, but I knew they would be wasted trips, and it wouldn't have made any difference. I knew where I wanted to go to school and play football and wrestle.

John Cooper had no problem with me wrestling, either. (Later, *I* was the one who had the problem with it.)

I was signed as a tight end, but the coaches moved me to defensive end in fall camp. I remember the first day in pads as a freshman when we were practicing three-on-two drills and I was doing a good job, Cooper kept repeating, "*Do it again! Do it again! Do it again!*" They couldn't move this young guy out of there, and I think it got the coaches' attention that day.

I really have to credit wrestling with making me become a much better football player. It's a one-on-one sport that helps you in the trenches. It helped me mentally and especially with gaining leverage on the guy trying to block me. On the inside, football is such a game of hand-to-hand combat and body positioning.

They quickly moved me inside, and I was playing along with Dan Wilkinson, who was a redshirt freshman. He was just Dan then, not yet "Big Daddy"—we didn't know yet how good he was going to be. In our first game of my freshman year, we were alternating every three plays against Louisville, and in the third quarter, [defensive coordinator] Bill Young came up to me and said, "I think we are going to leave Wilkinson in there for a while."

I thought, *I was wondering how long it was going to take you to figure that out.*

Dan had been moved over from the offensive line and he weighed about 310 pounds then. He was just an animal on the field—they couldn't block him.

I hurt my knee in the next game [against Bowling Green] and had to have it scoped [arthroscopic surgery]. I was out for about four weeks before I started working back into the mix during practices. The coaches told me I could still redshirt as long as I didn't play in four or more games, so I traveled with the team and dressed, but they weren't going to play me unless it became a necessity. It was the best of both worlds for me, because I got a whiff of playing time, traveled to every game that year, and got acclimated but didn't burn a year of eligibility. You don't realize it then, but redshirting can be a great thing.

In mid-January of my sophomore year, I started to realize juggling wrestling and football were too much for me. I would get up for 6:00 AM wrestling workouts, go to classes, have practice that afternoon, lift weights, and then try to study at night. My weight was going down—I probably dropped to 245—and so was my GPA. I had a 2.5 that quarter, the lowest of my college career. It was just too much and took its toll on me—not only the time demand it put on me, but I probably needed to maintain my weight in one sport, and add weight in another. That's a tough thing to do from season to season.

I realized that, to be decent in wrestling, I had to walk away from football and I didn't think that was the right thing to do. I needed to lift [weights] and be with the football team and at that point, my feelings for football overtook my love for wrestling. So I quit the wrestling team.

I started every game as a redshirt freshman [1993], and we rolled to a 10–0–1 record before heading to Michigan.

One disappointment that will always stick with me, no matter what happens in the future, is our performances against Michigan. In three of the four

295

years as a player, we went into the Michigan game undefeated, and yet we won just one game.

I can vividly remember how good it felt to beat them in 1994, celebrating after the game. It picks you up and carries you into the off-season, but those losses in '93, '95, and '96, when we were undefeated each year were just devastating. We had really, really good football players in '95 and were 11–0 but couldn't stop [Tim Biakabutuka]. My kids see that game replayed on the Big Ten Network and say, "That's the game Daddy got run over by Biakabutuka."

In '96 we went to Indiana, and I still can remember every part of it to this day. We had to win to clinch the Big Ten and the Rose Bowl berth, and we were struggling in the fourth quarter when Matt [Finkes] picked up that fumble and ran into the end zone to clinch it for us. The fence in that end zone came crushing down by the weight of Ohio State fans. The trip back to Columbus was great, but the fact is that we probably were not ready to play Michigan the next week. We were No. 1 in the country and led 9–0 at the half, and then got beat 13–9.

Fans remember [cornerback] Shawn Springs' slipping on their only touchdown, but I don't blame Shawn. He was a great cornerback. I just remember the same play they kept running to run out the final four or five minutes of the game—a counter back into the boundary. They just kept pounding Anthony Thomas at us, and we couldn't stop it to get the ball back for the offense.

No matter what happens in the series now, there will never be any love lost for Michigan on my part because of what happened when I was a player.

We still had the Rose Bowl to look forward to, but I tore my [chest] muscle in practice only two days before the game. It was very painful, but the bigger pain was thinking about not being able to play in the game. I didn't want to be out there if it hurt the defense. I got an MRI right away, and it was torn off the bone. I didn't tell anyone at first, but [trainer] Bill Davis knew it. The last thing they told me was, "See if you can handle the pain and tell us what you can do." The last thing I wanted to do was be out there and hurt the team. I mean, I couldn't push 10 pounds with that arm. I couldn't raise my arm above my chest, but they said I couldn't hurt it any worse, so I played.

We were leading 14–10 in the final minutes when [Arizona State quarterback Jake] Plummer scrambled into the end zone. I couldn't get to him, and I think Andy [Katzenmoyer] missed him on a blitz. He then slipped between

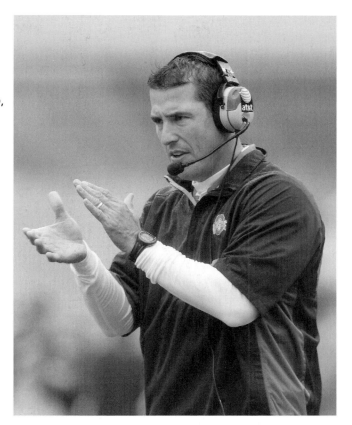

Luke Fickell, who started more consecutive games for Ohio State than any other player (50), served as interim head coach in 2011 and was retained as co–defensive coordinator under Urban Meyer.

Photo courtesy of AP Images

me and the other tackle, and I can still see him diving across the goal line, thinking we just had lost the game.

I hadn't given up hope, but it looked bleak. Then the offense started to move, and we got all of those pass-interference penalties. Once we crossed the 50, I thought we had a chance to kick a field goal to get to overtime. Then we got to the 10, and I thought, *Okay, win it right here.* We already had a field goal blocked, anyway, so the touchdown [a five-yard pass from Joe Germaine to David Boston with 19 seconds remaining] was real sweet. Winning the Rose Bowl was the highlight of my playing career.

I remember sitting there in the locker room, not wanting to take my uniform off for the last time. You just don't want it to end. All these years later, it has become so special to us. Mike Vrabel played 14 years in the NFL and in three Super Bowls, and he realizes how special that time in college was. It is a grind, but it is the journey that you remember forever. You never get that time back or the chance to do it all over again. That's why choosing your college is about as big a decision as you will ever make, just like marriage.

I found my best friends in life at Ohio State—guys like Mike [Vrabel], Bob Hoying, Matt Finkes, and Ryan Miller. I roomed with Mike for four years. I couldn't cook, and he didn't clean, so we made the perfect pair. He would cook, and I would clean up. Then I was the best man at his wedding. Bob was a roommate, too, and he and his wife, Jill, introduced me to my wife, Amy, who is Jill's sister. Now he and I are brothers-in-law, and our kids are the same age and go to school together.

There are so many things I truly love about the Ohio State tradition. I love singing "Carmen Ohio" at the end of each game. That really is an awesome tradition for us. It's become something that not only the football team embraces, but our fans also love. I must admit that when I was in school, I didn't know a word of our alma mater, but I know it by heart now, and my four-year-old son can sing it from memory. That is how much it has become a part of us.

I made a great choice. Ohio State became my home. I hope that I may become a head coach some day, but that will mean leaving, and I know it will be very hard. Right now, I want to work under Coach Meyer and learn as much as I can. This university and this football program are part of my family. I went to school here. I played here. I coached here. My kids don't know anything different than being part of 106,000 fans every Saturday in Ohio Stadium. Ohio State became a large part of me, and I can't say anything greater than that. And it will always be that way.

Luke Fickell is one of the greatest wrestlers in Ohio high school history, winning three consecutive state championships while at DeSales High (1990–1992). In football, he set an Ohio State school record with the most consecutive starts at any position (50). He was part of teams that finished 41–8–1 and played in the Citrus (twice), Holiday, and Rose Bowls. He finished his career with 212 tackles, including 26 for loss. He began his assistant-coaching career in 2002 with Ohio State under head coach Jim Tressel. When Tressel resigned in May of 2011, he was named interim head coach. The Buckeyes finished 6–7 before Fickell was named Ohio State co–defensive coordinator under head coach Urban Meyer.

MATT FINKES

DEFENSIVE END

1993–1996

I GREW UP IN PIQUA, OHIO, and my father was the principal at Piqua High School. As far as sports, I was a wrestler starting in elementary school and then started playing football in the seventh grade. I started as a quarterback and a linebacker, and I suppose I was always the biggest kid on our team.

We had some pretty good teams at Piqua when I played there and always made the playoffs, but we were the smallest school in Division I in the state of Ohio. We may have had 700 kids in the entire school. We lost to Cincinnati Princeton in the playoffs when I was a sophomore, Columbus Brookhaven when I was a junior, and Cincinnati St. Xavier when I was senior; and all of those schools are much, much larger.

I was being recruited as a wrestler by some Ivy League schools and some Big Ten schools such as Purdue and Wisconsin. Then I had a really good junior year in football and began to receive recruiting telephone calls for football. I guess I liked wrestling more, because I had been doing it longer and had a little more confidence in my wrestling ability. I knew I would be able to compete in college and be successful. Up until the day I suited up for that first practice at Ohio State, I questioned whether I would be able to perform at that level in football.

The recruiting process was so different back then. I didn't attend football camps in the summer like the kids do today. I started getting letters from all the schools but didn't have any strong feelings about where I wanted to go.

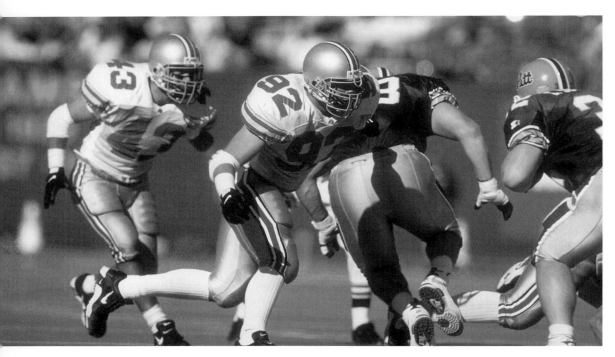

Matt Finkes (92) goes after a Pittsburgh Panthers player during the Buckeyes' 54–14 victory at Pitt Stadium on September 23, 1995. *Photo courtesy of Getty Images*

I was never a big fan of any college football team while I was growing up, and I wasn't a diehard Ohio State fan by any means. I probably rooted for the Wilmington College Quakers harder than any other team because my dad [Heinz Finkes, an All-American at Wilmington College in 1974 who was later inducted into the school's athletic hall of fame] played there, and the Bengals had their camp there in the summers. Dad would get us into the camp and go behind the scenes, so I became a Bengals fan, too.

I went to the spring games at Ohio State and Notre Dame, and [Ohio State assistant coach Bill] Young came to see me play in our final playoff game at the University of Dayton. I talked to him, and we set up an official visit to Columbus. I had a wrestling meet on a Friday, arrived on campus on Saturday afternoon, and packed a full visit into a day and a half. I knew Bobby and Tommy Hoying, and they were there that weekend, and I got to be friends with them. Mike Vrabel had been there the week before, and we were all going to play in the North-South All-Star Game. We all got to talking, and

I was asking about their intentions. They were all sold on Ohio State, and I felt very comfortable with those guys. I remain close friends with them to this day, along with Luke Fickell.

I also had visited Notre Dame, but I wasn't comfortable there. It's nothing bad about Coach [Lou] Holtz, but my personality didn't match his personality. Michigan came late to the party and started recruiting me after I committed to Ohio State. In the end, I wanted to stay close to home, too, so my family could see me play. My father had never missed a sporting event of mine—be it football, wrestling, or track—all through high school, and he continued that trend through college.

When I first arrived at Ohio State, there wasn't a lot of pressure to play right away, and I was thinking I would redshirt. I weighed 215 as a high school senior and was undersized as a freshman, but I started to put on weight once I was finished with wrestling. I spent the year working really hard on my strength and size, and I soon realized I could play with guys at this level. You take a lot of knocks as a true freshman going against older guys, especially in the trenches, but once you are able to earn their respect, you know you have made it.

As it turned out, I played more than any other true freshman that year, 1993. I know one thing: wrestling helped my football skills immensely. It translates very well to the offensive and defensive linemen as far as leverage, balance, and technique. Wrestling teaches you so much about discipline, weight management, and how to practice. I had a wrestling coach named Ron McCunn in junior high, and his favorite saying was, "Discipline is doing what you don't want to do when you don't want to do it."

That phrase got me through many two-a-day practices at Ohio State and in the NFL—and is still a philosophy I try to instill in the kids I coach today.

After one week of practice, they moved me from defensive end to the interior. I remember [strength coach Dave] Kennedy feeding me any kind of milkshake to put weight on me, and I put on 25 pounds that year.

Coach Young had told me before we played Rice [a 34–7 win] in the season opener, "Be ready, because you will get to play. Just relax, and you will be fine." On the first play I got into, I broke free, and I could hear the crowd roar as I made a tackle for a loss. That is probably the only time I ever heard the crowd when I played.

When we played at Purdue later that season, I got blocked so far out of the action on one play that I shouldn't have been a factor, but Craig Powell blitzed and hit the quarterback, and the football blew out of there and landed at my feet. I just fell on it for a touchdown. That was incredible. Most defensive guys don't get to score a touchdown in their lives, but I scored two—as I will get to later.

As the 1994 season started, they told me I would be starting at defensive end, but I was experiencing some shoulder problems: I had a huge calcium deposit at the end of my collarbone, and they told me I could have surgery immediately and redshirt, or I could wait until the end of the season since the injury wouldn't get any worse. I just wanted to block out the pain, gut it out, and play through it, so I did.

Mike Vrabel was on the other side, and we were both sophomores, both undersized at 250 pounds or so and facing tackles 315 pounds all the time. I think we caught a lot of people by surprise that year. That style of defensive end was just coming into vogue at the time. The Florida States and Miamis were having great success with smaller, faster ends, but you didn't see it in the Big Ten.

We had lost at Washington and to Illinois and got blown out at Penn State [63–14, the worst loss in school history], so not many people gave us a chance to beat Michigan. Rumors were going around that this would be it for Coach Cooper if we lost to Michigan again.

For the people who think Coach Cooper never had the passion or knew what the rivalry was about, I think he understood it that day. He gave us a passionate pregame speech and then destroyed a blackboard at halftime. He went into the Woody Hayes/Earle Bruce mode and took us to another level. I had a couple of sacks and a few tackles for loss, and it was the greatest feeling. Nobody was going to beat us that day, especially not Michigan. I still have a picture of my sack on Michigan's final play hanging over my desk [a 22–6 win].

I didn't realize I had set the Ohio State single-season sack record [11] until a reporter told me after the Michigan game. Then Mike went and had two sacks in the Citrus Bowl against Alabama to break my record, but he and I never paid attention to any of those numbers. We just wanted to win.

Our expectations were sky high in 1995. We had Bobby Hoying, Terry Glenn, Eddie George, and Orlando Pace on offense and almost the entire defense back. We destroyed Boston College [38–6] in the Kickoff Classic, and a few games later, the entire country was talking about our home game against Notre Dame. That was one of those games where I did notice the crowd. It was an amazing atmosphere that day, and the offense was unstoppable [in a 45–26 win].

We were 4–0 and had to play in Happy Valley for the second straight year. We just had been beaten 63–14 there the year before, and everybody knows Ohio State just doesn't get beat like that. I was looking forward to that game for a year. We were outgunned the year before—they had Kerry Collins, Ki-Jana Carter, Bobby Ingram, and all those stars. Now it was our turn. I remember Ricky Dudley making this great catch in between three Penn State guys on a third-and-long, and we scored late to win the game [28–25]. That was a sweet win for us.

We went to Ann Arbor with an 11–0 record and ranked No. 2, and it was just one of those things. It was their day. We couldn't do anything to stop them. That team was as talented as any at Ohio State in a long, long time, but we couldn't beat Michigan, and we couldn't stop Biakabutuka. [Tim Biakabutuka rushed for 313 yards in a 31–23 Ohio State loss.]

People ask me what happened that day. They lined up with two tight ends and ran the inside zone play and the counter all day long. We got behind and got to the point where guys were trying something extra to make plays and getting out of position. Whatever we tried, they had an answer. Whatever adjustment we made, they made a better adjustment. It was unbelievably frustrating.

303

The Citrus Bowl that followed was the only letdown game we ever had at Ohio State when I played there. Everybody felt like we should have been playing in Pasadena for the national championship. Instead we were playing against Tennessee in Orlando in the rain and mud. Everything about that game was a bad movie. The only thing good was that I sacked Peyton Manning twice, but when you don't win, it doesn't mean anything. [Tennessee won 20–14.]

We lost so many stars from that team that everyone on the outside said, "That was your shot at a national title," and nobody expected much from us in 1996. I think we were ranked very low [No. 10 in the Associated Press preseason poll], but I knew we had eight or so guys back on defense…guys with big hearts like Greg Bellisari, Rob Kelly, Ty Howard, Mike, and Luke. We had a chip on our shoulders and knew we would have a good defense, but we'd lost most of our offensive stars.

We won our first two games, 70–7 over Rice and 72–0 over Pittsburgh, so easily with these new guys on offense that we got people's attention. The next game, at Notre Dame in a rematch, was a really neat experience. It's a great place to play and a greater place to win. I still felt we had something to prove, even though we'd beaten them the year before. We ended up playing a great game and winning again [29–16].

We rolled to 10–0, and all we had to do to clinch the Big Ten championship and Rose Bowl berth was win at Indiana. And it proved to be much tougher than anyone thought. We were tied 10–10 with less than seven minutes remaining, and Indiana was driving on us when their quarterback dropped back to pass. I pressured him out of the pocket from our left side but lost sight of him when he scrambled to the other side of the field. I took an angle to get to where I thought he might be. When I came around a pile of people, Andy [Katzenmoyer] had wrapped him up, and the ball popped out. I just picked it up and started running. It seemed like it took forever. It was like living in a dream. I couldn't believe it actually happened.

That touchdown [of 45 yards] gave us the lead, and we ended up winning 27–17 to clinch a trip to the Rose Bowl.

Here's the neat story about that play: after I returned the fumble for the touchdown, I dropped the ball, and the guys tackled me in the end zone. We were celebrating in a pile, but there was still a lot of time left. This kid jumped over the fence, grabbed the football, and ran back into the stands. I saw it later on our game film. After the game, we couldn't get off the field because all of the Ohio State fans were celebrating the clinching of the Rose Bowl, and this kid came up to me, pulled the football from underneath his shirt, and handed it to me as a gift. I have it today on my mantle, and it has the Indiana logo on it because it was their ball.

Years later, I was about to play a round of golf at Little Turtle Country Club outside of Columbus when a bag boy grabbed my clubs from my trunk and took them to the 1st tee for me. He asked, "Remember me? I am the guy who gave you the ball at Indiana." I sent him a jersey and an autographed football. I always thought that was a neat thing for him to do.

Michigan came to Columbus the next week, as we had the Rose Bowl already locked up. I really don't think we celebrated too much from the week before or were complacent, either. We led 9–0 at the half and just didn't put them away. We had played with our corners matching up one-on-one outside, and as everyone knows, Shawn Springs slipped and we gave up the long touchdown that beat us [13–9], but that is the defense we played the whole year. Shawn was a lockdown corner and a great player. I just wish we could have scored one more touchdown.

Our teams finished 1–3 against Michigan, and I agree with the people who say that it became a mental thing. It absolutely became a mental block for us. When somebody has your number—whether it be in wrestling, baseball, basketball, or football—doubt creeps into your mind when something bad happens. A huge part of sports is confidence.

Knowing we would still play in the Rose Bowl took a lot of the sting out of the Michigan game, though. We would be playing against Coach Cooper's old team in Arizona State, but it seemed everything was working against us before the game: our practice field was absolutely terrible, Luke tore a [chest] muscle in practice, and Orlando [Pace] was sick all week. As we got closer to the game, I think we calmed down.

It was a back-and-forth game, and when Jake Plummer scored [to put ASU ahead 17–14 with 1:40 remaining], I looked up at the crowd and saw some Ohio State fans leaving. I was still confident we would mount some type of scoring drive to at least tie the game. Joe Germaine did an excellent job on that final drive, and every Buckeye remembers his touchdown pass to David Boston that capped the comeback. Watching that Rose Bowl clock hit double-zero was one of the highlights of my career, along with beating Michigan in my sophomore year and the fumble return at Indiana. I got great pictures from all those moments.

As a player, sometimes you don't realize what a special thing Ohio State football is until you have been removed from it for a few years. I go back to games now, sit in the stands, take part in the Tunnel of Pride, see the fans' passion, watch the band come out of the tunnel…all of that brings tears to my eyes. One of my greatest pleasures and greatest honors now is when someone will come up to me and say, "I really enjoyed watching you play."

To know that you have made an impression on someone like that and brought them joy is a great feeling. Now that I am older and more mature, I realize what an incredible thing it is. And to be a part of it, to be a part of that Ohio State family, is unbelievably special to me.

Matt Finkes finished his career with 162 tackles, 25 sacks, and 59 tackles for loss, including 20 in 1994. He was named All–Big Ten in 1994, '95, and '96, and also was named an All-American and Ohio State's Defensive Most Valuable Player in '96. In addition, he was a two-time Citrus Bowl Defensive MVP.

JOE GERMAINE

QUARTERBACK

1996–1998

FOR A WHOLE YEAR, MY FAMILY kept the tape of the message. It was John Cooper's voice. He had called my home, but we were out, and he just said, "Joe, just cancel all your recruiting trips…we want you to be a Buckeye." It was fun for me and my family to replay it and hear those words over and over again.

I was from Phoenix, and I had played one year at Scottsdale Community College, where I had set several junior-college passing records. One game against Arizona Western, I completed 49 of 60 for more than 600 yards, and we really couldn't figure out why I didn't have more offers. I visited Wyoming and Nevada-Reno, but Arizona State and the University of Arizona told me I could walk on. To this day, my family still wonders about it.

Then Larry Coker from Ohio State recruited me. He was the defensive backs coach at the time and then got appointed quarterbacks coach, so I was really excited about that. But suddenly, he left for Miami [to become offensive coordinator], and I remember talking to him over the phone, asking him, "What am I going to do now?" He said, "Joe, you need to be a Buckeye."

I never second-guessed my decision once I got to Ohio State in 1995. Walt Harris had arrived as quarterbacks coach after Coach Coker left, and I have to credit Coach Harris with my development. Bobby Hoying had a great year at quarterback while I redshirted, and I feel that year helped prepare me for the next three.

Right away, I really liked the campus. Those old stone and brick buildings with so much history…being from Arizona, I loved how green everything was. Believe it or not, I always liked the winter—I really thought the cold and snow were great.

During my redshirt year, before practice one Friday, President Clinton was giving a speech across the street at the Fawcett Center. Somebody came in and mentioned to us that the president would be driving down Olentangy River Road and we could walk out to greet him. We were strictly told not to bring anything with us. Later, somebody announced that he was leaving the Fawcett Center and now was our chance. In a hurry, we left the Woody Hayes Center and were walking out to the street. I realized then that I had a football in my hands, so I tucked it under my shirt. Well, we lined up along the street, and the president got out of the motorcade and started to shake our hands. I didn't know what do with this football, but I pulled it out and all of a sudden there were three Secret Service guys in my face. The president said, "Oh, you want me to sign that?" He signed it, and then Al Gore signed it, too. I later gave it to my roommate in Morrill Tower.

That following spring, Bobby Hoying was gone, so the quarterbacking job was down to me, Stanley Jackson, and Mark Garcia, another junior-college transfer whom Coach Harris had recruited personally. I think that is the time I really progressed, even though I was getting two repetitions to their four.

At the spring game, it turned out that the last rotation of the game was my turn. We drove down to the 5-yard line, and we had time left for one play. I threw this fade to Dee Miller, and he kept his feet in bounds and made the catch in the corner of the end zone. That sort of got the ball rolling for my career.

Mark Garcia had injured his knee, so he would miss the whole season. Then, as everybody knows, Stanley Jackson and I rotated for the next two seasons. There wasn't a set time when I would come in, and I definitely would have liked to have played more, but I didn't want to start any controversy. And there wasn't any, as far as the team was concerned. There was competition, but we got along fine. The coaches told us in camp, "Whoever separates himself from the other will get to play." I guess they really didn't think anybody stood out, so they just decided to play both of us.

Joe Germaine looks downfield against Minnesota in 1998.

I was never sure what the fans thought back then, if they ever favored one over the other, but I did receive a lot of support. The Ohio State fans were just great to me. All the same, I wonder what I would have done if I would have played more. For example, against Wisconsin, we were behind in the third quarter, and I threw an out route to Dimitrious Stanley, who made a guy miss and turned it into a touchdown. *Now we're rolling*, I thought.

But I got taken out, and I didn't play the rest of the game.

As the year went on and we won each game, I was keeping track of the Pac-10, and I knew that ASU was having a good year. I kept thinking that it would be ironic if we played my hometown team in the Rose Bowl. It couldn't have worked out any better.

The week we clinched the Big Ten, we played at Indiana. It had been so many years since Ohio State had played in a Rose Bowl, and there was a lot of pressure. Late in the game, we were leading Indiana in a close game [20–17], and I remember Matt Keller and I fumbling the exchange on a hand-off. I remember diving on the ball and all these linemen and linebackers landed on me. One of them told me, "Man, you guys are losing it."

A couple of plays later, Andy Katzenmoyer caused a fumble that Matt Finkes picked up and ran into the end zone to clinch it.

Even though we lost to Michigan the next week, we still went to the Rose Bowl to play Arizona State. Their quarterback, Jake Plummer, scrambled for that touchdown to put us behind 17–14, and there was just a little more than a minute [1:40] remaining.

The coaches had to make a decision about who was going to go in at quarterback. Later, I had heard the story: Mike Jacobs was the acting offensive coordinator because Coach Harris had already accepted the Pittsburgh job, but he had stayed to coach us through the Rose Bowl. When they came to deciding who would go in on that final drive, there was dead silence. Coach Jacobs didn't say anything. Finally, Coach Harris told them, "We've got to go with Germaine."

They just pointed to me and said, "Get out there."

We had practiced that two-minute drill each Friday all year. I got into the huddle and there wasn't a lot of talking. We just weren't going to let the game end like that. We had good field position to start, at the 35-yard line. We hit a couple of crucial third-and-longs, and then came the big play. We were on the 5-yard line, and we sent Dimitrious Stanley to the slot on the right and David Boston out wide to the right. The primary receiver was supposed to be Dimitrious, who would run a corner route. David would run inside on a hitch and then back toward the pylon. As I dropped back, I could tell they had Dimitrious defensed. They had cut him off. I looked down at Boston, and he was wide open. We won 20–17.

Being the Rose Bowl MVP, I couldn't describe a better ending. I will never forget standing up on that podium after the game with Orlando Pace and the seniors like Greg Bellisari, Luke Fickell, and Mike Vrabel. Those guys had always treated me well.

It was different to have the freedom in 1998, not to have to look over my shoulder. Stanley was gone, and I was now the starting quarterback. I think it was good for the team, too. They could get used to my style of play and not worry about who was in the game.

The Michigan State game that year was the only real disappointment of my Ohio State career. We were ranked No. 1 and were leading them 24–9, when…I still don't know what happened. I think we just tried to run out the clock and sit on the ball. It was just one of those things. That [28–24] loss cost us a national championship. We had some big dreams that year, but we still beat Michigan.

I will never forget being announced and running through that tunnel of former players before the Michigan game. All my family was there to see it.

I honestly can't think of a better place to go to school and play football. Ohio State was second to none. Buckeyes fans are the greatest in the world, and even though I came from Arizona, I am definitely a Buckeye.

Joe Germaine, the Big Ten's MVP in 1998, holds 12 Ohio State passing records, including most passing yards in a season (3,330), completions in a season (230), and 300-yard passing games in a season (seven). He played in the NFL for the St. Louis Rams, Kansas City Chiefs, and Cincinnati Bengals.

The
NEW
MILLENNIUM

JONATHAN WELLS
RUNNING BACK
1998–2001

BEING FROM RIVER RIDGE, LOUISIANA, the SEC schools and Louisiana schools like LSU and Tulane wanted me to play football, but my mind was always elsewhere. I remember watching TV and seeing Eddie George running through holes at Ohio State, and that was the image that stuck with me. I remember in 1995 when the Buckeyes beat Notre Dame and Illinois and Eddie had huge games. That team had Terry Glenn and Orlando Pace, and they put up a lot of points and made me an Ohio State fan.

I could have gone to Tulane and been the king of campus, or I could have gone to LSU and been a linebacker, but I didn't want to stay home—I wanted to go to Ohio State and be a running back.

When I first saw Ohio Stadium and the campus, I admit that I was in awe. I had never been away from home. That first day, I met Derek Ross and we became roommates for the next three years. Today, he is my best friend. My first real memory is coming up early before my freshman season and having [strength] coach Dave Kennedy put us through running and conditioning drills. I couldn't believe how tough it was. I stopped at one point, and he told me that if I ever stopped again, I may as well go home to New Orleans.

In that first game in '98, my first as a Buckeye, I scored a touchdown at West Virginia, and it was a huge thrill. We had such a great season that year but lost in that fluke game to Michigan State. We capped that season off in the Sugar Bowl, and I did get to go home to New Orleans. I had about 50

Jonathan Wells looks for a hole against Purdue in 2001.

friends and family there and got to carry seven times in the second half as we beat Texas A&M. That was a great thrill for a freshman.

I remember when we got back to campus after that game, I was so excited because it was the first time I got to see snow. We had a few inches on the ground, and there were a few guys in my class who had never seen it before, either, so we went out and played "snow football" without our shirts on.

I didn't redshirt that first season, and as it turned out, I would have been part of the 2002 national championship team if I had. But I have no regrets about that decision. I believe everything is done for a reason, and I was on the sideline at the Fiesta Bowl that night. I felt just as tired and as drained after that game as if I had played. That is the thing I learned—that you sweat and bleed for the guys you played with.

The one thing that was special at Ohio State is that the running backs all stuck together, even though we were competing against each other in a way. We pulled for each other. I never started every game until my senior year, because of injuries or for not always doing things right off the field, and I understand that. That is part of the great tradition that we have, and that's why I went there in the first place.

When we had the transition of coaches [when John Cooper was fired in January 2001], the whole thing was made a breeze and made very simple for me because of one man: Jim Tressel. I am glad Coach Tressel gave me the opportunity. He just told me straight up, "I'll give you an opportunity to do it, and it's up to you." It was all business with him, and I knew it was my last go-round. He just told me how to get it done. I really want to thank him for putting it on my shoulders.

I have to mention Coach [Tim] Spencer. He was hard on me at times, but I really appreciate him today. He got on me pretty good, but I knew it was to make me better, and I never took it personally.

One of my best memories is that night game against Northwestern [139 yards rushing]. I had been benched the week before against Indiana, and after that, my season was totally different. Coach Spencer sat me down and asked me, "If the season ended now, where would you be drafted?"

I answered, "In the fifth or sixth round."

He said, "No, the scouts who come in here say you wouldn't be drafted—you would be a free agent."

I was under a little stress at that point, and I just decided to play hard every down. Then in the Northwestern game, I broke loose on that run [71 yards], and things worked out for me after that. Against Illinois, I had gained 192 yards, but we lost. It was our last day in the stadium, and after the game, I just sat there and cried for about 15 minutes. I couldn't believe it was coming to an end like that.

But the next week was nothing but a pleasant memory. Under Coach Tressel, we had started preparing for the Michigan game back in the spring. When he was hired, we started watching tape on Michigan right away. He let us know that this was not a regular game, and it seemed like it was always on our mind. I liked the way he was confident about it, too. I think he knew he could come in and turn things around in the rivalry, and he put the pressure on himself by telling the crowd at the basketball game the day he was hired.

I took that game personally. I was a senior, it was my final game, and I considered myself a leader, so having three touchdowns in that first half up there was huge. Then my whole lower body cramped up, and I couldn't play in the second half. The important thing was that we won the game, and my class ended up with two wins over Michigan.

You know, it took me until my senior year to get the whole tradition thing at Ohio State down. We learned the alma mater and the fight song, and we wrote letters to our parents, and everything seemed to come alive my senior year. I really feel like I am part of the big picture at Ohio State now. I have no regrets at all, and I wouldn't change a thing if I could.

I am from Louisiana, I am living in Texas, but I love Ohio State.

Jonathan Wells, who rushed for 1,294 yards and 16 touchdowns in earning team MVP honors in 2001, was selected in the fourth round of the 2002 NFL Draft by the Houston Texans. He led the Texans in rushing during his rookie season. He played four seasons with the Texans.

CIE GRANT

LINEBACKER

1999–2002

MY DREAM BEGAN WHEN I WAS a quarterback coming out of New Philadelphia High School, and I was considering going to either Michigan or Michigan State. Jim Roman was an assistant coach on my high school team, and he was a member of Ohio State's 1968 national championship team. He just told me, "No, no, you just take your visit to Ohio State…just go to one game." I said, "Why? I know I am not going there." But I went to the ['97] Illinois game and had a real good feeling, and so did my parents.

Coach Cooper convinced me this was the best place for me.

I remember when I first got here, thinking how big this campus was. *Dang, I thought, this is a lot of walking, especially in the wintertime.* Then they showed us the bus system, and I learned to get around.

I redshirted during that '98 season, and now as I look back at it, with or without the national championship, it was the best thing for me. I hated to waste a whole year just playing special teams, and as it turned out, I am really thankful for that decision.

I started practices as a safety and then went to linebacker in the spring of 2000. That year was a crazy time. We lost to Michigan and then at the Outback Bowl, and they decided to go in a different direction, firing Coach Cooper. We had to get ready for winter conditioning, and we didn't know who the coach would be, but I remember [strength coach] Dave Kennedy working us out, telling us, "Don't worry, they'll bring a good coach in here. Just stay in shape."

We were coming off an 8–4 season, and we knew there was plenty of room for improvement.

After Coach Tressel got the job, he really made a good impression in that first meeting. He had a certain confidence about himself, and he said right away, "We are going to work to be the best." We all left that meeting and said, "Let's give him a chance."

He had given us something called "The Block 'O' of Life," which outlined goals of family, football, and education. What struck me was that he wasn't just a football coach—he wanted to know everything about you.

Later, we each had one-on-one meetings with him, and I told him, "I am a junior, and most of my work has been on special teams. I just want a chance to play. I need the opportunity because my time is closing. I don't want you to give me anything, just the opportunity."

He promised me he would.

Late that summer, I had missed one of our senior's presentations in front of the team. The seniors give reports on themselves to the entire team, and I missed Mike Collins'. Coach Tressel asked me, "How are we going to punish you? I know, you have to sing 'Carmen Ohio' in front of the team."

317

I had sung in the church choir a little, and he had made us learn all the school songs after he was hired. So I sang "Carmen Ohio" in front of the team that day—and I ended up singing it each Friday night in front of the team before our next game.

That fall, I was behind Joe Cooper at linebacker, and I asked [defensive coordinator Mark] Dantonio if I could get a chance to get on the field with the nickel [coverage] package. He said, "We'll see how you do in the nickel in practice." So I did pretty well, and then I did pretty well in one-on-one coverage, and they pulled me aside. "We're going to try you at corner," he told me.

Now this is only a week or two before the opening game. I went to corner, played well, and started 10 out of those 12 games. I got beat some games, such as that touchdown pass in the Wisconsin game, and the media was on me some, but at the end of the season, I ended up playing pretty well.

When we beat Michigan at Ann Arbor, it was just one of the greatest feelings I had experienced. We celebrated down in that corner with all of our fans, and to see most of those 111,000 fans quiet and dumfounded, we were

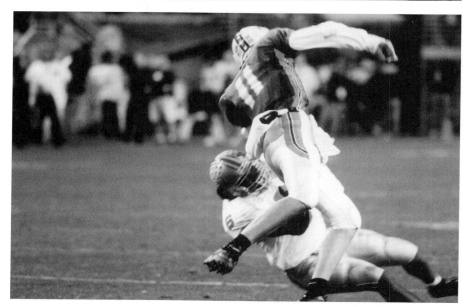

Cie Grant wraps his hands around Miami quarterback Ken Dorsey on the final play of the 2003 Fiesta Bowl, which brought the Buckeyes their first national championship in 34 years.

overwhelmed with emotion. Michigan had talked before the game about Michigan State being their rivalry now, not Ohio State.

In the locker room, Coach Tressel told us, "Now this one feels good, but we got to do it again next year."

I think what happened in 2002 actually began in the second half of the Outback Bowl. We were getting embarrassed 28–0 by South Carolina, and I looked over at [linebacker] Courtland Bullard. He said, "It's not about the fans, it's not about the coaches…it's about us. We have to play for pride—starting now!"

We came back and tied it and had the opportunity to win, but something changed in that second half.

Then, leading up to the season opener against Texas Tech, we had a players-only meeting. I told everybody, "I've been on a really good Ohio State team (that '98 team when I redshirted was one game from winning the national championship) and then a 6–6 team that didn't go anywhere for a bowl. We came to Ohio State for one reason. We want to win the national championship. I feel like we have what it takes to do it."

Coach Dantonio and I had talked, and we agreed it would be best for the team if I switched back to linebacker. That way, we would be able to disguise coverages and do so many things.

We all decided from the beginning to take one game at a time. It sounds like a cliché, but that's what we really did very well. Once we won our first seven games, nobody expected us to go to Wisconsin and win. After that game, we thought, *Yes, now we're on to something.* After beating Penn State at home, we said, "Yes, we can do this."

Then Coach Tressel told us, "Champions go undefeated in the month of November." We had Minnesota, Purdue, Illinois, and Michigan left. In that Purdue game, we were facing fourth-and-1 with the game on the line, and we went for it all. Craig Krenzel to Michael Jenkins. That's the kind of team we had. We took chances. And then we beat Illinois in overtime and Michigan again when the stadium was as loud as ever.

What can I say about our defense? We just knew that anybody at any time could come up with the big play. We were all capable of it. One time it would be Mike Doss. The next would be Donnie Nickey, or Kenny Peterson, or Will Smith, or Matt Wilhelm…I could go on and on.

The week before the Fiesta Bowl, you would have thought Miami was out there just for the joy of it. It was a given that they would be crowned national champions again. But we didn't go out there to roll over. We practiced like we knew we had to dominate that game. We practiced all week at game speed. And we knew that Miami did not really know how good our defense was.

Before the game, in the locker room, Coach Tressel told us, "Seize this opportunity. If you are a junior, sophomore, or a freshman, don't think you'll ever get here again and have another chance. This is it! Seize it! It has been 34 years since Ohio State last won a national championship. Know that you are playing for all of Ohio State's fans, alumni, and former players. Now go do it!"

I remember walking through that tunnel, and the adrenaline was pumping so much. I came out of the tunnel, and it was just like a home game. It was overwhelming. There was scarlet and gray everywhere. In pregame, I got so worked up that I couldn't breathe. I saw Eddie George, David Boston, and Jonathan Wells on the sideline. As the game went on, I would look over at those guys and hear them yell, "Come on!" We may not know each other on a personal level, but we knew that anybody who had ever worn the scarlet and gray was rooting for us that night.

There were so many big plays during that game. I remember Craig getting hit by their linebacker so hard, most quarterbacks wouldn't have gotten up. I remember Maurice Clarett stripping the ball on that interception. I remember Matt driving Ken Dorsey into the ground.

It came down to the final play, and when we got the call for our defense, I knew it was my play. I had stayed in the coaches' ears all night, "Bring me on the blitz, bring me on the blitz!" That was the call. I was thinking to myself, "This is big, this is big, this is really big." I remember seeing their tackle line up and thinking, *He can't stop me.* Then they brought some short motion, and I thought they might try to block me that way. There was a single back in the backfield, and I thought he might be the one assigned to me. I wondered why there was no tight end over there on my side. All these things were going through my head before the snap. I got the best jump on that snap that I ever had in my life. It was just me and Dorsey, and I told myself, *Don't miss him…just don't miss him.* So many times you see a guy who has a kill shot at the quarterback, and he ends up missing him.

I grabbed him and got him to the ground, and I saw that he didn't have the ball, but I didn't know what happened. I couldn't hear anything, but then I saw all the coaches running toward me. It wasn't until Coach [Mark] Snyder ran up to me that I realized it was over and we had won the national championship.

I just wanted to shout, "We are the champs! When we wake up tomorrow, we will be the champs! We will always be the champs!"

One of my fondest memories of the whole season will be our celebration in Ohio Stadium a few weeks later. On the bus ride over to the stadium, a few of the coaches asked me if I was going to sing "Carmen Ohio." I said, "My last time singing in front of anybody was the night before the Miami game." Then Craig Krenzel came up and asked me again. He wanted to get it on tape. I really didn't want to do it. Finally, during the ceremony, Mr. [Andy] Geiger said, "Would Cie Grant come to the front, please?" I told the other seniors, "We've always had each other's backs, so you got my back today. Don't let me down." It was cold and I hadn't warmed up my voice, but the rest is history. I am very glad I did it.

Who would have thought it would become a YouTube favorite all these years later?

This place means so much to me, I can't begin to put it into words. It's the winning tradition, the family, the teammates who I will remember until I am 70 years old. I will always be a big Buckeyes fan. I think all of us will bleed scarlet and gray for the rest of our lives.

Cie Grant had 71 tackles in 2002, including 10 for loss of yardage. He finished his career with 146 tackles and the most important quarterback pressure in Ohio State history. He was drafted in the third round of the 2003 NFL Draft by the New Orleans Saints, with whom he played four seasons.

KENNY PETERSON
DEFENSIVE LINEMAN
1999–2002

I GREW UP SORT OF UNUSUAL in the fact that I was never one of those guys who followed sports. I didn't follow college football or the NFL, so I never knew much about Ohio State. I am not ashamed to say that I was a big momma's boy, and when it came time to choose a college, I didn't want to go too far from my mom and family. I committed to Ohio State very early, at the end of my junior year in high school. I went to the football game at OSU, and Coach Pagac and Coach Cooper both told me, "Whenever you want to be a Buckeye, the invitation is open." Right then, I made my decision. In my senior season at Canton McKinley, I was a part of the team with Jamar Martin and Mike Doss that finished 14–0 and won the state and national championships.

When I arrived in Columbus, it was my first experience of living on my own, without my mom. It felt like freedom, but a scary kind of freedom. After the first few days of practice, I wanted to go home. I remember that after one afternoon practice, I was lying across the field inside at the Woody Hayes Athletic Center, and Jamar Martin was sitting on a bench with LeCharles Bentley. I looked up and said, "Man, Jamar, I am hurting!"

Jamar said, "My whole body hurts!"

LeCharles said, "I want to go home!"

We all wanted to go home. Then we all tried to figure out some injuries we had to get us out of practice…it was rough. We were ready to get right

Kenny Peterson sacks Miami quarterback Ken Dorsey during the 2003 Fiesta Bowl.

back on I-71 and head north to get back home. When I redshirted that season [1998], it was like falling off the face of the earth. I went from a highly touted high school player and from being an All-American to feeling like a nobody. We would come off the practice field, and these reporters would be there, and they would walk right past me. Nobody wanted to talk to me.

I got very discouraged, because I wanted to contribute. I didn't want people back home saying, "I knew he wasn't good enough to play at Ohio State."

One thing that really picked me up was when I found out that Cie Grant was my cousin. I knew I had relatives in New Philadelphia, but I didn't know Cie. Our moms got to talking, and we found out we were second cousins.

Anyway, by redshirting, I concentrated on my schoolwork, and I had a 3.2 GPA after my first year. As it turned out, I valued that year so much, and I learned the game of football.

There is no doubt that our class had some real tough times—the whole process of Coop [being fired], and then we didn't know who our coach would be. But that period brought us together as a team. At that point, all we had was each other. I have always been a firm believer that everything happens for a reason.

When I heard the name Jim Tressel, I knew we would be okay. I had several friends in high school who had played for him [at Youngstown State]. They told me that he was a great guy, and they said, "He will kill you with kindness." When he came in that first day, he met with us and didn't say one thing about football. It was kind of shocking to me—he came in and described what it took to be a champion and the importance of an education, our spiritual life, and how to be a good person. He hit on everything other than football, and that really impressed me. He said something like, "We want to be the class of college football, we want to be respected, and these people in this room will be a family."

He constantly stressed it was all about "we" and "team." It wasn't about "me" or "I." He had us read the book *Expanding Your Horizons*, about the 1942 national champion Ohio State team. He said, "This is part of the tradition." We always sang the fight song after games, and I knew we had an alma mater, but I never heard it until Coach Tressel came here. I never knew the words. Do you know what goes through my mind now when I hear "Carmen Ohio"? It almost brings tears to my eyes. Just thinking about it now, I am getting goose bumps on my arms.

Coach Tressel's game plan was this: "All great teams have to be perfect at home. After that, our goal is to become Big Ten champions. Then, we will compete for the national championship."

Before games, Coach Tressel wasn't the type to give rah-rah speeches. He would pace the floor back and forth like he was about to go out and play. And he was always encouraging. He would look at me before games and say, "Let's go, K.P.! Let's go, K.P.!" We would always say the Lord's Prayer and another prayer that got me so fired up. It went like this: "I am only one, but I am one. I can't do everything, but I can do something. What I can do, I ought to do. What I ought to do, by the grace of God, I shall do."

After the Washington State game, we knew what kind of caliber of team we had. I think we all realized that we had a good shot of doing what we did. We all believed that it wasn't about each individual—it was about us. Then we had so many nail-biters as the year went on. Mike Doss and I both talked about how it reminded us of Canton McKinley. We had so many close games and won the high school national championship.

In the past, bowl practices weren't the most crisp practices of them all. But at the Fiesta Bowl, we wanted to learn and improve every moment. We practiced at a fast pace, and we knew we had a group of guys who weren't going to be denied. When you get a group of guys willing to do whatever it takes, there is nothing else left but to succeed.

When we went out for warm-ups that night, we knew it was a home game. We were thousands of miles from home, but we felt like we were home. Everybody was so jacked up and ready to go. We were not being coached to come from behind, we were being coached to smack them in the mouth.

We didn't change anything about the way we played. We played physical and tried to dominate Miami from the start. I remember I got my first sack against [Miami center Brett] Romberg pretty early, and I knew right away we could play with them. Before that final play of the game, I was looking at everybody in the huddle, and I turned to Mike Doss, Donnie Nickey, and Dustin Fox. I said, "Let's go; this is what we've been waiting for." They were looking back through their face masks, and I could tell that they really wanted it. We had 11 heartbeats beating as one, and when it was over, I didn't know whether to cry or jump for joy. I didn't know my reaction until I watched the film—I started to walk off the field to the bench, but I turned around and saw David Thompson, and he had shouted, "We did it! We did it!" At that point, it started to sink in.

We all had been through so many ups and downs—to finish it like that is something you just can't describe. It seems like yesterday that I can reach out and touch the time I left my mom's house to head to Columbus.

That program means a lot to me. I can honestly say that if I had to do it all over again, I would do exactly the same thing. I have absolutely no regrets. Now I am so thankful that I did redshirt. I learned so much about myself in those five years. I learned how to be a man, and I matured so much. I don't know if I would have experienced those things at any other university.

I will always be a Buckeye.

Kenny Peterson, who had two quarterback sacks in the 2003 Fiesta Bowl, was drafted in the third round of the 2003 NFL Draft by the Green Bay Packers and played seven seasons in the NFL for the Packers and Denver Broncos.

CRAIG KRENZEL

QUARTERBACK

1999–2003

I PLAYED JUST ABOUT EVERY SPORT growing up in Sterling Heights, Michigan, which is an hour northeast of Detroit. It is the typical suburban, middle-class town—nice, clean, and a great place to grow up. My family still lives there.

My first sport was soccer, and I moved on to football, basketball, and baseball, but there were no sports at which I really excelled. When I started playing flag football at age seven, my dad, Allen, was our coach, and he wouldn't let me play quarterback. I remember being really ticked off at him, and he asked me, "Why do you want to be a quarterback?"

"I want to touch the ball on every play," I answered.

So that very first year, I became the center.

I finally got to play quarterback in tackle football in the sixth grade, along with fullback and linebacker, and then became a full-time quarterback soon after that year.

I admit I had just an average high school career at Henry Ford II High, playing football, basketball, and baseball, but I was blessed to have a very good head coach, Terry Copacia, who also was a very good quarterbacks coach. He started teaching me the position when I was a freshman and then put together a highlight video of my sophomore season. I got a lot of positive feedback from Mid-American Conference schools and had a few offers, first from Duke and Central Michigan.

Craig Krenzel led the Buckeyes to a perfect 14–0 season in 2002 and was named the MVP of the 2003 Fiesta Bowl win over Miami, as Ohio State claimed its first national championship in 34 years.

We never made the playoffs in my high school career—not once. We were 7–2 and 6–3 and used a pro-style, balanced attack. Then Terry left after my junior year, and the new coach implemented the run-and-shoot.

I was a tall, lanky quarterback, and I couldn't even tell you what star prospect I was. I went to the Michigan State, Michigan, and Ohio State summer camps and was put into the quarterback group with guys like Drew Henson. After my junior year, I got more and more offers and narrowed it down to those three schools. I have always had the personality where I like to plan ahead of time, and I wanted to get my decision out of the way and enjoy my senior year. Ohio State felt comfortable to me. I liked Coach Cooper and the coaching staff, so I committed to be a Buckeye in May 1998. I was a high school senior, and I remember watching Joe Germaine and the offense go up and down the field that season, putting points on the board—at least until Michigan State came to town.

The first thing I remember about my freshman year is my brother dropping me off at the Fawcett Center across from the Woody Hayes Center and meeting my roommate, Ben Hartsock. I couldn't ask for a better guy to room with. We hit it off right off the bat. He grew up in Chillicothe, and we both had the same mentality and outlook on things. On one of the first days, we were sitting in our room, and Ben looked at me and said, "Man, can you believe we get a chance to play football for Ohio State?"

329

Now, not being from Ohio, I never had looked at it that way. I just figured it was an awesome opportunity, but his comment put it into perspective for me. We were wide-eyed kids, nervous and anxious and not knowing what to expect in camp. We knew just to work hard, keep our mouths shut, and do what they asked us to do. We appreciated our scholarships, I know that, and getting an education was important to us.

Today Ben still is one of my best friends.

I was No. 3 on the depth chart my freshman year, behind Steve Bellisari and Austin Mocherman, and I traveled with the team just in case of an emergency. It was a year to adjust, learn, and soak it all up. It turned out to be a redshirt year.

In 2000, after Austin transferred, I battled Scott McMullen for the No. 2 job behind Steve, and we sort of went back and forth. It was a lost year for me, really, but I just tried to prepare as if I were going to play each week. I did everything I could to help Steve prepare, as well, but I wanted to play, and I wanted us to win. It was frustrating for me because we were losing [6–6 in

1999 and 8–4 in 2000], and still I didn't get a chance to play. I didn't think about transferring—that would be quitting. I did at times, however, think about walking onto the baseball team as a pitcher. I always had a decent fastball.

And, as everyone knows, Coach Cooper was fired soon after our Outback Bowl loss to South Carolina. When I heard the news, it was a little surprising, but not a complete shock. The good thing is, I didn't choose the university solely because of the coach, so I looked at it as a fresh opportunity under a new head coach. Then, when they hired Jim Tressel, I remember having a conversation with [former quarterbacks coach] Tim Salem, who was on his way out. I asked, "Who is this guy? I don't know anything about him."

He told me, "Hey, whatever happens, you will like him. He's your kind of guy. He gives everybody a fair chance to compete, and he's loyal to his players. He wants things done the right way, and he's a high character guy."

From the start, he was highly involved with the quarterbacks, and I had the mind-set that there would be an opportunity to earn some playing time even though Steve would be a senior. As I went through that first season under Tress, I didn't necessarily feel I was given a true shot to compete for the job, but I am sure Coach Tress would say that I didn't step up and do what I had to do to be the starting quarterback.

Then Steve had his problem. [With a 6–3 record, Bellisari was suspended after being charged with a DUI on the Thursday night before a home game against Illinois.] I wanted an opportunity to play, but in a million years, I never wished it would come the way it did. I always worried only about what I could control, and I couldn't control an ACL or a DUI to somebody else.

Scott started the Illinois game, and that was frustrating, but then I got in the game for the second half, and we came back and had a chance to win. We had fumbled the kickoff and were backed up on our own 5-yard line [trailing 27–22 with 9:41 remaining]. You have to come through as a quarterback, and I didn't. It was supposed to be a little five-yard out to the flat, and I threw it right to [Illinois linebacker] Ty Myers. It was a pick-six that I would like to forget but probably never will.

My feeling of frustration didn't stop just because I got onto the field that day. We lost. I could have made a lot of excuses, but I should have played better. [Krenzel completed 11 of 23 passes for 164 yards and one touchdown; he was intercepted twice in the 34–22 loss. Illinois went on to win the Big Ten championship with an 10–2 record.]

I got my first start the next week, going home to my old stomping grounds—at Michigan. If you would have said to me as a 10-year-old that my first start would be in Ann Arbor…it would have been a dream come true. I didn't do too much, but I got to ride the coattails of [tailback] Jonathan Wells in the first half, and we shot out to a big lead. [Wells rushed for three touchdowns as Ohio State built a 23–0 halftime lead.]

We held on to win [26–20] and walked out of the Big House with a win. That was a pretty cool experience. In the moment, it didn't seem as big as it does now. After the Michigan game, I looked at myself as the starting quarterback at Ohio State. I started the Outback Bowl, and it lasted about only eight plays of that game. I thought I would play more, but they went to Steve again, and he brought us back, although we lost [31–28 to South Carolina].

Come spring ball, Steve was gone, and there would be competition for the job. It wasn't just Scott and me—there was a new hotshot coming onto the scene in [incoming freshman] Justin Zwick. I thought, *I'll be damned if a freshman will win this job over me.*

Throughout the spring and heading into the fall, whether Tress made up his mind or not, he would just tell the press, "Well, if there was a game tomorrow, Craig would be our starting quarterback." But I never took that for granted—that's not the way I am wired.

Heading into 2002, I think we had the same three goals as Ohio State has every year: beat Michigan, win the Big Ten, and win the national title. In that locker room, Ohio State players expect nothing less than winning. If you don't, you are in big trouble.

I will say this about heading into that season: I could tell that Maurice Clarett was a special talent on the football field. His patience and vision as a freshman and his reliability as a pass blocker were amazing. When he was healthy, he was a complete player. And he showed that as the season wore on.

We also had a group of guys who were sick of being 6–6, 8–4, and 7–5. We didn't come to Ohio State to have records like that. After we started 3–0 with wins over solid teams like Texas Tech and Washington State, we went down to Paul Brown Stadium in Cincinnati and nearly let one get away from us. The field conditions were crap, and we played like crap. We really played poorly and didn't execute much offensively. At the end, I got into the end zone [a six-yard touchdown run with 3:44 remaining], and somehow we won [23–19].

Following wins over Indiana, Northwestern, and San Jose State, we were 7–0 and headed to Wisconsin. Camp Randall Stadium always is a tough place to play for us, but it is a fun place to play, an awesome place to play, and it always has a great atmosphere. We fell behind again in a really physical game, and I remember hitting Michael Jenkins on a post route on third-and-long at about the 50-yard line on our game-winning drive. I remember we were trailing 14–13, and the place was going crazy. I walked up to Clarett before we huddled, laughed, and said, "Look around this stadium—isn't this awesome? It doesn't get any better than this."

He looked at me like I had two heads, but I was always relaxed in situations like that. We scored the game-winning touchdown [a three-yard pass to tight end Ben Hartsock with 9:59 remaining] and got out of there with the win.

Next up was Penn State, and we struggled again before Chris Gamble made the big pick-six [returning an interception 40 yards] to win the game. We got to 10–0 on our trip to Purdue, and it was just like our game at Cincinnati—we didn't play very well. Clarett had that stinger [shoulder] issue and couldn't play much, and we weren't running it well. But it was one of those seasons in which we could beat you with defense and special teams.

I think Purdue had lost five or six games, but they were not your typical five-loss team. They took away our running game that day, and it came down to fourth-and-1 at their 37 with us trailing 6–3. We were just looking to get the first down, and they brought pressure at us and gave us a different look we hadn't seen that day. The play would have gone to Ben, but they had him covered. When you get Michael Jenkins one-on-one on the outside, if it's second-and-4 in the second quarter, or first-and-10 in the third, or even fourth-and-1 with the game on the line, that is where I am supposed to go with the football. So I did. It was perfect execution—the guys up front did their job, it was a good throw, a great catch, and great protection. I have seen it way more than 100 times by now, and people always ask me about that play. But, right after that game, we got back to the mentality of, *What's next?*

We were 11–0, but that touchdown wouldn't mean anything if we lost at Illinois or to Michigan. The Illinois game ended up as the first overtime game in Ohio State history, and again, we found a way to get the job done [a 23–16 win] and left Champaign with a victory.

Before the Michigan game, Ben and I looked out of our window at about 7:45 in the morning and couldn't believe the people everywhere. The anticipation and hype for that game was extremely high. Everybody knew what was at stake, and the whole country was talking about it. And we knew what was on the line—a chance to play for the national championship. We had a group of guys who were thoroughly prepared and really didn't feel any extra pressure. I think we were very relaxed.

Late in the game, I remember hitting Clarett on that wheel route, which we hadn't called all year, to get us down close. Then we got to the line of scrimmage at the 3-yard line [trailing 9–7 with 5:00 remaining], and the plan was for me to call a fake audible. We just knew Michigan always did a good job of scouting us, so we called a dummy audible, making them think we would run off-tackle. They were watching the B-gap, and we got the look we wanted and ran the option to the right. I pitched to Mo Hall, and he got into the end zone to give us the lead. Then Will Allen picked off the pass at the goal line at the end of the game to seal it for us.

It was a hard-fought football game, and we were 13–0. That was awesome. It was a surreal feeling, knowing we were going to Tempe to play for the national championship. I know our fans had waited a long time for a moment like that, and it was awesome when they rushed the field. There is a picture in *Sports Illustrated* of me being carried by fans, but I really don't even remember that happening. It was such a blur.

I used those first couple of weeks of bowl practice to get healthy. I had my knee worked on [arthroscopic surgery] that Tuesday to repair torn cartilage from earlier in the season. That time was beneficial to us, and plus, we were listening to the whole country say that we didn't have a chance to beat Miami. We knew we had the talent, the coaches, the players, and the opportunity. That is all we cared about, regardless of what the media or anyone else was saying.

Going into the game, I know defensively the plan was to get after [Miami quarterback] Ken Dorsey. Offensively, we knew they were a big cover-2 team, and they had the athletes to do it. They would match up underneath because their linebackers were very athletic and could cover tight ends and running backs. We knew in that defense that the one man they couldn't account for in the running game was the quarterback, so my carrying the football would be an integral part of the plan.

Typically, I've never really paid much attention to the crowd, but I do remember coming out for pregame warm-ups in that Fiesta Bowl and thinking, *Man, this is amazing. Our fans are making this a home game.* That is why it is special to be a Buckeye. There was unconditional support. Our fans do everything out of passion, and the turnout that night was a testament to who our fans really are.

Then we went out and turned the ball over, and they scored to lead 7–0. The first quarter was in their favor, definitely. Our guys took control defensively after that. They put a lot of pressure on Dorsey and got some turnovers. We came back and eventually took a 17–14 lead and had a chance to run the clock out at the end of the game. We called an out route to Chris Gamble, and he made the catch and rolled out of bounds, but they called the pass incomplete. That was a catch! And you can see it on film. People always ask me about the pass interference call in overtime, which I will get to, but I always point to this play in regulation. If there had been replay back then, we would have had a first down, run out the clock with a knee, and won the game 17–14. It would never have gone to overtime. But they called it incomplete, Miami got the ball back, kicked the field goal, and we went to overtime.

Now let me get to the play everyone talks about. It was fourth-and-goal, and we were down 24–17. We knew that they knew Michael Jenkins was our go-to guy on the goal line. We knew it would be tough to isolate him one-on-one, but we thought we could put him inside and get isolation on Chris [Gamble] outside. We didn't get the football in Chris' hands enough that year, if you ask me. We got the look we wanted and, sure enough, had Chris isolated outside to the right. It was a fade stop, and the timing had to be right. I admit the throw could have been better, more to his back shoulder, and Chris will tell you he should have caught the ball, but it's tough when somebody is pulling on you. We didn't execute the play. After the throw, I got hit and saw fireworks going off, and Miami was rushing the field. I threw my helmet and figured it was over.

Then somebody picked me off the ground and said, "It's not over! They threw a penalty! It's our ball!"

I had to go get my helmet and get back into the huddle. Those 10 seconds were the biggest roller coaster of emotions I have ever been through. Fortunately, we scored to send it to the second overtime.

After all was said and done, after Clarett scored to take the 31–24 lead, they still had a first-and-goal at the 1-yard line and couldn't get it in on our defense. I always point to that other third-down play in regulation, but I feel we deserved to win the game no matter what anybody else says.

We got into the locker room afterward, and Tress told us how proud he was of all of us, especially the seniors. I was with family and friends later and missed the bus back to the team hotel. What was really neat that night was that all of us—coaches, coaches' families, players, and players' families—celebrated at the hotel. It was a lot of fun. In college football, the coaches are under a lot of pressure, and they generally are high-strung individuals, but you could feel the weight come off of everyone's shoulders that night. It was done. And we were champions.

I have never worn my national championship ring once. It is so big and uncomfortable, but I have a place for it in my house. It means a lot to me because of what it represents. It represents what we accomplished as a team.

It's funny because people bring up my being on the cover of *Sports Illustrated* after that game—I was on the cover three times in my career. I always took pride in representing The Ohio State University in the best way I could. I wanted to be known as the guy who did everything to the best of his ability, the right way—in the classroom and on the field. That's how I want to be remembered, not that I was on the cover of *SI* three times. At the NFL Combine and through the draft process, nobody asked me about being on the *SI* cover three times. But now that I have three children, that stuff is cool for them and my family.

335

Looking at my senior year, we had all the pieces of the puzzle to win another national championship. We lost at Wisconsin but won the rest of them, and all we had to do was beat Michigan in Ann Arbor to get a chance. But our No. 1 problem all year was that we couldn't run the ball well enough, and it eventually cost us. It was the toughest loss of my career. Michigan hasn't beaten us since that game [until the 2011 season], and it seems like forever ago.

If I had to choose one word to sum up my career, it would be *blessed*. For a Midwest kid like me, not a top quarterback coming out of high school by any means, to do what we did, to play at a place like Ohio State, I was simply blessed. The No. 1 thing I take away from what it means to be a Buckeye—it's the people. The guys I played with and the coaches we played for, the fans, the community, the Ohio State family—the education I received and meeting my wife after my sophomore year—I can't imagine a better place to go to school than Ohio State or a better place to raise a family than the Columbus area.

I think about all those people I met, all the memories I have, how blessed I really am. I was blessed to be a Buckeye.

Craig Krenzel, who was 24–3 as a starting quarterback, completed 329 of 579 passes for 4,493 yards in his career. He passed for 28 touchdowns in his career, and in the 2003 Fiesta Bowl win over Miami, he led the team in rushing with 81 yards as Ohio State won the national championship.

BEN HARTSOCK
TIGHT END
1999–2003

I GREW UP ON A FARM OF SEVERAL HUNDRED acres in Chillicothe, Ohio, and I have to say I am more appreciative of that experience and the responsibility it taught me from an early age as each day passes. I spent countless hours with Dad, either in a pickup truck, in a combine, or in a semi headed down the road.

I got involved with 4-H in the third grade and remember taking my sheep and hogs to the Ross County Fair every summer. Any kind of toughness I have probably came from being around my uncle and my dad, who were rough-around-the-edges farm guys. They would roughhouse with you, and I like to think I learned a pretty good work ethic from them.

Mom and Dad were both Ohio State graduates, and they loved the Buckeyes. Dad always said one of his fondest memories was attending the Rose Bowl to watch the 1968 team led by Rex Kern win the national championship by beating USC. My brother and sister both earned degrees from Ohio State, so you could say Ohio State was ingrained into our family. As I grew up, we sat in front of the TV on Saturdays and watched the Buckeyes play football.

I started playing football in the third grade—the Scioto Valley Youth League provided my first flag football experience, and I was a member of the Browns. The distinguishing factor of that league was that the referees were prisoners at the local correctional institution. They would roll up in a van with bars on the windows, get out, ref our games, get back in that van, and head back to prison.

I played tight end from my freshman year at Unioto High School, and the coaches moved me around as much as possible, so I also played a little wide receiver, fullback, middle linebacker, and defensive end. In my four years, we had three different head coaches, but in my senior season we had an 8–2 record and won the league championship. That high school experience was the most carefree time for me. It was so much fun—wearing the jersey to school on game days, Mom cooking a pregame meal—it was just like *Friday Night Lights*.

There is a great story that I can't confirm isn't a myth, but Leroy Silvani is the man who started football at our high school in 1963. Leroy invited Woody Hayes to speak at a booster function of some sort after starting the program, but Woody had something come up and couldn't make it to the event, so he sent down an assistant with an official football from an Ohio State practice. He made a presentation and said, "Coach Hayes wanted to give you this football as a token from The Ohio State University, and it is to be passed on to the first player from your school who plays at Ohio State."

338

I started as a sophomore, and by the time I was a junior, I realized that recruiters were paying attention to me. I knew I wanted to play for Ohio State but wasn't sure I would get noticed. There were these recruiting services to help you, but my high school coach said, "Don't worry about those. They are for players who may not get noticed. You *will* get noticed."

From that point on, Dad and I did everything we could to get Ohio State to notice me. Whenever [athletics director] Andy Geiger or John Cooper would speak, we would go listen and shake their hands. I also went to the Ohio State camp every year, and it was at those camps where I was able to distinguish myself a little. Southern Ohio football isn't as well known as northern Ohio football as far as having as many powerhouse programs, so I knew those camps were my chance to play against the top talent.

I was in one tight-end drill, which was being watched by a graduate assistant coach named John Hill. I think he saw I was standing out a little bit, and the next thing I knew, [assistant coach] Bill Conley walked up and watched the drill.

When you are a sophomore, you are getting all the questionnaires from all the schools. Then when you start getting the handwritten notes from coaches, you know they are serious. Then you get the phone calls. I went

Ben Hartsock caught 58 passes for 519 yards and five touchdowns as a tight end for the Buckeyes. He was a three-time Academic All–Big Ten selection.

through my junior year and started getting heavily recruited. At that point, Purdue, Pittsburgh, West Virginia, and maybe Northwestern had been interested along with most of the Mid-American Conference schools. I figured I might go to Ohio University if Ohio State never offered me or asked me to be a preferred walk-on. But, at the camp before my senior season, I was performing well, and Ohio State coaches indicated an offer was forthcoming, though it still wasn't 100 percent.

Then two weeks into my senior season, Coach Conley called me and said, "It is a done deal. You will be a scholarship player."

I went to the nearest pay phone and called my parents. It was one of the most exciting moments of my life. My parents were just as surprised as I was about the entire process. It happened so fast. We were not a football family and not from a big football community. After Ohio State offered, that's when I received the anointed knightship, so to speak. Then all the Big Ten schools offered me scholarships, too.

But there was no decision to be made. I knew where I wanted to play football and get an education from an early age. And my high school presented me with the football that Woody Hayes had sent down 30-some years earlier. I still have it.

As my high school classmates packed up and went to Myrtle Beach for vacation, I packed up and headed to Columbus. As I drove out of our driveway, I thought everything happened a lot quicker than I had anticipated. That was my last day at home. I moved into Morrill Tower that day, and I know it was hard on Mom.

I jumped right into conditioning. Dave Kennedy, the Ohio State strength coach, was brutal on us. I know I was scared to death. That first summer day of conditioning, Eddie George of the Tennessee Titans was working out because he swore by Coach Kennedy's methods, but on this day, he collapsed and couldn't finish. I thought, *Well, if Eddie George can't do this, there is no way I am going to do this*.

I never made any of my [running] times, and Coach Kennedy would stand over me and tell me it was all in my head. "You can make it!" he would scream.

"I don't have the legs. I don't have the lungs," I would say.

He would play mind games with you and say things such as, "If I had a gun at your mother's head, and you had to finish, you could do it, right?"

I would tell him that, if those were the circumstances, I would just wait and spend the time with her saying good-bye, because there was no way I was going to make his predetermined time.

That summer, I was practicing in Pennsylvania the week of the Big 33 All-Star Game and broke my ankle. I was devastated. I was placed in a cast and thought my entire freshman season was gone, but that was my first exposure to advanced modern medicine. Back in Columbus, they whisked me into surgery with no waiting, with the best doctors and the best care, and I walked out of surgery with a plate on my fibula. I was on the field six weeks later.

Arriving at the Fawcett Center for fall camp, I remember rooming with Craig Krenzel and telling him how very few people get to be part of this. This is something that Woody Hayes and Archie Griffin were part of, and now we were, too.

We got beat by Miami in the Kickoff Classic in my first game that season and then came back for our home opener against UCLA. It was a night game at Ohio Stadium. I can still feel the sensation of running onto that field for the first time…the sound of the crowd, the darkness of the night with the lights cutting through it, the proximity of the fans right on top of you, my first time wearing that scarlet uniform with my name on the back of the jersey.

After I got hurt, I knew I wasn't going to play, and it took some pressure off of my shoulders. I figured I would be on the scout team and get adjusted to being a college student. Once I knew I would redshirt, it also gave me another year to be on the team down the road. One day in practice, I had one of those moments that was very encouraging. I beat [linebacker] James Cotton for a touchdown and Coach [Fred] Pagac told me, "You keep it up and you will be helping us very soon."

We finished 6–6 that year and didn't go to a bowl game, and there was a lot of disappointment. There were people calling for Coach Cooper's head, and we knew mediocrity was not accepted at Ohio State.

Everything I did for the first time, every milestone, I made a mental note about it. Like in the opener of my redshirt freshman season against Fresno State, they kicked a pop-up on a kickoff, and I was looking into the sun and couldn't see the football to save my life. It landed right in front of me, and I kicked it, the first time I touched the football at Ohio State. Fortunately, it went out of bounds, and I thought, *Oh, my gosh, thankfully I didn't cause a turnover.*

Then I caught my first pass for 11 yards and told myself, *Now I am going down in the history books that I caught an actual pass for Ohio State.* I knew it was something most people don't get to do. It was just a shallow crossing route from Steve Bellisari at the open end of the stadium, nothing fancy about it.

After we lost to Michigan, there was a complete sense of frustration, and we were headed to the Outback Bowl. It felt like the toilet bowl to us. We wanted to win, but it was a frustrating time for everybody in the program. There was controversy on the team and a level of discomfort. After we lost [24–7 to South Carolina], I knew things were bad. When Coach Cooper got fired the next day, my feelings then are the same as they are today: he was a successful coach and did a good job of keeping Ohio State nationally recognized, but his record against Michigan and in bowl games was not going to be accepted by the state of Ohio. He was a manager and let his coaches coach, and I think the university wanted a change from that style. I never felt like I wanted a new coach but understood why the university made a change. I was thankful to Coach Cooper for giving me a chance to play for Ohio State and feel fortunate to have played for him.

When we first heard the name Jim Tressel, nobody knew anything about him. I didn't know Youngstown State, but once Tressel got the job, somebody addressed us and said, "Don't worry. You will see what he is like soon enough. Just give it a chance."

Right after our first team meeting with him, I knew what they meant. In typical Tressel fashion, he was succinct and to the point and very focused. Then I was at the basketball game that night when he made the proclamation about fans being proud of his team at Michigan in 300-and-some days. I thought, *Wow, this guy is legit.* Nobody was nervous about his making that statement. We were all thrilled he made that statement.

I was still behind Darnell Sanders at tight end heading into that year [2001], and he and I got along real well. He wasn't threatened by me, and I wasn't into ruffling any feathers because I wasn't a starter.

I reached another big milestone with my first touchdown that season. It was against Purdue at home. It was a flag route to the corner of the end zone in the closed end of the stadium, and Bellisari just threw it up there. It seemed like it took forever to come down. It was play-action, the defense bit on it, and I was open.

Before we played at Michigan, it was obvious to us that Coach Tressel really embraced the scale of the game. He brought back former players and brought back Coach Bruce, who told us, "Everything revolves around this game. You have to beat Michigan!" We embraced it and rose to the occasion [winning 26–20].

Once Darnell decided to leave early for the NFL, I thought the job was mine. I knew we would have a good team in 2002, but going into training camp, nothing spectacular stood out in my memory. It wasn't until after the Washington State game [a 25–7 win in the third game] that I thought we may have a great team. There was a real sense of continuity. It was Coach Tressel's second season, our offense felt more comfortable, and the defense was dominant. We were developing an identity—Coach Tressel was always focused, and his demeanor was unflappable—and we became that way as a team.

Then we went down to Cincinnati, playing in a pro stadium for the battle of Ohio, and kind of laid an egg in that game. We were fortunate to win [23–19], and when I came back to our apartment, I remember telling my roommates, "Now I don't know if we are a good football team or not."

We went to Wisconsin and were behind 14–13 when I caught a [three-yard] touchdown pass in the fourth quarter. I knew it was important at the time, but there was still a lot of time left. I became so focused on the task at hand that I didn't realize how big it was until someone mentioned to me that I just caught the game-winner.

As that season wore on, and we won close game after close game, it symbolized "Tressel Ball." We played relentless defense, mistake-free offense, and won the kicking game. That was his recipe for winning.

The Purdue game and the "Holy Buckeye" play is still something many fans talk about. We trailed 6–3 late in the game and faced a third-and-15 when Craig hit me on a "Y Shallow" route. I got 14 yards. On fourth down, we called it again, and Krenzel was thinking he would come to me again for the first down. As I was running across the field, I could see his eyes as he went through his progression, and I was covered pretty well. He pulled off of me, and the pocket collapsed on him. I was thinking, *This is it*, when he stepped up and threw it over the top of me. Now everyone probably has seen it from the camera's perspective a hundred times, but to see that football flying over my head and landing in Michael Jenkins' hands for the touchdown was really an awesome viewpoint for me [resulting in a 10–6 win].

The Michigan game would be the biggest game of our lives, and we all knew it. There was no getting around it, but nobody was nervous. I have been on teams in big-game situations, and there is anxiousness and uncertainty, and we did not have that feeling at all. We were excited. We knew if we won, we were headed to the national championship.

I embraced the buildup and all the activities that go along with Michigan week, like when the band comes out to our practice and we get to grab an instrument and march with them. We had a pep rally, and there was a feeling of excitement all over campus. After winning the game [14–9], I think it took me 30 minutes to get to the locker room because it was sea of humanity on the field. It was like riding a wave. That was one of the high points for me, one of the coolest moments of my life. I always joked that I took a worse beating after the game than I did during it.

It was a sense of accomplishment being 13–0 and having beaten Michigan, and it felt like the entire state was celebrating with us.

We had a quiet confidence as we prepared for Miami, which was loaded with all of that NFL talent. We just put our work in for a month and let all of the talk about how Miami would dominate us take its course. We knew they were fast, but we also knew we would be more physical. We wanted to establish the run and the play-action on offense and knew our defense would do what it did every week.

We were ahead 14–7 in the third quarter and had a first-and-goal on the 6-yard line. I was running across the back of the end zone when Craig released the ball. I can still see it coming off of his fingers. I was open. Things just seem to slow down in those moments. I thought, *Here it comes. I can't believe I am going to catch a touchdown pass in the national championship game. Just look it in and catch it.*

In the course of a split second, [Miami safety] Sean Taylor came out of nowhere and took it out of the air. I was already planning a celebration with my teammates one moment and saw him streaking down the field with my football the next. That moment will be with me forever. Fortunately, Maurice Clarett tracked him down and took it away from him.

When the famous interference call happened at the end of the game, I was in the middle of the end zone, standing right under the uprights. I had such a unique perspective of it. I was not part of Craig's progression on that play. Everybody knew this play was it—do or die—and it seemed to take forever.

When the pass hit the ground, I thought, *Oh man, that's it.* But I also saw that there was a lot of bumping going on there, so let's see what happens. I swear that time stood still after that ball hit the ground. My view was, and still is, that the referee made the right call. Actually, it was a pretty easy call.

In the second overtime, when we had the lead, all the offense could do was stand and watch our defense take over. We had complete trust and confidence in those guys. As it played out, with Miami having a fourth down at the 1-yard line, on the last play of the national championship game, it was like a movie. It was the perfect culmination of the entire season. What did I do when the fourth-down pass hit the ground? I ran out onto the field like a screaming idiot, searching for someone to hug. Then we all just spent the next few moments running around hugging each other.

Here's the thing I remember most: remember when I referred to Dad being in college and scraping enough money together to attend the Rose Bowl when Ohio State last won the national championship? He once told me it was the highlight of his young life. And when I ran onto that field, I knew where my family was sitting and looked up to find them. My dad is not an emotional man, but I could tell that he was emotional at that moment. The university meant so much to him before he ever had children. Now to go through this moment again and to have a son playing for the Buckeyes...it was very, very impactful. I stood there and watched that stadium full of Buckeyes fans going absolutely bananas and locked in and found my parents, my future wife, and my brother and sister. I will never forget it.

345

When they rolled out that platform on the field moments later, only seniors were supposed to be up there, but I made sure to find my way up there on that stage to kiss that crystal football. I have watched every major sport in my life, and you see all these sports heroes holding up a trophy or a football on that stage and to be on the other side of that camera...it's hard to describe. It was a very real moment. I got my hands on that football, soaked it in, and marinated in the moment. I knew it didn't happen often and most likely wouldn't happen ever again.

In the off-season, my fiancée became my wife, and we were riding on Cloud Nine. I thought, *Well, we won one national championship, so we can do it again.*

During that fall camp, I hit my hand on Simon Fraser's helmet, kind of shook it off, and prepared for the next play. Then I noticed my pointer finger was pointing sideways instead of sticking straight up. I knew that wasn't good. My hand was broken, and it was 10 days before our first game going into my senior year. I was devastated. But this was another experience with modern medicine: I had surgery the next morning, and they put a plate on that bone. And I played in that first game, which was a night game against Washington at Ohio Stadium. We won 28–9 and then beat North Carolina State in three overtimes in a game in which I caught seven passes and scored a touchdown.

I had only five touchdowns in my career, so I can remember every one. It's funny because every summer the *Buckeye Sports Bulletin* did a story that Ohio State plans to use the tight end more during the upcoming season. I've never been the type of guy to lobby for more passes thrown my way, because I was just happy to have a role. I always joked with my friends when Craig was around, "If I wasn't buddies with him, I would probably only have five or six catches for the *season*."

We lost at Wisconsin and at Michigan in my senior season, and those were big disappointments. To not win that Michigan game as a senior really hurt, but we were excited to get back to the Fiesta Bowl because we all had such a great experience the previous year. Beating Kansas State and being in Arizona together for a week was a nice way for me to end my career.

I did pause for a moment before I took that uniform off for the final time. It really took me back to the first time as a freshman before picture day when I walked up to my locker and saw that jersey hanging there with my name on the back of it. All of us freshmen were just standing there at the Woody Hayes Center, as I thought, *This is my jersey. This is my locker. I have been chosen to be a part of this program's history*. I was taken back to that moment, and now I was wearing my jersey for the final time.

I am eternally grateful. I was grateful to wear that uniform. I got a tremendous education. I was taught not only by textbooks but by professors who *wrote* the textbooks. Ohio State was there decades before me and will be there decades after I am gone. I am grateful for the teammates I had. The tremendous thing about sports is that it brings different people from different backgrounds together for a common cause. I am grateful for Coach Cooper and Coach Tressel, and I learned valuable lessons from both. I appreciate that Coach Tressel always saw a bigger picture for us in addition to football. I look back on the entire experience with the deepest sense of gratitude.

I have two daughters now, and I can't wait to take them back to Ohio Stadium and back to campus some day, because I remember my experiences going to a game with Dad. I went back for the first time recently and realized what an incredible experience game day is. The marching band. The cheer-leaders. I have played in the NFL a long time now, and Saturdays are so much better than anything I have been around. Ohio State football is a matter of state pride. And it always gave me a deep sense of pride to be on that field, wearing the scarlet and gray.

I will always love this university.

Ben Hartsock started 31 games, catching 58 passes for 519 yards and five touchdowns, including 33 receptions in 2003. He was three-time Academic All–Big Ten and winner of the Big Ten Medal of Honor in 2003. He has played in the NFL with the Indianapolis Colts, Tennessee Titans, Atlanta Falcons, and New York Jets.

ANDY GROOM

PUNTER

2000–2002

THIS IS VERY DIFFICULT TO WRITE, knowing that my time being a football player at Ohio State is now over, but I think to myself, *What a way to go out.* From being a lonely walk-on, to a starter for the greatest team in college football, to All-American, to being on the 2002 national championship team, and to meeting the president of the United States...how could I have written a better script for myself?

My career will be something I will cherish for the rest of my life. I have met people who will be with me forever throughout life. Coaches, players, trainers, and academic counselors were some of the best people I have ever met.

The 2002 season was about the craziest season you could imagine. We had a few blowouts, but most of them were real nail-biters—from holding off Wisconsin on the road, to Chris Gamble scoring the only touchdown of the game to beat Penn State, to that gutsy throw from Craig Krenzel to Michael Jenkins on fourth down against Purdue, to the overtime win against Illinois, to the Michigan game everyone will remember...

There were so many big moments during the season, but I remember one especially. There were just a few minutes left against Penn State, and we were leading 13–7. We faced a fourth down from inside our 10-yard line, and the punt team was running onto the field. "Groom!" I heard Coach Tressel's voice, "Come over here!" I went over, and he told me, "Now you know the

348

punt is the most important play in football. I want you to show me why it's the most important play in football." From five yards deep in our end zone, I hit a 60-yarder that got us out of trouble. On the next possession, there was only 1:13 left, and we had to punt again. "Show me again," he told me. I hit a 58-yarder with negative return, backing up Penn State deep in their own territory. They didn't do anything offensively, and we won the game.

Then there was the national championship game that everyone said we would lose. I can honestly say that the one thing that this team possessed was that everyone cared for each other and loved one another. I would go to bat for anyone on that team. Whether it was a walk-on, freshman, nonstarter, or starter, I would always be there for them, and I knew they would be there for me.

We had something very special at Ohio State, something that not too many teams ever had.

The national championship game was truly unbelievable, as most fans know from watching it. But what people did not see was the behind-the-scenes things that the players got to see. The Fiesta Bowl treated us like kings in every way you could imagine. They had a hospitality room where we could all come together, relax, and play a number of different games. I can still see Darrion Scott sitting in there with his shirt off, playing cards with the guys, or Kenny Peterson talking junk all the way to the championship game of pool. These are the times I will miss most, the times that I will cherish forever. When you spend time with the fellas just being with each other and enjoying the camaraderie, there is nothing like it. Even though these times are over for me, I will never forget the good times I have had with all my teammates.

Before the Fiesta Bowl, I don't think there was one reporter who said we could win that game against Miami. The main thing was, everyone on that team knew we were going to shock the world. We had heard that we did not have enough team speed to beat Miami. We had plenty of that. Not to toot my own horn, but I'd like to race their punter and see if he ran a 4.4. All of that can be thrown out the window, because we came to Tempe to win, not to lose. We were just quiet about it, though, and didn't shoot off our mouths like some players from Miami.

At that final practice at the Fiesta Bowl, Mike Tomczak addressed the team this way: "I have never been this excited and pumped up since I played at Ohio State. I want each and every one of you to go back to the hotel tonight

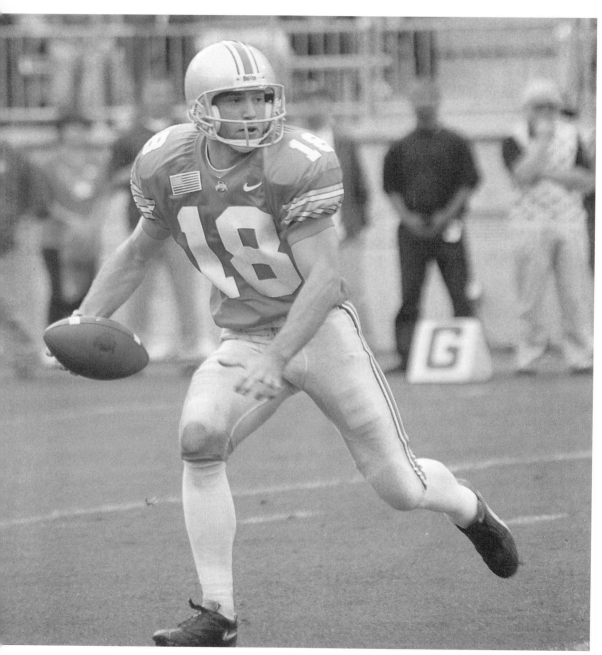

Andy Groom, a former walk-on, became one of Ohio State's greatest all-time punters.

and write this down: '2002 national champions,' because if you don't write down your goals, they won't come true." I know I did it and others did it. I think Donnie Nickey even put his inside his helmet.

As I think back to that magical night, everything about the game was breathtaking, and I took it all in so I would remember it the rest of my life. Seeing the sea of scarlet in the Fiesta Bowl was a sight for sore eyes, and I felt like we were back at home in the 'Shoe. All I know is that when the silver bullets stopped Miami on fourth-and-goal on the game's final play, I just sat down and cried, because I knew what we had done was special.

At the same time, I was also saddened because I knew that my time at Ohio State was over and that there would be no more Buckeyes football for me. It was a bittersweet feeling, knowing that we had accomplished something that so many of the teams before us had tried to accomplish, and so many teams after us will try.

Weeks later, we had the celebration in the 'Shoe allowing the seniors to be together one last time. It was a very emotional day to have all of us come together as a team for the last time. The seniors, as many know, got to dot the *i* in "Script Ohio" and then listen to linebacker Cie Grant sing "Carmen Ohio."

351

All of that, and seeing my father cry for the first time in my life, was too much for me to absorb all at once, and I began to cry like a baby. It was so hard to say good-bye to something that I have known and loved for so much of my life. It was truly a day to remember, seeing more than fifty thousand fans sitting in freezing temperatures to see their beloved Buckeyes.

Our trip to the White House was something I'll never forget. About 30 minutes before we were supposed to meet President Bush, Coach Tressel pulled me aside and said, "Groomy, you're my man."

I said, "What do you mean?"

He just said, "You're our guy who will present the helmet to the president. Don't screw it up. Don't talk politics. Just call him 'Mister President.'"

Now I knew I had come a long way from being a walk-on, but talking to the president of the United States was something I never could have imagined in my wildest dreams. I could not believe he picked me to do this, and I have to admit I was a little nervous—it's nothing like before a crucial punt.

Well, everything went well at the White House. I gave the commemorative helmet to President Bush, and when we were leaving, Ben Hartsock decided that he wanted to make a snow angel on the front lawn of the White

House. As he was doing this, the Secret Service popped out and screamed at the top of their lungs at Ben. Well, he didn't hear them and continued in his mission on the lawn. While this was happening, Coach Tressel was dying with laughter, but Ben didn't understand what the fuss was about. He got scolded by the Secret Service and was a little red in the face. It capped off the day, making it one to remember for the rest of our lives.

I am very honored I am a Buckeye, and I will take these memories with me wherever I go in life. I truly think that winning the national championship will not sink in until sometime down the road. But I do know one thing—the 2002 national champion Ohio State Buckeyes did a lot of people around the country very proud, and we did something that many OSU teams before us could not do. My time at Ohio State honestly has been the best time of my life, and I am so proud to be a part of Buckeyes history.

Andy Groom averaged 45.0 yards per punt in 2002 and was named to several All-America teams.

MIKE NUGENT

KICKER

2001–2004

Growing up in Centerville, Ohio, I had a great family life, great friends and coaches, and was always exposed to sports—it shaped me as a person. I wanted to play football, but when I was five years old, my parents thought soccer would be better for me. So every year I asked, "Can I play football yet?"

I was a defender in soccer and played other sports throughout the year, and as I started junior high, I finally got the chance to play football. I started off at running back and also became the team's kicker. Not many teams kicked at that level, so our team definitely had an advantage.

By the time I got to Centerville High, I was kicking, playing running back, and, before my senior season, I became the quarterback. The highlight of my career was kicking a 52-yard field goal against Wayne, although we lost that game. It was the final kick of my high school career.

I was a big Bengals and Ohio State fan growing up, and I had dreamed of playing college football for the Buckeyes. There were plenty of times, however, when I didn't think it would become a reality.

The summer before my sophomore year, I had attended [former Ohio State kicker] Tim Williams' camp, and he told Dad he saw some real talent in me. He asked if I was headed to the Ohio State kicking camp and provided the information for us to make arrangements. That summer, I attended the camp, and it was amazing. I met Bill Conley, then Ohio State's tight ends

354

Mike Nugent holds the all-time Ohio State record for points scored with 356. He was a two-time All-American and won the 2004 Groza Award as the nation's top kicker.

coach and recruiting coordinator. And I also met Dan Stultz, Ohio State's kicker at the time, and we hit it off right away. The great thing for me was that Dan took me under his wing and began mentoring me.

After that summer camp, I realized those camps were a way to get exposure and experience. Dan had put me in contact with a man named Dick Pierce, who operates kicking and punting camps, and that is where I learned most of the techniques and fundamentals I use to this day.

Following my junior year, I headed back to the Ohio State summer camp and started getting more attention. I began to think that realizing my dream of becoming a college football player could become a reality—and I even thought I had a remote chance of playing at Ohio State, which is most every Ohio high school football player's dream.

I had a goal, and that was it.

Dan was due to finish his Ohio State career, and I knew there would be an opportunity the following season [2001], but they had signed Josh Huston, who was a year older than me. At that point, I was thinking there was no way I would become a Buckeye. In the meantime, I was attending camps at Michigan State, Notre Dame, and Purdue. I had a great camp at Michigan State, and one of the coaches working the camp was Mark Dantonio [Michigan State's defensive backs coach]. He told me to look for an offer soon from Michigan State.

Unfortunately, when the call came, Coach Dantonio said the head coach [Bobby Williams] told him, "We have to take the kid from Michigan [Dave Rayner]."

I was devastated.

Oddly enough, when Coach Cooper was fired and Jim Tressel was hired at Ohio State, he hired Coach Dantonio as defensive coordinator. During one of their first meetings, he asked them, "How are we doing for a kicker?" They said they were set, but Coach Dantonio's next words were, "Get Mike Nugent."

I was headed to Pittsburgh for an official visit when I got the call—it was a scholarship offer from Ohio State, and I committed right on the spot—about two weeks before signing day.

Today, Coach Dantonio [now Michigan State's head coach] always reminds me that he is responsible for me going to Ohio State. I will always be grateful to him, and we still stay in touch.

My career didn't start so well, mainly because of nerves. It was amazing to run onto that field at Ohio Stadium for the first time and to see the stands full, but then I missed my first field-goal attempt—a 35-yarder that I pulled to the left against Akron—in Coach Tressel's first game.

After September 11 happened, we had a game postponed and then went to UCLA at the Rose Bowl the following week. My knees were shaking, and I missed an extra point and a 28-yard field goal, and we lost 13–6. That was four points right there, and I was down on myself, knowing I just had to work harder to become a good kicker at this level.

I hit a 44-yarder at home against Northwestern and slowly started gaining confidence as I felt more comfortable. Then I hit the biggest one of all that season—a field goal that put us up by 10 at Michigan [in a 26–20 win].

The following spring, I just felt more comfortable. I felt more relaxed and was getting everything figured out after my freshman season [7-of-14 in field goals, 27-of-29 PATs]. I admit it had been a mental thing.

As we started 2002, the job was mine, and I kicked 23 field goals in a row [an Ohio State record]. By the time we got to Illinois, we were 11–0, and the wind was blowing crazily. I missed a 42-yarder into the wind, and that was the end of the streak. I was 3-for-5 that day, but most important, we won the game [23–16 in overtime]. It was really surprising to me, not knowing what it was like to miss a kick since the Michigan game of the year before, but I can't control the weather.

Since I started kicking, I had wanted to win the Groza Award, given to the nation's best kicker, and I was a finalist, but the award went to [Iowa's] Nate Kaeding. I admit I was devastated. I knew it was so tough just to become a finalist, and figured I might never get another shot at it.

But we had a national championship game to prepare for. Heading into the Fiesta Bowl against Miami, they were such an enormous favorite that few people gave us a chance. I made one kick in the third quarter [44 yards to give Ohio State a 17–7 lead], but then I had a chance to put us ahead 20–14 late in the game. It was a 42-yard attempt from the right hash, and once I looked at the film, my [pre-snap] walk-off wasn't good. I just kicked it straight down the right hash and pushed it a little.

Fortunately, we still won the game in double overtime, and the whole night was amazing. I can still picture the sun setting that night in Arizona. Nothing is better than winning a national championship, and I remember thinking how lucky I was to be a part of this. It is an experience I will never forget.

We expected nothing but a national championship in my junior year, but we lost tough games at Wisconsin and at Michigan. The highlight for me was kicking a 36-yarder in overtime to beat Purdue.

Heading into 2004, it was really an honor to be elected as a team captain. I know there haven't been many kickers who have held that position. I had three misses that year [24-of-27], and I can remember them all: I missed a short one early in the season, a 40-yarder in overtime at Northwestern that went right over the upright, and a 48-yarder that was blocked by Penn State.

Every kicker's dream is to hit a game-winning field goal, and I got that opportunity in a home game against Marshall with the game tied 21–21. I knew my range was 58 to 60 yards, and as the clock ticked under 1:00, the offense drove us into position. Hearing that "Nuuuuuge" from our crowd, I lined up for a 55-yarder on the final play. As the ball went off of my foot, I knew I had hit it well. It seemed like it took forever, but the crowd let me know it was good.

The defining moment for me came on Senior Day against Michigan. The field was lined with alumni players, and I was the last one out of the tunnel. That hug from Coach Tressel meant everything to me and said it all. I looked up at the crowd and could hear the "Nuuuuuuge" and realized then what Ohio State football meant to our fans.

By the time we got to the Alamo Bowl the next month, I realized I needed seven points to tie [Pete Johnson as the all-time Ohio State scoring leader], and I thought it would be cool to have that record.

Fortunately, I got the chance, making four of four field goals and three extra points. It is awesome when I hear somebody say that I have scored more points than anyone in Ohio State history. It isn't an individual game, and I have to thank Kyle Andrews, who was the long-snapper for three years, and Kyle Turano, my holder for my senior season.

And I won the Groza that year, which was very exciting for me.

Ohio State became another family for me. Coach Tressel treated us like family, and we acted like it. From the first day at camp, we had to learn everyone's first and last names, their jersey numbers, and where they went to high school. Ohio State is so full of tradition, and Coach Tressel was all about creating it and preserving it. Little did we know when he had us learn the words to "Carmen Ohio" that we would sing it at the end of every game and continue to do so for the rest of our lives.

I think I got out of my career what I put into it. I put in plenty of hard work, but it also was a matter of timing and good luck. What if Coach Tressel didn't get the job? What if Ohio State already had a sophomore kicker and I never got the chance? I feel so lucky those things happened for me. I have to say that it is not a right to play football at Ohio State—it is a privilege—and I had that privilege.

So is getting an education at Ohio State. I was eight classes short of a degree when I left for the NFL, and I continued to go back in the off-season, earning my business degree in 2007.

I went back for a home game in which Devin Barclay hit the game-winner against Iowa to win the Big Ten championship [2009]. I tailgated with my parents, and once I heard that fight song and our alma mater, it brought back so many memories. I appreciate all of it now that I am so much older and I know that I will always want to stay connected to Ohio State. To be able to say I played at such a first-class program and to meet the people I consider friends today, it will always be special to me.

Mike Nugent is Ohio State's all-time leading scorer with 356 points. He made 72-of-88 field goals and 140-of-143 PATs. He was twice named an All-American and also won the 2004 Groza Award as the nation's best place-kicker. Through his first seven seasons in the NFL with the New York Jets, Arizona Cardinals, Tampa Bay Buccaneers, and Cincinnati Bengals, Nugent made 127 of 157 field-goal attempts. He became one of the league's best kickers during the 2011 season, making 33 of 38 field goals for the Bengals.

NICK MANGOLD
OFFENSIVE LINEMAN
2002–2005

MY FIRST MEMORY OF PLAYING FOOTBALL goes way back to the third grade. It was the night before our first practice, and Dad and I had just picked up all the pads. Sitting at home eating dinner, I was like a kid on Christmas Eve. I couldn't wait for the next day and my first practice.

I played soccer, basketball, baseball, track, football, and swam while growing up in Centerville, Ohio, but as I got bigger and less athletic, I couldn't play all of those sports. Sooner or later, they all gave way to football.

I was a big Ohio State fan, going way back. I went to my first game at Ohio Stadium when I was really young, like six or seven years old, because my Uncle Doug was swimming for the Buckeyes. Then, when we were at my grandma's house in Washington, D.C., for Christmas in 1996 when I was 12, Dad somehow got hold of two tickets for the upcoming Rose Bowl. We flew to California, watched the Tournament of Roses Parade, and went to the game [Ohio State defeated Arizona State 20–17].

The next time I saw an Ohio State game, I was playing in it.

I went to Archbishop Alter High. We never played Centerville High after my freshman year, but I knew about A.J. Hawk and Mike Nugent a little. I played on every play—center on offense, first linebacker and then defensive tackle on defense—except kickoffs and punts. I got more attention for my play at center and started every game there since the seventh grade, so I guess it was natural that my recruiting focused on that position. Tom Meyer, my high school line coach who played at the University of Dayton, coached me up as we went along. He taught me the fundamentals and the footwork I would need and gave me an insight into what it would be like in college.

I went through all of those college questionnaires, Mom typed them all up for me, and I visited Clemson and Ohio State. Notre Dame also offered me a scholarship, and that is where it got difficult. Mom was pushing Notre Dame, while Dad told me, "Everybody in Ohio wants to go to Ohio State and play football. You wouldn't be a good Ohio boy if you turned down the Buckeyes."

So I committed to Ohio State before my senior season. I think Mom still has all of the recruiting letters. After I eventually signed my letter-of-intent, I was talking to my high school coach one day, and I said, "You know what's weird? I got something from every Mid-American Conference School and every Big Ten school but one. Michigan never sent me a letter or anything."

Coach looked at me and said, "Well, yes, they did. They sent you a whole bunch of stuff, but I threw it all away."

I just laughed. I probably wouldn't have considered them, anyway, but it is a funny story.

360

You know of those moments when you realize how different college football players are than high school players? Mine came in the spring when I visited Ohio State and LeCharles Bentley was working out. He had some ridiculous amount on the bench press. I was peeing down the side of my leg, and I thought, *How in the world can I come here and compete with guys like this?*

Once I got to Columbus, I became close with A.J. and roomed with him all four years. Bobby Carpenter was fantastic. Mike D'Andrea was fun to be around. The whole linebacker group got along well, and Robby Sims became a good friend. We just had a good group of guys, and we worked hard together. It was something special that we had together.

When we started practices, [offensive line coach] Jim Bollman gave me some advice that I tried to follow. He said, "Don't compare yourself to the other guys who have been here for three or four years and are 22 or 23 years old. Don't do anything against somebody else. You compete with yourself. Try to get yourself to improve day after day."

It turned out to be great advice.

That first game [2002, against Texas Tech], I didn't play a snap, and it was different for me standing on the sideline, after going through high school and playing every play on offense and defense. I didn't really think too much about it until after the game when Dad mentioned it. "Thanks, Dad," I told him.

Nick Mangold started 34 games at center for the Buckeyes from 2003 to 2005. A first-round NFL Draft pick of the New York Jets in 2006, he has made four consecutive Pro Bowls through 2011.

But as the season went along, I got to play a decent amount and ended up playing the entire second half at Illinois in a crazy, cold game that we won in overtime. That was an amazing season. We just listened to the older guys, and those guys always had the belief that we would win, no matter the situation. We never gave up, and we always won. The way I looked at it, it was my opportunity to play with the Buckeyes, and we were making a run at the national championship.

The Fiesta Bowl against Miami was a crazy, crazy experience. I got put in on the goal-line package in the second quarter when they moved [Alex] Stepanovich to guard. On the first play, Vince Wilfork jumped offside and just destroyed me. I thought, *Well, shoot, this is going to be quite ugly.* It was another of those eye-opening moments, but we scored two plays later.

I think I played 10 plays that night, but I didn't care. I just wanted to be a part of it. It was unbelievable. Going through high school, I never got a chance to win a state championship, so to win a national championship in my first year, the way the people of Ohio reacted to it when we came back from Arizona—how excited everybody was—it was an amazing, awesome time.

We had the celebration at Ohio Stadium, and it was so cold, I don't know how Cie Grant was able to sing "Carmen Ohio" that day. It was the best time to be a Buckeye.

Going into the 2003 season, I was just biding my time. I think I had made a huge step in my freshman year. And the way Jim Bollman taught the offensive linemen was perfect for me. He didn't yell at you, but you knew you messed up by the way he looked at you. He paid great attention to detail. I always thought I was a cerebral player, to know what every lineman should be doing, and that is what drew me to center in the first place.

So when Alex injured his ankle [in the season's second game against San Diego State], I was ready to play. When he returned later, they moved him to guard, and I started the final 11 games as we went to the Fiesta Bowl again and beat Kansas State.

We started 3–0 my junior year but then went through a real tailspin [losing three games in a row]. That Iowa game [a 33–7 loss] was miserable. We couldn't do anything right. They got out to a big lead and never looked back. We had four losses that season after having had only two the previous two years. Michigan came in riding high and headed to the Rose Bowl.

I remember, after we fell behind in the Michigan game, we had that 99-yard drive that was the turning point of the game. It seemed like we were out there on the field forever. It was neat. I would like to go back and watch tape of that to relive it. We all knew Troy [Smith] had the physical talent, but watching him do it on the field against Michigan that day was fantastic. We wanted to hold our blocks that extra second for him. [Smith rushed for 145 yards and one touchdown and passed for 241 yards and two touchdowns in a 37–21 win.] We sent our seniors out the right way.

We went down to San Antonio for the Alamo Bowl and practiced outdoors in 40-degree weather all week, knowing we would be playing in the dome. But that win [33–7 over Oklahoma State] was a good jump start for our senior year.

Our expectations were huge—nothing less than a national championship would satisfy us as seniors. Then the Texas game…it was a real shame. We had it right there for us to take, a night game at Ohio Stadium, leading the whole night. But to lose that one was really tough. Then we lost another close game at Penn State during one of their whiteouts.

Luckily for us, we learned how to bounce back after some losses during our junior year, so we wouldn't go down that path again. We ran the table to get to Michigan. We fell behind, but I knew we would find a way to win that game, and I remember Gonzo [Tony Gonzalez] making that catch down near their goal line. It was a great experience for us to beat Michigan at Michigan. I got an awesome picture of that scoreboard as it ticked to zero reading OSU 25, Michigan 21.

I loved every minute of the Fiesta Bowl, my last game as a Buckeye, on the same field where we won the national championship. I thought that week, no matter which path I went in college, even if I had gone to Notre Dame, my career would have finished in that game. I never got to play in a Rose Bowl, which would have been an awesome experience, but we did play in three Fiesta Bowls.

Being selected as a captain my senior year was one of the greatest honors I ever received, especially from that team and all the great seniors we had. Going to the Captains' Breakfast before the Michigan game last year was a really special time for me.

My class came in with a purpose, and we were able to do some great things together. I cherish my memories with my teammates, and we all know that if anyone ever needs anything, we are only a phone call away. I knew, from the moment I had an opportunity to go to Ohio State, that it would be a remarkable experience. With the tradition and the people who have come before me, and developing that bond with them and the guys I played with, it is barely describable to me.

I am very honored to call myself a Buckeye.

Nick Mangold played in 46 games and started 34 at center from 2003 to 2005. He was a first-round pick of the New York Jets in 2006 and became the highest-paid center in NFL history heading into the 2010 season.

BOBBY CARPENTER

LINEBACKER

2002–2005

I WAS FORTUNATE GROWING UP, because my dad, who played 10 years in the NFL, didn't put any pressure on me at all to play football. In fact, he didn't let me play football until I was 13 years old, and he never went out of his way to force it on me or my three brothers. He wanted me to love it on my own, and I am not even really sure he wanted any of us to play the game.

But he knew the sport very well and knew a lot of players and coaches in college and the NFL, so we always watched and talked a lot of football when I was a kid. I played soccer and basketball, and I was a skinny kid growing up in Lancaster, Ohio. Dad was coaching football at New Lexington, about 20 miles from Lancaster for six or seven years by the time I reached the seventh grade. He then coached me in junior high at Lancaster and later became the head coach of our high school team, so I was fortunate that he got to coach me for six years.

It worked out for the best for me, because he did a great job rebuilding the program. Before he got there, the high school team had been 1–9. Dad's teams were 2–8 during my freshman season, then 5–5, 4–6, and finally we had a winning record of 6–4 during my senior year, when we lost three or four games by less than a touchdown—and they still have not had a losing season since. Dad's teams were 73–27 the last 10 years.

I played safety as a freshman, and he didn't want me to play on the varsity, but I learned this much later: his assistant coaches threatened to walk out on him if he didn't play me after we started 0–3. I was about 6′2″ and only 165 pounds, but I put on weight every year.

The other sport I loved was swimming, which was my mom's sport. I practiced in the pool every day at 7:00 AM from the age of six to 13, and if my football career had not been going well enough, I would have put my future in swimming. But as you get bigger for football, it is harder to swim. I graduated at 235 pounds, and it's hard to swim at that weight.

Mom also played field hockey, and I always told Dad that my athletic ability came from her.

When I was about seven or eight years old, we went to Columbus for a 5K run for charity for the adults, and I remember getting to run on the field at Ohio Stadium. I thought that was the coolest thing in the world, but other than that, we never had any emotional connection to Ohio State as a lot of people in the state did. After all, my dad played at Miami of Ohio.

I went to the Ohio State football camps after my freshman and sophomore years, and [Ohio State assistant] Coach [Bill] Conley offered me a scholarship on the last day of camp as a sophomore. It was a Friday, I was 16 years old and very excited. Randy Walker, the head coach at Northwestern, had been Dad's roommate at Miami of Ohio, and he also offered me a scholarship. So did Michigan State and North Carolina.

365

When it came to making a decision, Dad made a list of 10 factors in choosing a school, and the biggest factor to me was being close to home. Then he asked me, "If you get hurt for good on the first day of practice, would you still want to go to school wherever you are?"

I finally committed to Ohio State a week before signing day, as one of the last guys in that class [2002]. That was a really strong class, with Mike D'Andrea, who was one of the top recruits in the country, A.J. Hawk, Stan White, Doug Datish, Ty Everett, Nick Mangold, Justin Zwick, and Nate Salley. I really liked all of the guys in my class. I can honestly say there is not one guy in our class whom I disliked. We still all get together whenever we can.

We opened with Texas Tech in my first game as a freshman. I remember running down the field on the opening kickoff, and the guy blocking me got out of position. Then the kickoff returner caught it about eight yards deep in the end zone and brought it out. I was thinking, *What is this guy doing?* I tackled him at the 10-yard line [the first official tackle of the 2002 national championship season].

Bobby Carpenter drops into pass coverage at Ohio Stadium during one of his 26 career starts at outside linebacker.

Not many freshmen contributed on that team because we were so deep with veterans. I played behind Robert Reynolds at linebacker and tried to make my mark on special teams. I made a few tackles here and there, and we were winning, so I had to be happy with that. It was tough as a freshman, though, because you wanted to play and contribute. I felt then like I was one of the better players and should have been on the field. But the reality is that I was competing against guys who were 22 or 23 years old with experience and who knew the game.

The coaches were riding us hard every day in practice, and sometimes I wondered, *What did I get myself into?* I even talked to Dad about transferring about once each week, but he said, "You are sticking it out at least two years. And if you leave, don't come back to our house. You are on your own." Looking back, I am forever indebted to him. I know now that staying was the right decision.

As you get older, I learned, the coaches have respect for you once you buy into the system and work hard. Practices become more fun, you have a good time, and you earn your playing time.

Winning the national championship was so special for Ohio State. It meant a lot to me, even though I was a freshman and not a starter.

I played more and more as a sophomore, and then Robert Reynolds had that unfortunate incident with Jim Sorgi [Reynolds was suspended one game after choking the Wisconsin quarterback in the sixth game of the 2003 season, a 17–10 loss that snapped Ohio State's 19-game winning streak]. I got my first start in the next game against Iowa, and I was so amped up that I didn't play as well as I would have liked. Then I kind of split time with Robert before they moved him inside, and I started the last three games.

We weren't ready to play that day at Michigan, even knowing we could have played for another national championship if we had won that game. We were down 21–0 before we realized what was happening. We sure got ripped at halftime that day [by the coaches] and got ripped for the next month [after the 35–21 loss]. I remember walking out of the weight room, and I would see Coach [Mark] Dantonio. He would have that Michigan game film on and still be pointing to guys, so angry that we lacked passion that day. He was just seething for a month.

That is why I think we played so well in the Fiesta Bowl win over Kansas State. They had just destroyed No. 1 Oklahoma and had some great offensive players in Darren Sproles and Ell Roberson at quarterback. But we played one of our best games [a 35–28 win in which Carpenter had five tackles, two and a half tackles for loss, and two sacks].

My junior season started well as we came in ranked in the top 10 [ninth] and won our first three games. Then we went to Northwestern and turned it over a few times and got beat in overtime [33–27] in a night game. Then we lost to Wisconsin [24–13] and got dismantled at Iowa [33–7]. We were the first Ohio State team to start 3–3 or worse since 1988.

I really think that moment in time forged us to get better over the next couple of years. We found a way to win three in a row before we lost at Purdue. Then Michigan came in, ranked seventh, and they already had a trip to the Rose Bowl clinched. They went up 14–7 right away before our offense put together a 99-yard drive that changed the game. Brandon Joe had a big day pounding them with the run, Troy Smith was scrambling around and lighting them up, and the offensive guys put on a show [in a 37–21 win]. We then beat Oklahoma State pretty easily [33–7] in the Alamo Bowl and had a lot of fun doing it.

I knew we would be pretty good in my senior year, and it was a national championship–or-bust mentality for us. I don't know if we ever played a better game and lost than what happened at home against Texas. We just couldn't put them away. People ask me all the time, "What was the most exciting game you ever played in?" That was it. We had them beat but missed a 50-yard field goal that would have put us up by nine. Then Justin Zwick threw into the end zone to Ryan Hamby, and he bobbled it just a second before getting hit. If he'd caught that, Zwick may have started the rest of the season.

I have to admit that tackling Vince Young was like trying to tackle a horse. We pounded him all night, and eventually he stopped running in the second half. I once talked to him when we were in the NFL about that game, and he said, "Man, you all tried to knock the crap out of me." Texas [which won 25–22] went on to win the national championship, and we got beat a few weeks later at Penn State.

We had a 3–2 record and were down 17–7 late in the first half against Michigan State when they lined up for a field goal. If I remember right, they had only 10 men on the field when Nate Salley blocked it, and Ashton Youboty picked it up and ran 72 yards for a touchdown. We came back to win [35–24], and that one play saved our season.

We won the rest of our games leading up the game at Michigan. On our first defensive play, I was playing down on the end, and they ran a draw play. I tried to squeeze it and turn, but I couldn't get my right foot out of the turf. Plus, I had [Michigan tackle] Jake Long leaning on me, and I felt it break right away. I never wanted to be down on the field and have to be carried off, so I hobbled off and hoped they could tape it up and I could go back in, but I couldn't put any weight on it. Then they didn't even have a cart on the sideline to take me up that steep ramp at Michigan Stadium to the locker room. I had to hobble uphill for about 10 minutes to get there. The doc looked at it and said there was nothing they could do. It was broken. (I talked to Jake about it years later when I played at Miami in the NFL, but there was nothing dirty about it. Jake's one of the nicest dudes I know.)

It was my last game, I wanted to go out with a win at Michigan, and I thought, *Is this the summation of my college career? It all ends on the first play of the game?*

Right then, I wanted to shower and put on my street clothes, but I knew this would be my last chance to wear that uniform. So I kept it on, got back to the sideline, and watched the game. All the guys I had been with for four years now were great that day, coming up and encouraging me and telling me, "Don't worry, we got this for you. We won't lose." James Laurinaitis went out and played in my spot. I told him, "Just relax, and those guys will help you out." He played a solid game and did his job, but we were down by nine points with only six minutes to go.

369

I stood over there on crutches, wondering, *How in the world are we going to win this game?* Then Troy did his magic that day and led us back with two late touchdowns, and we won [25–21].

What I remember most is how much fun we had that night back in Columbus. We had about 50 guys, went to a bar, hung out, and had fun together. It was a great, great night, even though I was hobbling around in a big boot. I remember waking up at about 4:00 in the morning when the painkiller wore off and screaming in pain.

I rehabbed my tail off, hoping I could play in the Fiesta Bowl against Notre Dame. It was a mild break, and the doctors said I would be active in two or three months, but I tried everything to play—even one play—but I risked blowing my knee out if I couldn't move or get out of the way. I tried to run and just couldn't do it. I was so frustrated. Anyway, we won easily over Notre

Dame [34–20], but my career ended with me rooting on all my teammates from the sideline.

That was one of the best things about my four years—making lifelong friends and being around a group of great guys. We were all very close and joked around constantly. I have so many stories of all the good times and the good people, such as Anthony Schlegel. "Schlegs" transferred in [from Air Force] and was a Texan and a big cowboy. He loved to hunt and always told us all of his wild hunting stories about killing boar or deer with his bow and arrow. He used to practice with it at the Woody Hayes [Athletic Center] until Coach Tress put a stop to that. I always joked with him, telling him I never saw pictures or any proof that he ever shot anything with that bow and arrow. So one day we came back from lunch, and there was a small box in my locker. I opened it, and there was a note that read, "Bobby, Anthony got me—he's the best hunter in the world!" Inside was a dead squirrel. I had to get proof, and sure enough, one of our equipment managers confirmed that he dragged that thing in there on the end of one of his arrows. Twenty minutes later, Schlegs walks in with a big ol' grin on his face.

Those were the best times, even though you don't always realize it when you are playing.

I could live anywhere now, and I still go back in the off-season. I love being around the program and the guys who play there and have played there. When we played, guys like Mike Vrabel and Eddie George would be there, talking to me just like we had played together. And that's what I plan to do, too: help out the current players if I can, especially the linebackers.

It was a life-changing experience for me. My dad had told me once, "If you play at Ohio State and don't get into trouble, there will always be opportunities for you after college." I know now what he meant. I made some of the best friends in my life, I met my wife there, and it shaped who I am and what I am today. Ohio State was a great place for me—the perfect place for me.

Bobby Carpenter finished his career with 191 tackles, and 14½ sacks. He also had three interceptions and 23½ tackles for loss. He was a first-round pick of the Dallas Cowboys in 2006 and also has played with the St. Louis Rams, Miami Dolphins, and Detroit Lions.

A.J. HAWK
LINEBACKER
2002–2005

I WAS BORN AARON JAMES HAWK, but they always called me A.J. because my grandpa was a big fan of race-car driver A.J. Foyt. I was the youngest of three boys growing up in Centerville, Ohio, and I pretty much did everything my older brothers did—whatever sports they played, I played, and wherever they went, I went.

Centerville was an awesome place to grow up. Being only 25 minutes from Cincinnati, it was natural for me to become a Bengals fan, and I also rooted for Ohio State. I was not a diehard fan like most people in Ohio—I also liked Florida State, so I rooted for both schools.

When my brother Ryan, who is two years older than me, became the starting quarterback [at Centerville High], he paved the way for me, and I just tagged along to all of the varsity workouts. Then I became a starter on the varsity in the third game of my freshman year, playing tailback—we were running the triple option—and, of course, linebacker on defense.

But I knew that, no matter how many yards I gained and touchdowns I scored, if I wanted to play offense in college, my options would be limited to fullback. So I knew my future was at linebacker.

I really wasn't highly recruited. I went to Ohio State's camp as a freshman but wasn't on anybody's radar at such an early age. Then I was getting some letters from the Mid–American Conference schools. But, when I went to the Ohio State camp the summer before my senior year, they offered me a scholarship. It is what I had been waiting for. I got an offer from Penn State the next week, but I knew all along I would go to Ohio State if they offered.

I injured my knee in the first game of my senior season and was worried about my future, but the Ohio State coaches weren't worried. They told me to rehab it and get ready to play, and everything would be fine. I [underwent arthroscopic surgery], sat out five games, and then came back and played the final four games of the season.

Once I graduated, I went to Columbus and started working out with the guys in seven-on-seven drills. All of the seniors that year [2002] were great to us freshmen—guys like Cie Grant, Donnie Nickey, Mike Doss. I give them so much credit for involving us in everything and helping us getting ready to play.

They were all very close—the same way my class became. Bobby Carpenter and I hit it off right away, and then Nick Mangold and everybody in my class became good friends.

I think we were in the last class that was allowed to have freshman camp before the varsity reported. Then the NCAA changed the rule the following year so everyone reported at once. But it was brutal at first. We had 20 guys scrimmaging and doing drills with little rest. We were dead tired by the time the upperclassmen reported.

I didn't have any expectations about playing time during my freshman year and was unsure if they wanted to redshirt me. As we got further into practices, I was backing up Cie Grant [at outside linebacker] and starting on special teams.

Running out of the tunnel onto the field that first game against Texas Tech was awesome. I remember running down the field on kickoff coverage, and Bobby made the first tackle. Then I got in the game because we were blowing them out, and it was great to be playing for the first time in that stadium.

The next game, against Kent State at home, I don't remember what they were running offensively, but we dropped into our zone coverage, and I made the read, picked it off, and scored [on a 34-yard return]. It was awesome. It was icing on the cake for me.

The other highlight for me that season was after Cie got hurt. I played the entire second half against Wisconsin, and it was fun to be a part of those types of games. They were all close, hard-fought, and we always found a way to

One of the greatest defensive players ever at Ohio State, A.J. Hawk is one of the few to have played on both national championship and Super Bowl–winning teams. He was a two-time All-American and winner of the Lombardi Award.

win. Then, the next week against Penn State, there was a tipped ball, and I got the pick. It was such a close game that every play made a difference. In the end, Chris Gamble returned an interception to win the game for us [13–7].

We were winning every game and winning most of them so close—I was so young as an 18-year-old freshman—I had no feel for how big it was. I remember the seniors never panicked, no matter what the situation was, and I think we all learned from that. We just kept winning, and after we beat Michigan [14–9], knowing we were going to play for a national title—it's hard to describe that feeling. I think it took me 40 minutes to get off the field and into the locker room because of the fans on the field that day.

Going into the Fiesta Bowl against Miami, we never felt overmatched. They were rolling [having won 34 games in a row], and we knew it would be a huge test, but we still felt confident. We wanted to pressure Ken Dorsey. We hit him a lot in the first half, and it got him feeling the rush as the game went on. The defensive line did a great job that night, and that set the tone for the game. Winning that night was an awesome experience. That's all I knew so far at Ohio State—winning every game. I just planned on coming back to the national title game every year, but we never got back. It definitely makes me respect what it was and what it meant, even to this day.

I never wore my national championship ring and never have been a jewelry guy, so I can't see myself ever wearing my Super Bowl ring, either.

Bobby and I started to grow our hair out in the spring of our junior year, and people started to make a big deal about it, but we did it to honor Pat Tillman. Bobby and Schlegs [linebacker Anthony Schlegel] and I were big fans of his, and after he got killed [April 22, 2004, in Afghanistan], we talked about doing it but didn't want to make a big deal about it. We just started growing our hair, and it stuck.

Later, when I got into the NFL, I got a chance to talk with Dave McGinnis, who coached Pat with the Arizona Cardinals, and he told me so many stories about him. He said, "A.J., he was your kind of guy."

By the time our senior year started, we had big expectations. Winning. Winning every game. Winning a national championship. Going into every season that was our goal, but this was our senior season, we had a lot of starters back, and Troy Smith was a junior and had some experience. We had a fun training camp and figured we would have a big season.

Everybody was talking about the Texas game all summer long. It would be a night game at Ohio Stadium, and we felt like we were ready, but Vince Young had a heck of a day. It was close, but for whatever reason, we couldn't get up by two scores and put them away. For sure, it was the worst loss of my career. It was early in the season and tough to accept that we let it get away from us.

Then we lost at Penn State and were 3–2. We were obviously upset, but our confidence wasn't shot. We just had to win out to go to a BCS game, and that is what we did.

At Michigan, Bobby got hurt on the first play, and I felt horrible for him. It was tough looking over at the sideline and seeing him standing there cheering us on the whole game. Our offense brought us back that day, and it still is amazing that our last loss to them was my sophomore year. Tress said before the game to the seniors, "Hey, it's much better to be 3–1 against Michigan in your career than 2–2," and he was right.

That put us in the Fiesta Bowl against Notre Dame, and the media was making a big deal about my dating Laura [Notre Dame quarterback Brady Quinn's sister], but we knew we were pretty serious, and it wasn't just a fling at the time. It was a fun thing at the time to play against Brady and Notre Dame, but after that game we never talked about it much. [Ohio State won 34–20, and Hawk had two quarterback sacks of Quinn, now his brother-in-law, and was named Fiesta Bowl co-MVP.]

People have asked me at times how I seemed to be in the right place at the right time, or have so many tackles or make All-America, and all I can say is that anytime you play off the ball like I did, you learn to read the schemes and rely on your instincts. I always read what the offensive line was doing, what the running backs were doing, so I had a feel of where the ball was going. I really believe you can be born with those instincts, and I watched a lot of film, too. We always had great defensive lines at Ohio State, so that helped.

I was never big on individual awards, but it was pretty neat winning the Lombardi Award and then getting drafted by the Packers right after that. But I know that playing at Ohio State, with the teammates I played with and the coaches I played for, put me in position to achieve those types of things.

I can't say I have any regrets, other than not winning four national titles, but I wouldn't change anything else. As a kid, I always dreamed about playing at Ohio State, and I looked at those guys like movie stars, but it's hard to put into words once it happens to you. I think it becomes bigger as the years go by. Every day is a journey, and when you are playing, you are working to become better for the next day. What it took to get there and what it means to you hits you later on after you are gone.

One neat thing is that after every game on Sunday, I seek guys out from the other team who played at Ohio State. Some of them I never knew, but they are part of the program, sort of like one big fraternity.

I look forward to when we have the national championship reunion some-day, and all the guys will come back to town and we can relive our memories. That will be awesome.

A.J. Hawk started 38 games and finished his career with 394 tackles, including 41 for loss. He recorded seven interceptions and scored two touchdowns. With the Green Bay Packers winning Super Bowl XLV, Hawk also joined the elite club of players who played on both national championship and Super Bowl–winning teams. He was a three-time All–Big Ten player and a two-time All-American, as well as the 2005 winner of the Lombardi Award.

BRIAN ROLLE

LINEBACKER

2007–2010

I GREW UP IN A SMALL TOWN in South Florida called Immokalee. It wasn't a bad place by any means, but you could get in trouble if you went to the wrong part of town. It is a town of about 30,000 people, and there is not much to see there. You have to work hard for everything you get, and most of the people worked in agriculture. I loved growing up there, and it is still a place I call home.

And football is everything there.

During my freshman year, I was a better offensive player as a fullback than I was a linebacker. Then my coach told me, "You have something special, and you can be great some day," and it was like a light bulb went on in my head. That sophomore year, we won the Class 2A state championship, and I began to think I had a future at middle linebacker at the college level.

Being so close to Miami, I naturally became a Hurricanes fan. They played with that swagger, and I just wanted to be a part of it. Guys like D.J. Williams and my cousin, Antrel Rolle, always played with emotion, and I loved that. I went to most of their games during my junior and senior seasons in high school, and when I started to get recruited, I just figured I would be at home at Miami. I thought it was a great fit for me.

Then their head coach, Larry Coker, got fired, and it seemed the new coaching staff didn't want me. Florida recruited me, and I loved my visit there—I went to the LSU-Florida game and I totally understood why people go there to play football. I have to admit that I was leaning their way a little bit.

Ohio State became interested during my senior season, and Tim Beckman, who later became the head coach at Toledo, recruited me. Honestly, I didn't know much about Ohio State, I just thought it was another average university. I now know that I didn't know anything about anything. I didn't know about Ohio State–Michigan. I didn't know about the great linebackers who had come through the program, and I didn't know about players like Archie Griffin.

I had watched the Northern Illinois–Ohio State game in the 2006 season opener, and [NIU] had a running back, Garrett Wolfe, who ran wild that day. I thought, *Ohio State is supposed to be good? They can't even stop this little Northern Illinois running back.*

But then I visited Columbus during the Ohio State–Michigan game at the end of the season. I was wide-eyed from the moment I stepped off of the airplane. Game day was something else. The skull session at St. John Arena, the Tunnel of Pride on the field before the game, the game itself [a 42–39 Ohio State win]…everything was unbelievable.

378

The campus was like a city itself, and the stadium just blew me away that day. People were going crazy. It was an unbelievable atmosphere, and that's what sold me to come to Ohio State. It felt like home.

I told my mom after the game, "I am coming to Ohio State!"

When I arrived in Columbus in the summer of my freshman year, I expected to be another big man on campus. I got a slice of humble pie right away when I saw James Laurinaitis. He was a real man playing linebacker. I have to thank Doug Worthington and Nader Abdallah because they took me in just like a brother and took care of me for a few weeks until I moved into the dorm.

That's one thing I love about the Ohio State program under Coach Tressel: the older guys treat the freshmen like they had been there for three years with them. They treat them like brothers, and that's the way it should be.

Everything seemed so much bigger to me. It took me a while to adjust to the college life and being away from home. It was my hardest year in college, as it is with most students. I missed my family a lot, but I never wanted to be back home. I just wanted my family to be with me in Columbus. My brother had played football at Illinois State, so he had prepared me on what it would be like to be away from home, to play football in the north.

One thing that never bothered me much, however, was the cold and snow. That first winter wasn't that bad. The first day it snowed, it was about 1:00 AM and I was asleep when it started to fall. I woke up and went outside and thought it was the most beautiful thing in the world. Sometimes it got irritating when you had to bundle up every day, but we never had to play football in anything colder than 25 degrees.

I soon learned about Ohio State's tradition. I learned about all the great linebackers who played wearing my No. 36, such as Chris Spielman and Marcus Marek, and how prestigious that number has become at Ohio State. I learned about the Michigan rivalry and what it means to beat Michigan.

I didn't want to redshirt my freshman year. I told the coaches, "I could have gone to Florida to redshirt. I came here to play," and I played special teams and learned my position. There was nobody better to learn from than Laurinaitis. If James ever made a mistake, he didn't make it twice. He would practice the right way. He would beat the defensive backs in running and agility drills. He worked like nobody else worked. That's how he became a two-time All-American and a Butkus Award winner.

By the start of my junior season, I became a starter at middle linebacker, and one of the highlights of my career happened on Navy's two-point conversion attempt to tie the game in our season opener. We had practiced the play Navy ran and talked about it the entire week leading up to the game, and sure enough, as their quarterback started to roll out, I thought, *This can't be the play they are running now, is it?*

It was. I read it and intercepted it and headed down the left sideline. Once I got the ball in my hands, I saw the end zone, and all I could think was, *I am the man! I am THE MAN!"*

Anyway, that play helped put away the 31–27 win over Navy.

That play just shows how well our coaches prepared us. They prepared every player, starter and backup, to be mentally prepared and to know what the other team was going to do in about any situation. This was a two-point conversion to tie the game, near the end of the game, and Navy did just what we had prepared for.

Midway through the 2009 season, we lost at Purdue, and something just didn't feel right from the beginning of that game. I could tell from the kickoff that we were not ready. We didn't play Ohio State football that day and lost. But we went on to win the rest of our games, and of course, the highlight was beating Michigan 21–10 at Ann Arbor.

Brian Rolle tackles Michigan tailback Vincent Smith during the Buckeyes' 21–10 win in Ann Arbor in 2009.

What can I say about the Rose Bowl? It is just one of those experiences you hope to get a chance to play in. Everybody had a chip on his shoulder because the experts were picking Oregon and saying their offense would go up and down the field. We heard all week how we couldn't keep up with them. They came in averaging 40 points per game. In watching film of them, I did wonder, *How are we going to stop this guy Jeremiah Masoli?* I knew he wasn't big, but he could sling it and he could run.

We had fun out in California, seeing the Hollywood sign and things like that. I remember being on the Rose Bowl field before the game, it truly gave me goose bumps. The grass was so crispy and perfect. The mountains were in the background. When our offense had the ball to start the game, I stood on the sideline and the sun was setting—it was the most beautiful thing I ever saw. I just took a deep breath, stood there and soaked it all in.

That day, we mainly just played our base defense. It was "assignment" football—"gap" football to us. We may have blitzed only a couple of times, and everybody did their part and stayed disciplined. After Cameron Heyward sacked Masoli once, [Masoli] got up and slammed the ball down to the ground, and I knew we had 'em. He was frustrated. Looking back, it was a great win [26–17] and an awesome experience.

Every year, I felt like any of our Ohio State teams have a chance to win a national championship, and the 2010 team was no different. We just had to keep our heads right, and through the first seven games, we did all the right things.

I told all my coaches and teammates before the Miami game, "This is personal to me." I talked to people back home all week. I knew we would play well and win that game, although the special teams' breakdowns let them stay in it. The score [36–24] should have been worse than it was.

I admit that our heads were not in the right place at Wisconsin, for some reason. Guys weren't playing as physically as we needed to. Wisconsin came out and did what they did, and we fell behind 21–0. It was the toughest loss [31–18] of my career. I couldn't stop crying after that game, knowing we would not win a national championship in my senior season.

We picked ourselves up and finished strong again. We played hard at Iowa and rallied for a big win, and I took real pride in the way I played that day. I let it all go that day [making 10 tackles, 3½ for loss]. Coaches gave me a 90 percent grade and told me what a great game I had played.

On Senior Day against Michigan, I couldn't hold back my tears. Leading up to it, the previous three years, you watch guys cry, and you think, *Man, I got a while before that happens to me.* But it goes fast. As they called my name to run onto the field, I thought, *I can't believe this is really it. This is my last time in the 'Shoe.* The game itself was so much fun. Michigan came in averaging 540 yards per game, and it was a tremendous feeling to shut them down [a 37–7 win].

There are a lot of great players in Ohio State history who have one pair of gold pants, maybe two. I am proud to say I am one of the guys who has four. We did not break the streak. And my parents have all four of them.

We also accomplished one more thing I am proud of—we beat an SEC team in a bowl game by beating Arkansas. That ended that streak.

The highlight of my career was being around so many great people and players, like Cameron Heyward. All the seniors on my team were very, very close. We came in together and played for each other.

I have no regrets at all. I feel very blessed that I came to Ohio State.

Brian Rolle, one of six captains in 2010, finished his career with 206 tackles and four interceptions, including a 30-yard return for a touchdown in the 2010 season-opening win over Marshall. He was a sixth-round selection of the Philadelphia Eagles in the 2011 NFL Draft. He started 13 games for the Eagles during his rookie season.

CAMERON HEYWARD
DEFENSIVE LINEMAN
2007–2010

I WAS BORN IN PITTSBURGH before we moved around a little bit as a family because my dad, Craig "Ironhead" Heyward, was an NFL player who played in New Orleans, Chicago, and Atlanta, which is where we finally settled. And that is the smartest decision my family made—I loved growing up in Atlanta.

We didn't want to keep traveling, and sports was a big part of my life, so no kid wants to keep moving. The thing is, Dad didn't want me to play football. He knew it was a violent game and wanted me to stay away from it, but all my friends were playing, and I loved the game.

I started playing football in the fifth grade, but I admit that I was very awkward and clumsy. I had no control over my body. As I grew, I also played basketball and thought for a time that I would become a basketball player. By the time I got to high school, I was a defensive end and tight end, and they also tried me a little at fullback, but Dad didn't want me to play running back like he did.

I guess I was stubborn as a child because I didn't want to listen to anything he had to say when it came to football. He was always there to support me and offered some advice for technique and things like that, but he never forced it on me. Now that I am older, I understand everything he was trying to tell me.

The great thing was, after Dad's games, he would pick me out of the stands and take me into the locker room with him. It's pretty neat being a kid and hanging around an NFL locker room, getting to know guys like Jamal Anderson and Eric Metcalf, the guys Dad hung out with.

I played at Whitfield Academy as a freshman and sophomore and then at Peachtree Ridge High School for my junior and senior years after Dad became sick again [Craig Heyward was diagnosed with cancer in 1999 and died May 27, 2006—three weeks after Cameron turned 17 years old].

Recruiting was overwhelming and very stressful at times for me, not having Dad around. It was very difficult, but I couldn't have done it without Mom. She was like my agent. She would ask defensive coordinators, "How many defensive ends and tackles do you have? What schemes are you playing?" All the coaches were astounded because they never expected a woman to know that much about football. She wanted a school that would take care of me and not let me fall behind in school if I got hurt.

Pitt was the first to offer me a scholarship, and I did consider them a little bit early, but Pitt was my dad's school. I wanted to branch out and try someplace new and make my own mark. I knew I couldn't follow my dad's legacy. I wanted to leave a legacy of my own and not live in his shadow. He was a great player and always will be in my heart.

Eventually, I had narrowed it down to Florida, LSU, and Ohio State. In the end, Ohio State had everything I wanted. The coaches were down-to-earth guys, and it has one of the most beautiful campuses I have ever seen. I knew a little about the tradition, and I knew to get a degree from Ohio State would be a great thing to have. I also could tell that Coach Tressel was a man of his word and a great spiritual leader. He is a great family man, and the football program was a family I wanted to be a part of.

People asked me all the time how a boy from Atlanta could live in Ohio, but I considered myself a northern boy. It was not a problem for me. My roots were in Pittsburgh.

Once I got to Ohio State, I got caught up to speed really quickly. I saw Mirror Lake and the Skull Session, dotting the *i* and Buckeye Grove. It was unbelievable to me, and now I was part of it.

Those first few weeks, I was known as the guy who was always sleeping. You could ask my roommates—Solomon Thomas and Nate Oliver—and they would tell you I was like a bear in hibernation. Workouts were rough, and I wanted to get my rest.

Cameron Heyward returns an interception against the Miami Hurricanes during the third quarter of the Buckeyes' 36–24 victory on September 11, 2010, in Columbus. *Photo courtesy of AP Images*

As my freshman season started, I knew [defensive coordinator] Jim Heacock was a man of his word because he had said, "The best players are going to play," and I appreciated that. You can have seniority, but the coaches are trying to win. I loved that because I knew it gave me a chance to see the field.

I got a sack in our season opener [a 38–6 win over Youngstown State] and was getting playing time through those first five games. Then I became a starter at Purdue that season. I didn't play my best game that day, but I was ecstatic to be starting. You couldn't tell me anything before that game, because I was in the clouds. I knew it was on ESPN and my family would be able to watch it.

The [28–21] loss to Illinois that season broke my heart. We were ranked No. 1 and having a heck of a year, but I took that loss really hard. I didn't play well and was very sorry for that loss. I laid a lot of that loss on myself.

In my first Michigan game, I had a chance to go against [Michigan tackle] Jake Long, and I knew he would be a top pick but had no idea he would be the No. 1 pick of the draft. I put him on his butt and got him off-balance a couple of times, and I thought, *Hey, I might have a chance.* When you win by a score of 14–3, you know it was one of those great defensive games on our part. It was my first rivalry game, and I wanted to win it so badly.

My sophomore year I went through a bit of a funk, and it just didn't feel right. Something told me it would be a hard season for me, and it was. We went to USC, and that was not pretty at all [a 35–3 loss]. We were missing Beanie [Wells] that day and going through the transition from Todd Boeckman to Terrelle [Pryor] at quarterback.

386

We went on to beat Michigan that year 42–7 in RichRod's first trip to the 'Shoe and should have beaten Texas in the Fiesta Bowl. There was that questionable spot at midfield [on Texas' game-winning drive], but Colt McCoy hit the throws he needed to at the end to beat us. We had a bend-but-not-break attitude, and they found a way to get it into the end zone.

I worked my butt off going into 2009 and had big expectations. I wanted to play like I was going into the NFL the next year and didn't want another season like my sophomore year. I knew 'SC was coming back to see us, this time in Ohio Stadium, and wanted to be ready for it. I had one of the best games I ever played that night, and we were controlling the game, but we couldn't get up by two scores. They hit that third-and-16 late in the game, and if we had made that play and stopped them, we would have been sitting fine. It was a tough, tough loss [18–15].

We were 9–2 going to Michigan later, and I got my first touchdown in that game. Tate Forcier was their quarterback, and we just wanted to keep him contained. On their first series, he cut back and dropped the ball, and I jumped right on it, seeing that I was over the [goal] line. That is an amazing feeling to score a touchdown against Michigan. The coaches always told us how everything is magnified in that game—a yard is like two yards, a first down is like a touchdown. Everything is so much greater.

The last time we went to California, we got our butts spanked, so we definitely were motivated to play Oregon in the Rose Bowl. They were putting up about 50 points per game and [quarterback Jeremiah] Masoli was just rolling over guys all season. We just wanted to shut up everybody who said we couldn't win those big games. We got after them that day, and everyone maintained their assignments. They had a couple of spurts up the middle, but other than that, we shut them down. It was a totally fun game [a 26–17 win].

After the game, I had a decision to make about the NFL, but there were not a lot of cons to staying in school. I wanted my degree, and I was looking forward to being a senior. I wanted to lead my team and be a captain, and once I was, it really was a great honor.

I had great expectations for my senior season. I expected so much. It almost drives me crazy not playing well and not winning every game. I expected to win every game. The Miami game would be our first test, and when they put together that long drive in the second half, it was hot and we were getting exhausted, but the coaches called the right play for us. It was a man blitz, and I got a good break on the ball, caught it, and took off running. I really should have scored, and I still get abused [by teammates] for not scoring, but I did break a few tackles. [Heyward's 80-yard interception set up the game-clinching touchdown in Ohio State's 36–24 victory over Miami.]

387

We were No. 1 by the time we got to Wisconsin, but it was a rough game for us. We didn't play our best, and they were a great team. They loved to run the ball, and we didn't react well to the running game that day. It was tough. We had one of the best chances at the national championship but didn't make enough plays. After that game, we knew we didn't control our own destiny.

Before the game at Iowa, we all got together, and I told the guys, "Let's play for each other. Don't let anything get you down, block out all of the issues, we are all in this together. Now let's win it together."

It was one of those up-and-down games, and I knew we would have a chance if we stayed in it. Winning it [20–17] was very satisfying, especially for all the seniors. Those seniors are like brothers from another mother to me. We hung out together. We got along really well, and I would do anything for them.

Senior Day was very tough for me and tough for my mom, not having my father there with us. It was a chance to go out with another win over Michigan, and that meant a lot to me. I remember Doug Worthington once telling me, "You don't want to be that team that loses to Michigan and breaks this streak," and we weren't. We seized the moment, and I feel very lucky to be part of that rivalry. I gave all four of my gold pants to Mom. She deserves them.

We faced another challenge in the Sugar Bowl against Arkansas, hearing how we were 0–9 against SEC teams in bowl games. We needed to answer the call, just as we had a year earlier when people said we couldn't beat a Pac-10 team in the Rose Bowl.

In the second quarter, I was making a pass-rush move and sort of caught myself as I landed and somebody fell on top of me, badly hyperextending my elbow. It was painful to play with, but I wasn't coming out. I had to get into a four-point stance just to take some weight off of it at times. [Heyward had three and a half tackles for loss in Ohio State's 31–26 win over Arkansas].

When it was over, and we had won our final game, I had no regrets. I knew I made the right choice in coming to Ohio State. I gained so much from it. I got a great education and made many great relationships. All the moments—from practices to the times in the locker room with the guys—are very special, and they hold a big place in my heart.

I am blessed to get my degree in education and look forward to teaching third-, fourth-, or fifth-graders some day. That's the right age for me to teach—they know enough, but not too much. That's another part of what Tress taught us. He wanted us to be more than football players. He wanted us to be complete persons with good morals and a spiritual side. He wanted us to succeed as family members and to contribute to society.

I know my experiences at Ohio State will help me do that.

Cameron Heyward started 47 games on the defensive line, making 163 tackles, including 37½ for loss in his career. He was named first-team All–Big Ten in 2010 and also was a Lombardi Award semifinalist. Ohio State had a 44–8 record in his four years and played in the BCS Championship Game, the Fiesta Bowl, the Rose Bowl, and the Sugar Bowl. He was drafted in the first round of the 2011 NFL Draft by the Pittsburgh Steelers, 31st overall.

LIE REAM · JAMES LANGHURST · CECIL "CY" SOUDERS · HOWARD

Y · ROBERT "ROCK" JOSLIN · HOWARD "HOPALONG" CASSADY · C

E · PAUL WARFIELD · ARNIE CHONKO · DWIGHT "IKE" KELLEY · M

BAUGH · JIM STILLWAGON · JOHN BROCKINGTON · DICK WAKE

EGEL · BRUCE ELIA · DOUG PLANK · BRIAN BASCHNAGEL · TIM

TOM SKLADANY · CHRIS WARD · JEFF LOGAN · TOM COUSINEAU

MARCUS MAREK · VAUGHN BROADNAX · KIRK LOWDERMILK · M

CARTER · CHRIS SPIELMAN · JEFF UHLENHAKE · CARLOS SNOW

AINE · JONATHAN WELLS · CIE GRANT · KENNY PETERSON · CRAI

BOBBY CARPENTER · A.J. HAWK · BRIAN ROLLE · CAMERON F

RD TEIFKE · BOB BRUGGE · JOE WHISLER · WILLIAM "BILLY" NEV

DY · GALEN CISCO · AUREALIUS THOMAS · JIM MARSHALL · JIM H

· MARK STIER · DIRK WORDEN · JIM OTIS · TED PROVOST · RE

WAKEFIELD · STAN WHITE · TOM DeLEONE · JOHN HICKS · R

NAGEL · TIM FOX · CORNELIUS GREENE · ARCHIE GRIFFIN · BOB

COUSINEAU · KEN FRITZ · DOUG DONLEY · CALVIN MURRAY ·

OWDERMILK · MIKE TOMCZAK · KEITH BYARS · THOMAS "PEPPER

CARLOS SNOW · JASON SIMMONS · EDDIE GEORGE · BOBBY HO

PETERSON · CRAIG KRENZEL · BEN HARTSOCK · ANDY GROOM ·